1991

Modernism and the fate of individuality examines the complexities and transitions of the idea of the self in the modernist period. Michael Levenson addresses the problem of individuality, structuring his argument around detailed readings of eight major novels by Conrad, James, Forster, Ford, Lewis, Lawrence and Woolf, and his discussion engages with the extensive body of modern theoretical writing on the topic. The book addresses issues such as the crisis of liberalism, the challenge to Eurocentrism, the advance of bureaucracy, and the contest between men and women. Central to its concerns is the problem, in locating the self within the entanglements of a community, of defining formal concepts whilst preserving a moral value.

Modernism and the fate of individuality

Modernism and the fate of individuality

Character and novelistic form from Conrad to Woolf

MICHAEL LEVENSON

University of Virginia

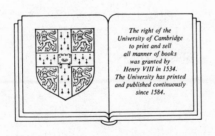

CAMBRIDGE UNIVERSITY PRESS

Cambridge

New York   Port Chester

Melbourne   Sydney

Published by the Press Syndicate of the University of Cambridge
The Pitt Building, Trumpington Street, Cambridge CB2 1RP
40 West 20th Street, New York, NY 10011-4211, USA
10 Stamford Road, Oakleigh, Melbourne 3166, Australia

First published 1991

Printed in Great Britain at the University Press, Cambridge

British Library cataloguing in publication data
Levenson, Michael H.
Modernism and the fate of individuality: character and
novelistic form from Conrad to Woolf.
1. Fiction in English 1900–1945. Forms. Novels.
Characters. Critical studies.
I. Title
823.9120927

Library of Congress cataloguing in publication data
Levenson, Michael.
Modernism and the fate of individuality: character and novelistic
form from Conrad to Woolf / Michael Levenson.
p.   cm.
ISBN 0–521–39491–0
1. English fiction – 20th century – History and criticism.
2. Characters and characteristics in literature. 3. Modernism
(Literature) – Great Britain. 4. Individuality in literature.
I. Title.
PR888.C47L48   1991
823′.9120927 – dc20   90–1694 CIP

ISBN 0 521 39491 0 hardback

GG

For Karen, my fate

Contents

Preface

This thing we name the individual, this piece of matter, this length of memory, this bearer of a proper name, this block in space, this whisper in time, this self-delighting, self-condemning oddity — what is it? who made it? Ours may be the age of narcissism, but it is also the century in which ego suffered unprecedented attacks upon its great pretensions, to be self-transparent and self-authorized. It discovered enemies within and enemies without; walls within, mirrors without; it no longer perched securely on the throne of the self; it no longer sat confidently at the center of the social world. The wandering "I" is the protagonist of this study whose chief interest is to read eight big novels (big even when they are little) which move between the longing to recover some figure of the self, to preserve some vessel of subjectivity, and the willingness to let it go, to release the knot of subjectivity.

Accordingly, the main current of argument in this book will follow the diverse fortunes of individuality in modern English fiction: its changing verbal aspect, its historical limits and symbolic resources, its political dispossession, cultural displacement and psychological self-estrangement, its uneasy accommodation of mind and body, its retreat from the world and its longing for community. Cast in the broadest terms, this study attempts to chart the lambent movements of post-Romantic subjectivity as it endures the heavy pressures of modern history and modernist literary experiment. As the subtitle implies, the issue that organizes this general concern is the relationship between character and form, and this relationship has two pertinent aspects.

The first involves the relation of fictional character to narrative form. In the preface to *The Golden Bowl*, James observes that in the course of his novel Maggie Verver "duplicates, as it were, her value and becomes a compositional resource . . . as well as a value intrinsic." The idea of a "duplication" emphasizes one distinction that my title means to suggest, the distinction between the "intrinsic" values that characters are made to embody and the "compositional" laws to which they must conform. The issue becomes most sharply defined in the fiction of James, Ford, Lewis and Joyce, but it has bearing on all the works to be considered in this study. One of the great concealed dramas of the modern novel is the struggle between certain enduring traits in literary character and certain innovations in narrative structure, the contest between a notion of fictional self inherited from nineteenth-century precedents and the new literary forms designed to contain it. The Romanticism of Stephen Dedalus, the liberalism of Margaret Schlegel, the Victorianism of John Dowell — to name just a few instances — stand in uneasy relation to the forms which surround them, and part of my historical claim is that the modern novel had to negotiate between conventions of character sustaining traditions and principles of structure attacking them. I shall argue, that is, that the struggle between character and form often takes the aspect of a conflict between tradition and modernity and that one way to understand this moment of transition in the history of the novel is in terms of nineteenth-century characters seeking to find a place in twentieth-century forms.

The second aspect of the problem concerns the relation of character, not to narrative form, but to social form. A repeated movement in these novels is the portrayal of a dense web of social constraints followed by the effort to wrest an image of autonomous subjectivity from intractable communal norms. The motif of exile is a conspicuous expression of this concern, but what is most notable about the aspiration to exile is how frequently it leads, not to an escape from the community, but to a withdrawal to its interstices. This common pattern establishes a subject that will be prominent in the study, the ambiguous boundaries between "I" and "Other," the chief thematic problem here being the attempt to construct a figure of individuality from within the rigid confines of community.

Although I describe this emphasis separately, in fact the pressures of social structure stand in close and provocative analogy to the pressures of literary structure. The dislocation of the self within society is recapitulated, reenacted, reconsidered, in the dislocation of character within modernist forms. And yet part of what makes these novels so tense and nervous is that they pursue their formal disruptions of character even as they so often sustain nostalgic longing for a whole self. A set of works that engage in self-conscious assault on a notion of character persistently associated with the nineteenth century continue to cherish nineteenth-century ideals of the autonomous ego, free and integral.

One methodological principle should be acknowledged here, namely that the strategy for reading these works is to invert the usual metaphoric relation between text and context, according to which "context" resembles a large backdrop behind and above and around the players who move within its horizons. It is true, or at least figurally well established, that novels participate "in" history, but it is at least as figurally significant that history unfolds "in" novels. The style of reading here is to see these novels as dense environments which have incorporated an historical artifact – seen in one description as a concept of individuality dislocated by social pressures; seen in another as a traditional method of characterization unsettled by new formal commitments – and which adopt revealingly diverse techniques for digesting the history they have swallowed. The crisis of liberalism, the challenge to Eurocentrism, the advance of bureaucracy, the contest between men and women – these are problems that enter my work as they entered these novels, but it should be said from the first that they receive nothing like a degree of attention proportionate to their magnitude. Their mention gives only a telegraphic sign of the full-scale social history that I once thought could stand among these pages.

It should also be said that this study refuses the artifice of thematic coherence, and that on those several occasions when an issue other than the fate of individuality rises to prominence it is not (at least not often) because the author has a subtle argumentative connection well in mind; it is because the author happens to find it interesting. To the question that will occasionally occur to a reader, "How does he intend to fit *that* into the larger structure of the book?" the answer often is, "He doesn't."

Acknowledgements

Always there are many incalculable debts, and always the greatest is to my family. But with this book I owe just as much to my graduate students at the University of Virginia. There are too many to name (too many called Ann, too many called Richard) but not too many to remember. At every stage they nodded and frowned, chatted and swatted, encouraged and chastened. From out of the fertile context they created, my ideas developed first into essays. Early versions of the material appeared in *Nineteenth-Century Fiction, Studies in Short Fiction, Modern Language Quarterly, Twentieth Century Literature, Papers on Language and Literature*, and *Modern Language Studies.* The essays then returned to the classroom, and under new generous scrutiny they reformed themselves until they settled into the chapters that follow. The quality of this book aside, the process of its composition has been for me a justification of academic life. Speech and writing, private thought and public exchange, intellectual detachment and emotional engagement, all flowed together and carried me in their stream. For their splendid teaching I thank my students.

CHAPTER ONE

Two cultures and an individual
Heart of Darkness and
The Ambassadors

I

The first rude act in this frequently wilful study is its opening act, the decision to place *Heart of Darkness* and *The
Ambassadors* side by side and to introduce a problem in modern
English narrative by passing from one to the other. Admittedly, it is an almost absurdly comic picture to imagine Strether
among the alligators of the Congo or to envision Captain
Marlow in a tête-à-tête with Marie de Vionnet. And yet the
incidents of these narratives, like the works themselves, belong
to the same historical moment, and it is instructive to imagine
that just as Marlow was pressing deep into the jungle, Strether
was crossing the Tuileries, and that while Strether was loung-
ing on a Parisian balcony, Marlow dodged arrows on an
African river. The incongruity of these pictures gives us some
feeling for the incongruities of the nineties, when the middle
classes had perfected both the habits of leisure and the methods
of colonialism. To enjoy the delicacies of a long cultural tradition and to overstep the boundaries of that tradition, to witness
civilization at its most finely wrought and to confront its rude
origins, to contemplate the refinements of social convention
and to watch such conventions dissolve – these are concur-
rent historical possibilities that will allow us to locate modernist character within the expansive context that it demands.

Two novels so unlike in subject, tone and style should
generate a warm friction when they are brought close together,
and part of the point of this opening chapter is to take advantage of some marked dissimilarities in order to establish the
range of issues that the rest of this study will pursue. But a
deeper point is to show where dissimilarity yields to likeness.

1

These works that so decisively brought the English novel into the modern century contain frequent improbable echoes of one another, echoes so persistent that they establish the sound of literary change.

A man leaves his native country to travel to another, where he hopes to retrieve an unaccountably estranged member of his community. He finds himself entering a much older culture which deprives his own of its moral inevitability. With some difficulty he finds the object of his quest only to discover that a startling change has occurred in the man he seeks, who has taken on the manners and the morals of this alien community. As his own certainties waver, he finds himself drawn into unanticipated solidarity with the renegade, and his original errand seems to lose its point. Obliged to make a choice between the values he has inherited and the values he discovers, he chooses the latter; but having renounced his old measures and standards, he is still unable to live among these new ones. He decides to return home where he will live as a stranger among his neighbors.

This, in outline, is Marlow's story — and Strether's. And lest it seem my own unwarranted abstraction from imaginative detail, James's early description of *The Ambassadors* may be recalled. In his first notebook entry on the novel James decides that his hero will travel abroad in order "to take some step, decide some question with regard to some one, in the sense of his old feelings and habits, and that the new influences, to state it roughly, make him act just in the opposite spirit — make him accept on the spot, with a *volte-face*, a wholly different inspiration." From this situation of high generality James begins a slow descent into particularity. Suppose this man's mission involves "some other young life in regard to which it's a question of his interfering, rescuing, bringing home." Suppose our protagonist promises to restore the young man to his family, and then suppose that under the new influence he "se range du côté du jeune homme."[1] With only a few more details this outline will give the plot of *The Ambassadors*, but what is more significant is how readily it might have given the plot of *Heart of Darkness*. James's synopsis applies, with very little discrepancy, to Conrad's tale. As we shall see, Con-

2

rad did not derive the principles of his plot so systematically, but the final consequence is that Marlow too sets out to inter-fere, rescue, bring home; he too finds that old feelings yield to new influences; like Strether he accepts a different inspira-tion, makes a *volte-face* and forms a surprising alliance.

The formal congruence of these two plots should get us started. It should remind us that the difference between an African canoe and a French rowboat is not a final difference and that beyond their manifest contrasts the two works share certain primary features, most notably, the confrontation bet-ween cultures, the "sharp rupture of an identity," and the transvaluation of values.[2] To recognize these submerged parallels is to identify a shared narrative paradigm whose finer points it will be my task to elaborate.

Still, if the works met only on this plane of abstraction, their relationship would have a limited interest. The large issues that will be pursued through this study – the connection between character and form, self and society – will oblige me to move continually from such austere structures to concretely thematized detail. As a first instance, we may turn briefly to Marlow and Strether themselves in order to recall some homely facts that will gain in importance as we proceed.

One is a sea captain, the other an editor. No doubt if we could look at their hands, we could quickly tell them apart. And yet neither of them would have dirty hands – which is to say that both Marlow and Strether take exceptional pains to preserve their integrity within morally suspect contexts. Both find themselves entangled in the unrestrained economic activity of the period; the "great industry" of Woollett, a "big brave bouncing business" (I, p. 59), finds its complement in the immense trading concern that arranges Marlow's journey to the Congo. And each work places a single profitable com-modity in the foreground: the notoriously unnamed object manufactured at Woollett and the ivory pursued so obsessively in Africa. Indeed, it is tempting to fancy another subterranean connection, a secret unmarked trade route that brings Kurtz's ivory to Woollett where the Newsomes fabricate it into their vulgar domestic artifact.

"I don't touch the business" (I, p. 64), Strether points

out, and while Marlow cannot be so fastidious, he too keeps his distance from the eager pursuit of private fortune. Surrounded by great wealth and economic opportunity, neither seeks personal gain, and their own labors have distinctly pre-industrial pedigrees, stretching in the one case back to an heroic naval past and in the other to a tradition of humane letters. At the same time it is evident that they owe their positions to those who pursue profit without such fine scruples. Strether's journal is financed by Woollett's "roaring trade" (I, p. 59), and Marlow, who conceives his journey in a spirit of uncalculating adventure, can only carry it through by hiring himself to that Company for which he professes such contempt.

They are, if you will, members of the *lumpenbourgeoisie* who retreat to the interstices of the community even as they are conditioned by its values. Strether enters the novel with a "New England conscience" but a "double consciousness" (I, p. 5) and Marlow endures the old English version of this self-division. Neither romantic exiles nor revolutionists, the two figures are rather "aliens" in Arnold's sense — of, but not with, the cultures they inhabit. Possessing little authority and no power, they place themselves in the service of others; they are indeed *portable* sensibilities whose essential passivity makes them susceptible to change. James and Conrad are interested in those who can still move within a rigidifying social order, but this interest accompanies a recognition of the weight and inevitability of communal norms.

We may set out the opening problem of the study by bringing together these structural parallels and these thematic analogies in order to ask what relation obtains between individual experience and collective representations. This is the general form of a question that has many particular aspects, but as an initial step we can usefully divide it into two parts. The first concerns the integrity of personal values as set against the integrity of culture; the second concerns the relation of collective forms, especially language, to the form of individual character. These issues must be separated in order to keep their contours distinct, much as James and Conrad must be separated if their *rapprochement* is to be meaningful. I turn first to *Heart*

4

of *Darkness*, then to *The Ambassadors*, then alternate between the two, hoping in this way to establish the harsh lights of contrast by which surprising similarities may be seen.

II

During the trip upriver just before the attack on the steamer, a dense fog settles upon the water, with the result, recalls Marlow, that "What we could see was just the steamer we were on, her outlines blurred as though she had been on the point of dissolving, and a misty strip of water, perhaps two feet broad, around her – and that was all. The rest of the world was nowhere, as far as our eyes and ears were concerned. Just nowhere. Gone, disappeared; swept off without leaving a whisper or a shadow behind."[3] And later, when Marlow remembers his desperate attempt to prevent Kurtz from returning to jungle savagery, he remarks that "There was nothing either above or below him – and I knew it. He had kicked himself loose of the earth. Confound the man! he had kicked the very earth to pieces. He was alone – and I before him did not know whether I stood on the ground or floated in the air" (p. 65).

These two instances signal a condition that persists all through Conrad's work, a radical *disorientation* that obliterates any stable relation between the self and the world, and that raises the question of whether there *is* a world to which the self belongs.[4] The fragility of identity, the barriers to knowledge, the groundlessness of value – these great Conradian (and modern) motifs appear most often in terms of a sensory derangement that casts the individual into unarticulated space, a space with no markers and no boundaries, with nothing behind, nothing above, nothing below.

In the face of this dizzying formlessness, the first word of Conrad's title has been a reassuring spatial index, a signpost directing readers Inward. Whatever ambiguity stirs and confuses the surface of experience, the heart promises a center of meaning (however dark), a psychological source, an inner origin. And in the view of *Heart of Darkness* that has prevailed until recently, the fiction has been regarded as a paradigm, almost a defining instance, of interior narrative. Within this conception Marlow's journey only incidentally involves movement through physical space; in essence it represents a "journey into self," an "introspective plunge," "a night journey into the unconscious."[5] The African terrain is taken as a symbolic geography of the mind, and Kurtz as a suppressed avatar lurking at the core of the self.

Certainly the tale offers abundant metaphoric support for this standard line of interpretation. Marlow is first attracted to the Congo because it stands "dead in the center" (p. 13) of the map; he wonders what lies *behind* the coast and *beneath* the sea. When he arrives in Africa he travels to the Central Station, but it then happens, comically, cryptically, that the center is not near enough to the core. Marlow must travel hundreds of miles farther on until he reaches the Inner Station, where he meets a man whose soul "had looked within itself and . . . had gone mad" (p. 65). Kurtz's own passage into the wilderness is described as a "fantastic invasion" (p. 57) — a phrase that applies equally well to the received way of reading this fiction, according to which selfhood is seen as a central essence, a deep interior, a concealed core that must be penetrated before it will yield its meanings. As a first appraisal of modernist character we may begin with this familiar picture, sketched in the very phrase "heart of darkness," which renders the self as a kind of oblate sphere whose deceptive surface encloses the inwardness which gives the truth of personality.

In the last several years, however, a reaction has set in against the prevailing introspective approach. A number of readers have asked just what Inner Thing lurks at the mysterious center. The heart, after all, is a heart of darkness; Kurtz is "hollow at the core" (p. 58); the Manager suggests that "Men who come out here should have no entrails" (p. 25); and when Marlow listens to the venomous brickmaker it seems to him that "if I tried I could poke my forefinger through him and would find nothing inside but a little loose dirt, maybe" (p. 29). Confronted with images such as these, some critics have begun to argue that *Heart of Darkness* dramatizes no confrontation with an inner truth but only a recognition of the futility of truthseeking.[6]

In an essay called 'Connaissance du Vide" Todorov has

claimed that the tale addresses a problem of interpretation rather than action and that having meditated on the nature of knowledge it concludes that knowledge is unattainable. He emphasizes how little we know about Kurtz, who is eagerly anticipated and vividly remembered but scarcely ever present. Marlow seeks to interpret, to understand, to know Kurtz, but "Que la connaissance soit impossible, que le coeur des ténèbres soit lui-même ténèbreux, le texte tout entier nous le dit." Marlow journeys to the center only to discover that "le centre est vide."[7] Meisel concurs, arguing that *Heart of Darkness* enacts a "crisis in knowledge": "Rather than a psychological work, *Heart of Darkness* is a text that interrogates the epistemological status of the language in which it inheres." The conclusion of that interrogation, the real horror in the tale, is "the impossibility of disclosing a central core, an essence, even a ground to what Kurtz has done and what he is."[8] In this view Conrad's representation of character is the representation of an absence.

The introspectivist identifies the heart as an emotional plenitude; the sceptical epistemologist looks in the same place and finds an emptiness. Both are preoccupied with this one site of meaning, this one region of experience; and while its importance cannot be doubted, more is necessary to account for the intricacy of Conradian characterization. Indeed *Heart of Darkness* draws another diagram of experience that is just as prominent and just as necessary to its interpretation. In the description of Kurtz's final moments Marlow notes that

he had made that last stride, he had stepped over the edge, while I had been permitted to draw back my hesitating foot. And perhaps in this is the whole difference; perhaps all the wisdom, and all truth, and all sincerity, are just compressed into that inappreciable moment of time in which we step over the threshold of the invisible. (p. 69)

Here then is a second way to understand the crux of character: to cast it in terms of the end, the limit, the threshold, the edge, the border. Alongside the figures of penetration and invasion the tale offers these figures of *extension*, a reaching towards some distant point on the limit of experience.

Early in the tale the frame narrator describes the Thames waterway as "leading to the uttermost ends of the earth" (p. 8), and when Marlow begins to speak, he describes the terminus of his journey as "the farthest point of navigation" (p. 11). "I went a little farther," says the Russian, "then still a little farther — till I had gone so far that I don't know how I'll ever get back" (p. 54). Kurtz, who has passed "beyond the bounds of permitted aspirations" (p. 65), understands the consequences "only at the very last" (p. 57). And when Marlow visits the Intended, he hears a whisper "speaking from beyond the threshold of an eternal darkness" (p. 74).

This second imaginative emphasis must be recognized for the distinct alternative it is. Suppose truth does not lie submerged in the deep interior; suppose it stands on the far side of a permanently receding horizon. Suppose that Africa was the "dark continent" not only because it was seen as a mirror of the darkness within but because it was seen as a window to the darkness beyond; and suppose that Kurtz's last words have their extraordinary effect on Marlow because they indicate the scarcely conceivable point that connects the "inside" of life to the "outside" which is death. Such considerations suggest that it is insufficient to look towards the center and to ask whether it is psychologically replete or epistemologically vacuous. Too much in *Heart of Darkness* occurs over the edge, at the last, across the threshold, at "the end — even beyond" (p. 65).

Early in the work, in a much-quoted remark, the frame narrator describes Marlow's peculiar method of narrative.

The yarns of seamen have a direct simplicity, the whole meaning of which lies within the shell of a cracked nut. But Marlow was not typical (if his propensity to spin yarns be excepted), and to him the meaning of an episode was not inside like a kernel but outside, enveloping the tale which brought it out only as a glow brings out a haze, in the likeness of one of these misty halos that sometimes are made visible by the spectral illumination of moonshine. (p. 9)

The representation of meaning as outside, "like a haze," awkwardly overlays the picture of a dark heart beating within the world's body. These conceptions are more than rival metaphors; they give two ways of orienting the ego, two ways of understanding the crux of character. Unlike the images of penetration, the images of extension suggest that the secret of character must be sought at the antipodes; only at the most distant extreme of navigation, on the point of death, in the utterance of one's last words, is the truth of the self disclosed. Center and edge identify decisive moments in individual experience — confrontation with its source or its end, accession to the innermost core or the outermost boundary — and in any description of the modernist temper these two moments must figure prominently. Still they remain in important respects antithetical: what is further from a center than an edge? And in order both to broach the problem of modern character and to illuminate *Heart of Darkness*, it is necessary to ask how such incompatible forms of representation can be accommodated within a single imaginative structure.

In the tale's opening descriptive passage the frame narrator notes the nautical instincts of the Director of Companies and observes that, "It was difficult to realize his work was not *out there* in the luminous estuary, but behind him, *within* the brooding gloom" (p. 7, my emphasis). This conjunction of the two motifs within a single sentence establishes their intimacy, but here, in this first example, the relations between them are perspicuous and undisturbing. "Out there" lies in one direction; "within" lies in the other. All through this prologue London appears as the originating interior, "the biggest, and the greatest, town on earth" (p. 7), a moral source from which emanate "messengers of the might *within* the land, bearers of a spark *from* the sacred land." The narrator invokes the English naval past which he represents as an heroic movement "*from* Deptford, *from* Greenwich, *from* Erith" and "*into* the mystery of an unknown earth" (p. 8, my emphasis).

As soon as Marlow begins to speak, he inverts this stable and heroic relation of "from" and "to." He invokes the memory of a Roman soldier in Britain, "Imagine him here — the very end of the world" (p. 9); and suddenly London, which had been the generating center, becomes the distant frontier.[9] Moreover, the specific formulation of this point is highly disquieting. "Here" always locates a perceptual center, the place one presently occupies, the standpoint from which one looks onto the universe. To speak of "here" as the "end of the world" is to unsettle the categories of perceptual experience, a task at which Marlow excels. Thus he represents the Congo as both the end of the world and the center of the earth; when he arrives in the very heart of darkness he finds himself "on the edge of a black and incomprehensible frenzy" (p. 37); and he claims that it is when Kurtz steps "over the edge" that he is able "to penetrate all the hearts that beat in the darkness" (p. 69). The relationship between center and edge grows obscure, and the distinction between inside and outside unsteady, with Marlow at one point confusing the beating of the native drums with the beating of his heart. The ambiguity culminates in the tale's final image when the narrator entangles his original spatial perception within the figure that he has learned from Marlow: "the tranquil waterway leading to the uttermost ends of the earth flowed sombre under an overcast sky — seemed to lead one into the heart of an immense darkness" (p. 76).

Within the uncanny geography of darkness these two antithetical images fuse into a spatial paradox. A tremendous sensation of movement informs *Heart of Darkness*, a hurtling towards some fateful destination far removed from customary haunts, but what makes the journey so confounding is that movement outward and movement inward coincide. To travel to the end of the earth is to find oneself at the heart, and to occupy the inner core is to stand on the outer edge. Faced with the claim that *Heart of Darkness* represents a journey within, one must respond that it does so only by representing a journey without; the "introspective plunge" only becomes possible in the act of crossing a frontier. Contrary to all logic, the center is on the circumference; the middle is on the periphery; the heart of darkness lies on the border of experience.

It is possible to situate, if not to explain, this paradox, by connecting it to a particular moment in the history of the European mind. One of the unintended consequences of neocolonial expansion at the end of the nineteenth century was the accumulation of anthropological insights. The search for new commodities inadvertently uncovered new cultures. Marlow travels to Africa as part of the new economic imperium, but his own deportment, as James Clifford has pointed out, is closer to the imperialist's ideological cousin, the ethnographer.[10] Marlow looks at the natives "as you would on any human being with a curiosity of their impulses, motives, capacities, weaknesses" (p. 43), and he comes to a perception that contemporary ethnographers were painfully sharing: namely that, faced with those who are called primitive, "what thrilled you was just the thought of their humanity — like yours — the thought of your remote kinship with this wild and passionate uproar" (p. 38).

This recognition suggests another form for our spatial conundrum. In the age of anthropology the European mind can only discover truths about its origins by going outside the physical limits of its culture. It can only learn all that it contains by passing beyond its own boundaries. The doctor who examines Marlow before his departure remarks that "the changes take place inside, you know," and then smiles, "So you are going out there" (p. 11). The cryptic observation epitomizes the relations between edge and center. "Out there" changes occur "inside."

The doctor's odd remark reminds us of the often uncomfortable intimacy between anthropology and psychoanalysis, two modern disciplines that matured together and that frequently have trespassed on one another's domain. The anthropologist travels to the farthest point of navigation only to discover home truths that the psyche had not recognized for itself. The psychoanalyst presses to the deepest reaches of the self only to find the stranger whom the anthropologist is seeking abroad. The experience of the individual in *Heart of Darkness*, Marlow's experience, follows the nervous course of this intimacy: a transcendence of the self that ends in immanence, a self-encounter that culminates in confrontation with the Other.

In a visionary moment Marlow acknowledges that "The mind of man is capable of anything — because everything is in it, all the past as well as all the future" (p. 38) — a remark that should be set against the Russian's repeated assertion that Kurtz has "enlarged [his] mind." The conjunction of these two pregnant observations gives rise to an awkward question: If the mind of man has everything in it, how can it be enlarged? Here is another form, an explicitly psychological form, of the dance between inner and outer in *Heart of Darkness*. Marlow, one might say, exceeds the boundaries of his mind only to discover that there is no novelty in psychic life; there is only renewed acquaintance with permanent possibility. The mind enlarges until it is wide enough to contain what it always has.

The phrase "heart of darkness" itself suggests this double extremity. Turn the phrase one way, and the "of" is the compositional "of," identifying the metaphoric stuff that makes up this awful heart — "heart of darkness," then, as in "heart of stone" or "heart of gold." Turn the phrase another way, and the accent falls on "darkness" rather than "heart," and the "of" is a spatial index: Where is the darkness? — here at the heart. In the changes that Conrad works on his central phrase he wrests both implications from the metaphor and turns them to their separate purposes. An expression such as "the darkness of its heart" emphasizes the monstrous substance of which this heart is made; alternatively, an expression like "the heart of an immense darkness" marks out a particular place within this murky expanse. Notice that in one case the danger appears as a dark interior, a black point in the center of experience, while in the other it is an enveloping field, a dark immensity surrounding those at the center. Marlow moves between these distinct but equally charged perceptions: a horror at what we enclose, a terror at what encloses us.

The meeting of these two horrors, the *inseparability* of these two terrors, engenders the metaphoric alchemy that I have been describing and that one might call, in a necessarily clumsy phrase, "the beyond within." What stands beyond the threshold lies within the heart. Little wonder, then, that subjectivity is so elusive in Conrad and little surprise that the attempt to render this paradoxical state leads to such strains in literary form. If character can no longer be defined through a disjunction between inside and outside, if what is most distant is also most intimate, if what occurs on the fringes of human community resides in every mind, then there can be no discontinuity between the condition of others and the condition of the self.

Perhaps the most significant formal consequence is the most

conspicuous: the division of attention between Kurtz and Marlow. Later in this study more will have to be said about the two protagonist structure in modernist fiction; here it only needs to be noted that in *Heart of Darkness* (as in *Lord Jim*) the vision of the periphery in the heart, the limit at the middle, suggests that the only way to represent the individual mind is to represent two individual minds.

"It is not my own extremity I remember best," says Marlow, "No. It is his extremity that I seem to have lived through." This sentiment contains all the charged ambiguity of the beyond within. Inside oneself is another's extreme. And Marlow immediately goes on to acknowledge that Kurtz "had made that last stride, he had stepped over the edge, while I had been permitted to draw back my hesitating foot" (p. 69). One foot strides over the edge; one draws back. *Heart of Darkness* requires two such different feet in order to make one imaginary body. It requires two protagonists – one to speak from beyond the threshold, the other to feel a quickening within the core.

III

Although they occupy similar places within the pattern of journey, quest and reversal, the savage Mr Kurtz and the refined Chad Newsome could never be mistaken for one another, and the distance between them marks out the expanse we must now cross. Kurtz, who set out to "climb to the top" (p. 33), will later seem to be "lying at the bottom of a precipice where the sun never shines" (p. 68). Somewhere in this long fall he must have passed Chad who was rapidly ascending from his former vulgarity to the dizzying elevation of a Parisian gentleman. The contrast in moral trajectory corresponds to the distinct geographies of the two works, the movement in *The Ambassadors* from America to Europe and in *Heart of Darkness* from Europe to Africa. The common term is Europe, but in one case it is a destination and in the other a point of departure, in one the site of the civilized mind, in the other the veneer over primitive emotions.

Our initial concern being to orient modern literary character within the forms of fictional experience, and our first subject being the "beyond within," the late novels of James pose a sharp challenge. The standard charge against these works, less troubling in recent years not so much because it has been answered as because it has been ignored, is that the Jamesian domain reaches no extremes, either beyond or within, but folds upon itself, closed against the world. H. G. Wells put this criticism in its most uncompromising and colorful form, complaining that James

sets himself to pick the straws out of the hair of Life before he paints her. But without the straws she is no longer the mad woman we love ... These people cleared for artistic treatment never make a lusty love, never go to angry war, never shout at an election or perspire at poker.[11]

The ascendancy of Jamesian over Wellsian values has prevented such a perception from receiving the attention it deserves. But the question of literary domain, and in particular the pressure towards an imaginative narrowing, is central to the problematics of modern narrative.

Where is the body in *The Ambassadors*? Where is the material world? These are almost rude questions given the unfailing civility of the novel, but it may be the inexorable civility that tempts one to rudeness, until even the most sympathetic reader of late James is liable to echo Waymarsh's blunt imperative, "Look here ... quit this" (I, p. 109). One does not find many objects in the novel, and the objects that one finds are most often *objets* — relics, medallions, miniatures, books, pictures — composing the great "empire of 'things' " (I, p. 119). These artifacts dwell within larger artifacts: drawing-rooms, studios, theaters, churches. On the single notable occasion when the natural world enters the novel, Strether's ramble in the French countryside, he pictures himself, as every reader remembers, within "the oblong gilt frame" of a landscape by Lambinet, which disposes its lines and brings the trees, reeds, and rivers "into a composition" (II, p. 247). Not for James to imagine the earth "monstrous and free" (*Heart of Darkness*, p. 37); here there is no wilderness, no confrontation between the human body and the physical world; nature is framed, composed, aestheticized.

What is true of nature is *a fortiori* true of human nature — this is the substance of Wells's complaint, that Jamesian

14

character is as attenuated as the world it moves through. A good place to begin meeting this issue is a dialogue between Strether and Maria Gostrey that occurs near the end of book seven. Strether has just declared that the "work" of his rediscovered "youth" is to "see [him] through" — to which Maria responds,

"But through what?" — she liked to get it all out of him.
"Why through this experience." That was all that would come.
It regularly gave her none the less the last word. "Don't you remember how in those first days of our meeting it was I who was to see you through?"
"Remember? Tenderly, deeply" — he always rose to it. "You're just doing your part in letting me maunder to you thus."
"Ah don't speak as if my part were small; since whatever else fails you — "
"*You* won't, ever, ever, ever?' — he thus took her up. "Oh I beg your pardon; you necessarily, you inevitably *will*. Your conditions — that's what I mean = won't allow me anything to do for you."
"Let alone — I see what you mean — that I'm drearily dreadfully old. I *am*, but there's a service — possible for you to render — that I know, all the same, I shall think of."
"And what will it be?"
This, in fine, however, she would never tell him.
"You shall hear only if your smash takes place. As that's really out of the question, I won't expose myself" — a point at which, for reasons of his own, Strether ceased to press. (II, pp. 51–2)

It is almost a love scene and bears the usual marks of emotional heightening in James's later fiction, the intensifying adverbs ("tenderly," "deeply," "drearily dreadfully"); the pointed emphasis of personal pronouns and the verb "to be" ("*I*," "*You*," "*will*," "*am*"), the self-consciously sentimental repetition ("ever, ever, ever").[12] The passage intimates rigorous unstated conventions, a chivalric code of the drawing-room that allows the characters to speak in elliptical suggestions, periphrasis on periphrasis, catching at one another's hints, finishing one another's sentences. And yet the implication of perfect intimacy is offset by the high generality of the diction: "this experience," "my part," "your conditions," "a service." Moreover, as is typical in such exchanges, the mutual transparency becomes abruptly clouded, and the conversation ends in a familiar Jamesian abyss. In short, the scene creates a distinctive combination of intimacy and distance, the product of an elaborate rhetoric that seems to mark the characters as immaterial conversationalists without physical needs and desires, indeed, without bodies.

However, one other aspect of the scene should be noted. For while the verbal exchanges undoubtedly predominate, James offers some modest but significant stage directions. First we learn that although "she liked to get it all out of him," his terse answer is "all that would come." In the context of this super-sensuous dialogue, here is a comparatively concrete image of extraction or absorption, even (one shudders to say it, but someone must) an image of sexual voracity. Moreover, after Maria's next response we read that Strether "rose to it" − not, of course, that he gets to his feet; he only rises conversationally. But then in the following exchange the figure amplifies − he "took her up" − and indeed through the mist of conversation one can almost see him making the bold physical gesture, rising to it and taking her up. Finally in the last exchange, after Maria has chosen not to "expose" herself, Strether, as though at the end of a passionate embrace, "ceased to press."

Beneath the incessant chatter of these garrulous friends there appear, then, not bodily movements but bodily metaphors. It would be melodramatic to claim that they provide the suppressed truth of an elusive scene, but neither are they mere idle ornament. Rather, they are the shadows which the physical world casts upon the smooth plane of polite discourse, and all through *The Ambassadors* these shadows pass. An incorporeal emotion sows a material image, and the image buds and blooms. Life is a train; freedom is a ticking clock; consciousness is a helpless jelly; youth is a waving of wings. John Paterson has aptly pointed to the many violent images that recur throughout the novel and that create what he calls "the language of adventure."[13] But these represent only a special, though important, instance of the more general phenomenon: the construal of highly abstract human relations in terms of concrete physical activity. In one extravagant eruption of wilfully mixed metaphor, Strether reflects that to explain a personal relation was to live by the sweat of one's brow, and "the sweat of one's brow was just what one might buy one's self off from by keeping the ground free of the wild weed of

16

delusion. It easily grew too fast, and the Atlantic cable now alone could race with it" (I, p. 141). The realm of matter of-fers a running commentary on the affairs of mind; consistently the bodily world is neglected, suppressed, tamed or conceal-ed, only to reappear in metaphor; indeed it is remarkable how strenuously the novel avoids matter and how robust is its metaphoric return.

Before attempting to draw consequences from this fact, we should consider another series of figures.

"I've been sacrificing so to strange gods that I feel I want to put on record, somehow, my fidelity – fundamentally unchanged after all – to our own. I feel as if my hands were embrued with the blood of monstrous alien altars – of another faith altogether." (II, pp. 167–8)

"I moved among miracles. It was all phantasmagoric." (II, p. 301)

Still he could always speak for the woman he had so definitely promised to "save." This wasn't quite for her the air of salvation; but . . . (II, p. 204)

The spiritual life lies even more heavily upon the novel's metaphors than does the material world, and Strether's drama is consistently interpreted in terms of mystery, miracle, apostasy and faith, the losing and finding of souls.[14] To the language of adventure we must surely add the language of salva-tion; indeed perhaps the central question of the novel is: Who will save whom? Strether himself sets out to save Chad but then finds himself using "the exorbitant word" with Madame de Vionnet, "I'll save you if I can" (I, p. 255). Elsewhere Waymarsh gives Strether a deep look that "fairly sounded out – 'to save you, poor old man, to save you; to save you in spite of yourself'" (II, p. 103). Mamie Pocock had hoped to preside over Chad's salvation, but she is "too late for the miracle" (II, p. 172); as Strether points out, Marie de Vionnet has already "saved him." "I thought that was what *you* were to do," says Bilham. "I'm speaking," explains Strether, "of his manners and morals, his character and life. I'm speaking of him as a person to deal with and talk with and live with – speaking of him as a social animal" (I, p. 283).

This last remark not only celebrates Madame de Vionnet's achievement; it tersely recalls a familiar description of James's fictional domain: the manners and morals of the social animal.

This, one is tempted to say, is what the metaphors qualify, what they aim at, what gives them their point. But such an opinion is in important ways highly misleading. The great provocation of James's late work lies in its disrespect for the boundary between literal assertion and metaphoric figure, its mischievous teasing of the line that tries to separate them.

In conversation with Waymarsh, Strether describes his first visit to Chad's handsome apartment; "I stayed, I dawdled, I trifled; above all I looked round. I saw, in fine; and − I don't know what to call it − I sniffed" (I, p. 105). "Do you mean a smell?" asks Waymarsh. He is not wrong to ask; the metaphors can, and often do, accommodate a comfortably literal interpretation. Frequently, in fact, an image born as a metaphor goes on to lead a literal life. Having reflected that Chad's alteration is "marked enough to be touched by the finger," Strether in the next sentence "put his hand across the table and laid it on Chad's arm" (I, p. 152). One of the novel's recurrent images depicts characters at sea in small craft, a conceit that is abruptly literalized at the climactic moment when Chad and Madame de Vionnet row towards Strether and disclose the truth of their intimacy.[15] In the dialogue quoted earlier Strether metaphorically "rose to it," "took [Maria] up" and "ceased to press" − predicates that need not have been only metaphorical in this emotionally charged relationship. Indeed, in other exchanges, Strether takes a literal first step; he develops the habit of rising from his chair during conversation and pacing as they talk.

A measure of James's radicalism is shown in his willingness to carry this movement through, to let the imaginative figures entirely displace the literal assertion. "Do you mean a smell?" is just the sort of question which readers find themselves asking − but with no more hope of an answer than the exasperated Waymarsh. Regularly, the turnings of plot, the motives of character, the meanings of event, receive a metaphoric characterization which is not dependent on, derived from, associated with, or referable to, any independent nonmetaphoric judgment; which is often the *only* form of representation which the fiction offers. The image of salvation does not substitute for some more direct utterance, some more forthright expression which a fastidious James refuses to offer. It is the unique characterization of an elusive relationship; it does not qualify, so much as it invents, the experience it describes.

The life of the social animal thus assimilates experience whose origin lies within other realms. In the midst of exacting refinements in the drawing-room, the bodily image ascends from below and the spiritual image descends from above, investing manners and morals with an aspect they could not otherwise possess. Occasionally the figures meet in a single image, as in Waymarsh's "sacred rage" or in Strether's appeal to Maria after his first meeting with Chad: "He repeatedly knocked at her door to let her have it afresh that Chad's case . . . was first and foremost a miracle almost monstrous" (I, p. 167). And in a finely comic, though deeply serious, conceit we read that when Strether has to "swallow" the intimacy between Chad and Madame de Vionnet, their deception "disagreed with his spiritual stomach" (II, p. 265). Spirit and stomach collide on the plane of manners, transforming it into a highly variegated expanse. The attenuation of the material world, the remoteness of a spiritual world, do not prevent matter and spirit from defining the social animal. James does not imply that moral experience *is* spiritual or physical; he is offering neither a naturalist reduction nor a theological deduction. But his method displays the conviction that there are subtleties of feeling for which we have no language but the language of physical extremity or spiritual crisis.[16]

Moreover, within the expansive domain of metaphor James's Europe discloses further surprising continuities with Conrad's Africa. In the midst of Gloriani's garden party – elegant, subdued, civilized – Strether feels something "covertly tigerish, which came to him across the lawn and in the charming air as a waft from the jungle." Gloriani himself appears as a "glossy male tiger" (I, p. 219), while Miss Barrace paints the American Bilham in the image of a failed missionary: "You come over to convert the savages . . . and the savages simply convert *you*." "Not even," replies Bilham, "They've simply – the cannibals! – eaten me; converted me if you like, but converted me into food. I'm but the bleached bones of a Christian" (I, p. 205).

If we only see irony in these metaphors, we miss the way they establish the terms of emotional response and give content to otherwise impalpable social relations. Strether finds violence beneath Parisian civility; he finds "the fierce, the sinister, the acute" (II, p. 271); he even finds, again metaphorically, an example of human sacrifice – young Jeanne de Vionnet immolated on the altar of an arranged marriage, while her mother remains "exquisitely remorseless" and Strether recoils in "sensible shock." Through the reach of Jamesian metaphor Madame de Vionnet's *"vieille sagesse"* – "something ancient and cold" (II, pp. 128–30) – can be as deep, as harsh, as primitive, as that other form of *vieille sagesse* that Marlow discovers in the Congo. And if someone should say that reliance on images and conceits makes James's vision of extremity "unreal," we need to ask why the imaginary perspiration of Conrad's characters has a greater purchase on reality than the imaginary metaphorical perspiration of characters in James.

At issue is a distinctive notion of the relations between language and experience, an idea that dates from early in James's career and that is given pointed expression in an essay of 1865. Reviewing Harriet Prescott's *Azarian* James attacked the author's verbal license, her fondness for inventing new words and combining old ones to make exotic phrases.

If the dictionary were a palette of colors, and a goose-quill a brush, Miss Prescott would be a very clever painter. But as words possess a certain inherent dignity, value, and independence, language being rather the stamped and authorized coinage which expresses the value of thought than the brute metal out of which forms are moulded, her pictures are invariably incoherent and meaningless.[17]

An instructive oddity informs this definition of language: "value" stands on both sides of the identity. Words possess an "inherent" value, but this is only because language "expresses the value of thought." The formulation, strained as it is, summarizes James's attachment both to the priority of human thought and to the independence of linguistic forms: both are "valuable." The complex metaphor registers this taut dualism – words are "the stamped and authorized coinage" of thought. Humanity, that is, endows its language with value; but once this procreative act has occurred, then, like the system of currency to which James compares it, language becomes an independent system of meaning, with values "inherent" as well as "authorized." Although its origin and its sanction lie in the human mind, it resists any attempt to make it serve private expressive whim.

Language is the most human and least individual of artifacts, yielding its secrets not to those who coerce it, only to those who submit to it. It does not register the history of individuals; it registers the history of a community; and the particular soul can only express itself through a surrender to this collective form. Words cannot be cast into any shape, as though they were raw materials (like paint or metal) susceptible to personal stylistic will; language cannot be turned to just any formal purposes because its forms have already been assigned. Another passage from the review of *Azarian* makes the point eloquently.

If Miss Prescott would only take such good old English words as we possess, words instinct with the meaning of centuries, and, having fully resolved upon that which she wished to convey, cast her intention in those familiar terms which long use has invested with almost absolute force of expression, then she would describe things in a manner which could not fail to arouse the sympathy, the interest, the dormant memories of the reader.[18]

For James linguistic nuance is no rarefied verbalism distinct from human experience; experience inheres in language; words embody the history of action − in his fine phrase they are "instinct with the meaning of centuries." Furthermore, they can restore that record, because to retrieve a verbal distinction is to recover a cultural memory. And in this general thought about language we have a key to Jamesian metaphor.

Most often, James's metaphors have nothing intrinsically figural about them. They do not defy common understanding ("mute cry"), do not depict physical anomalies ("heart of darkness"), do not test the boundaries of our concepts ("unruly sun"). The force of the images lies in their proximity to literal utterance; they suggest how what we call metaphor may come to be called truth. Swimming, sweating, chasing trains, incurring debts, yearning for salvation − unlike a "mute cry," such activities have many familiar non-metaphoric contexts which continue to echo in their metaphoric use. Indeed the metaphors frequently have the tone of quotations drawn from other texts, and as if to enforce this point, James occasionally places single quotation marks around a phrase in tacit acknowledgment of its source: "his coming out, all solemnly appointed and deputed to 'save' Chad" (I, p. xvi). The most important figures in *The Ambassadors* have their origins in literal assertions from other modes and genres. The violent images which Paterson collected – a runaway car, a shipwreck, a tiger, a woman buried alive, a pirate's cove – derive from an adventure genre in which they would have been put to sensationally literal purposes. Similarly, the spiritual conceits – miracle, salvation, sacrifice – descend from a devoutly serious religious discourse. In these and so many other instances, James looks for metaphor not in what may be imaginable, but in what has been actual, what people have done, have believed, have written.

Novelty, it is commonly said, is the great virtue of metaphor. Certainly when Shakespeare's Antony describes Caesar's blood as "rushing out of doors" or when Eliot's Prufrock sees the yellow fog rubbing its back upon the windowpanes, they are drawing new contours for experience. James's metaphors, however, serve tradition before novelty; within the intangible web of social relations they preserve a human past which lies far from the drawing room. And if James's characters often seem estranged from a tradition of human activity, the metaphors hold a place for history, in both its most exotic and its most banal forms. They awaken "dormant memories," memories of the forgotten heroism, the archaic belief, the anachronistic gesture, the verbal cliché, and in this way they revive a waning tradition.

In a luminous observation made early in *The Ambassadors* James writes that a man such as Strether "might have . . . an amount of experience out of any proportion to his adventures" (I, p. 227). This may be taken as almost a statement of literary program, a definition of the Jamesian method of characterization, whose aim is precisely to convert meager adventure into gorgeous experience. The constraints on his characters – the cramped social space, the narrow psychological domain, the limits of decorum – are not final or irrevocable; they are

22

merely incitements to the recovery of experience; and the chief device in that recovery is metaphor. The *disproportion* between experience and adventure is the disproportion of a metaphoric perception which restores to the imaginative realm those possibilities that have been lost in the realm of fact.

When Strether realizes that Madame de Vionnet places all her hopes in him, he decides that since "she took him for a firm object . . . he would do his best to *be* one" (II, p. 11). This response belongs to a standard pattern: throughout the novel characters attempt to be what they are taken for, to make their metaphors literal, to *live up* to acts of imagination. Perhaps the most intricate and remarkable example occurs in a passage from book twelve, in which Strether visits Madame de Vionnet after their climactic encounter in the countryside.

> With this sharpest perception yet, it was like a chill in the air to him, it was almost appalling, that a creature so fine could be, by mysterious forces, a creature so exploited. For at the end of all things they *were* mysterious: she had but made Chad what he was — so why could she think she had made him infinite? She had made him better, she had made him best, she had made him anything one would; but it came to our friend with supreme queerness that he was none the less only Chad. Strether had the sense that *he*, a little, had made him too; his high appreciation had, as it were, consecrated her work. The work, however admirable, was nevertheless of the strict human order, and in short it was marvellous that the companion of mere earthly joys, of comforts, aberrations (however one classed them) within the common experience, should be so transcendently prized. It might have made Strether hot or shy, as such secrets of others brought home sometimes do make us; but he was held there by something so hard that it was fairly grim. This was not the discomposure of last night; that had quite passed — such discomposures were a detail; the real coercion was to see a man ineffably adored. There it was again — it took women; it took women; if to deal with them was to walk on water what wonder that the water rose? And it had never surely risen higher than around this woman. He presently found himself taking a long look from her, and the next thing he knew he had uttered all his thought. "You're afraid for your life!"
>
> (II, pp. 284–5)

The passage concludes with another dizzying convergence of spirit and matter upon the unquiet realm of manners. To deal with women is to walk on water; here is another miracle; but then that miraculous water begins to rise like any profane fluid and threatens to drown Madame de Vionnet in her own drawing-room. When Strether finally speaks, his remark

— "You're afraid for your life" — places the agony of romantic love in the context of physical pain and spiritual desolation. But what gives special point to this climax, and what lends the passage its great interest, is a recognition that occurs earlier within it. Chad, acknowledges Strether, is only Chad; and this is a recognition of some consequence. It had after all been his conviction that Chad was no longer Chad, that he had suffered the "sharp rupture of identity" (I, p. 137) and had become "an absolutely *new* quantity" (I, p. 150). Now Strether understands the limits of transformation, indeed the limits of value: "better" and "best" are possible, but "infinite" is not. Chad is again a "mere earthly" companion who belongs to "common experience" and who remains, despite all, within the "strict human order."

Yet a mystery remains, (something "appalling," something "marvellous"); it is not (any longer) that Chad appears transcendent but that he is "transcendently prized." Here we should think again of Kurtz. Like Kurtz before the Africans, Chad is granted the "might as of a deity" (*Heart of Darkness*, p. 50), and Madame de Vionnet in her suffering is perhaps closer to the "barbarous and superb" (p. 67) native woman than to the guileless Intended. In both Kurtz's African passion and Chad's discreet Parisian license, spirituality and sexuality come into powerful conjunction. But Chad, we might say, is a false Kurtz. His deathless passion, his paganism, the "rupture" of his identity, are imaginary, and by the end of the novel an essential vulgarity has crept back into his temperament.

For James, though, the interest lies precisely in the imaginary, not the real, change, and hence he directs his attention to the adorer rather than to the false god. Madame de Vionnet is neither deceived nor blinded with devotion. Because she has caused whatever change has occurred in Chad, she knows its origins and its limits — and still she worships what she has made. She loves a living metaphor, her own metaphor, by which she is nonetheless subdued. She adores her earthly companion as though he were divine and ignores the bitter terrestrial truth, that Chad is, literally, only Chad. But this is not mere illusion. Who can doubt, certainly not Strether, that

24

her trope expresses the force of her emotions? What makes her case so illuminating is that it shows how "common experience" can beget the perception of transcendence — how transcendence, if you will, is immanent. Madame de Vionnet thus discloses the furthest reach of Jamesian metaphor. Through metaphor the emotions are nourished by a tradition of experience written into our language and therefore into the structure of our feelings.[19] The sentiment of religious belief persists even when belief is gone; Chad may only be metaphorically transcendent, but the image gives the truth of Madame de Vionnet's response. Indeed this is the fateful implication of metaphoric perception in James: in creating figures for common experience, the imagination must endure what it has made.

Metaphor is thus the surprising source of James's own Transcendentalism, which originates not in the Emersonian soul but in the worldly experience of the social animal. Emerson asked what difference it would make if "Orion is up there in heaven, or some god paints the image in the firmament of the soul?"[20] James raises another, but no less Emersonian, question. He asks in effect what difference it makes whether Chad is infinite or infinitely adored. This is the "queerness" of manners and morals, that although they are rigorously circumscribed within the "strict human order," they contain all the possibilities which language can register. Chad can be transcendently prized, because language preserves the concept of transcendence. By pursuing this thought, James engenders extravagant imaginative possibilities from within the confines of common experience, much as Madame de Vionnet engenders an infinite Chad. In neither case is it a "real" transcendence, but from the standpoint of the emotions "as if" has the force of "as."

The phrase, the "strict human order," may be taken as one expression of the realist commitment, and for James language is of all human activities the most strict and most orderly. But it is also the transcendental ground. It is what allows the plane of manners to become a region of sacred rages, spiritual stomachs, and doors slamming upon miracles. There often seems to be a startled recognition in James, which he transmits

25

to the startled reader, of the astonishing heterogeneity of our discourse. It is, after all, a fact of some note, which we should not accept as casually as we do, that one language, one grammar, can accommodate such a miscellaneous nomenclature as the one we possess — that objects, sentiments, ideas which belong to such distinct categories of thought can be placed within the narrow confines of a single sentence. We should not take it for granted that spirit and stomach can rest side by side within a metaphor. Language is that human instrument which contains within it signs of the extra-human. Whether or not one sustains religious faith, and however remote one feels from the violent surge of the physical world, these experiences leave their traces in our speech and therefore in our lives. To possess the word "miracle" is not of course to possess the thing, but it is to retain the idea, which in James is prodded, nudged, urged and encouraged, until it yields the emotion.

IV

"Nothing is more easy," writes James in his preface, "than to state the subject of 'The Ambassadors' " (I, p. v), but in fact nothing is harder. *The Ambassadors* is a novel whose every detail can be registered and which can still leave the reader wondering, "What is it finally about?" This is not a question about the plot but about how to engage with the plot. The earliest notebook entry on the novel identifies the protagonist as a man who hasn't "lived" — "in the sense of sensations, passions, impulses, pleasures" — and then struggles to give content to this vague conception. "He has been a great worker," decides James, "a local worker. But of what kind?" Various possibilities present themselves: clergyman, journalist, lawyer, doctor, artist, and finally, editor of a magazine. Notably and characteristically, he begins with the genus and then derives a species. A local worker who hasn't lived — this is the wide class that interests him, and the choice of an item within that class appears almost a matter of indifference: "He may be an American — he might be an Englishman,"[21] with James settling on the former, "of sufficiently typical New England origin."[22]

26

"Sufficiently typical" is a standard requirement in James's late phase in which no imaginative reflex is more marked than the desire to be free of the contingent particularities of a fictional subject. In later reflections upon *Roderick Hudson* James regrets his decision to identify Northampton as the initial setting of that novel, attributing this misstep to the influence of Balzac: "I 'named' under his contagion" – with the result that the novel represented a "particular local case" when it required only "a peaceful, rural New England community *quelconque*."[23] He returns to the subject in recalling his decision to set *The Ambassadors* in Paris, calling the city a "mere symbol for more things than had been dreamt of in the philosophy of Woollett," and adding that "Another surrounding scene would have done as well" if it could have precipitated Strether's crisis (I, p. xiv). Particulars, at least some particulars, are interchangeable, and for James it is a matter of high aesthetic principle to ascend staunchly from a thing to its kind. What he writes of Strether might easily pass as self-description: "However he viewed his job it was 'types' he should have to tackle" (I, p. 53).

The great provocation of James's late work is its refusal of what one may call the novelistic norm of descriptive specificity – a norm of descriptive precision, which takes as its foundation material things of medium scale, in J. L. Austin's phrase "moderate-sized specimens of dry goods."[24] James is blandly indifferent to these dry goods, these concrete objects, these particular local cases which populate the fiction of the nineteenth century. Certainly one of his oddest gifts is his ability to imagine drama at any level of typification, and this is what makes it so difficult "to state the subject of the *The Ambassadors*." Who, after all, is Strether? That he is an editor from Woollett, Mass. describes but does not define him. That he has a "New England conscience" gives him a dramatically relevant trait and sets the plot in motion, but to stop at this level of generality is still to stop too soon, sooner at least than James himself. That he is a "man of imagination" allows him to raise those portentous questions – "life," "freedom," "goodness," "beauty" – which exceed the boundaries of a regional morality. And that he has a state of mind which "might have

27

been figured by a clear green liquid," which "had begun to turn from green to red, or whatever, and might, for all he knew, be on its way to purple, to black, to yellow" (I, p. xii) – this image places him in the broadest of categories: the set of things that change.

James not only assigns his individuals to types; he sorts his types and classifies his sorts, achieving at times such a high level of abstraction that characters and events melt into concepts and forms. Anticipating how Strether's difficulties in Paris will be presented, he writes, "Well, he finds himself sinking, as I say, up to his middle in the Difference – difference from what he expected, difference in Chad, difference in everything; and the Difference, I also again say, is what I give."[25] James blithely prescinds from differences to Difference: Strether expected one thing, now he finds another. Remarkably, James can derive lively emotions from a thought so abstract, and more remarkably he can inspire lively emotions in us (in me). One can also imagine him saying of Strether what he said of Paris, that his hero is a mere symbol and that another entity, another organism, would have done as well if it could only have shown the Difference.

Part of what makes the late Jamesian project so daunting is that despite the abstract generality of the verbal forms, the drama turns on the concrete singularities of human response. James may be indifferent to the particular local case, the accidents of geography or physique, but he remains devoted to the resonant instant of perception, the unparaphrasable specificity of certain privileged moments, and perhaps his most urgent stylistic task is to find some accommodation between the immaterial type and the lived experience.

In the preface to *The Spoils of Poynton* James speaks of "a vivid enough little example, in the concrete, of the general truth,"[26] and in *The Ambassadors* Strether marvels at women of "highly developed type in particular" (I, p. 273) – two remarks that establish the issue before us, the transaction between the encompassing forms of experience and its individual precipitates.

Not long after completing *The Ambassadors* James wrote to Hugh Walpole that "the whole thing" is "a picture of relations."[27] Indeed the reader learns early that Strether "had wanted to put himself in relation, and he would be hanged if he were *not* in relation"(I, p. 93), and learns later that Madame de Vionnet makes "a relation of mere recognition" (I, p. 252), while Maria Gostrey offers "the essential freshness of a relation so simple" it was "a cool bath to the soreness produced by other relations" (II, p. 292). This prominent Jamesian term is clearly another expression of the desire to avoid the contingencies of experience; "relation," as it stands, bestows no content on any human tie; it escapes the definition of love, envy, respect or loathing, and allows James to arrange his characters as though they were colors and masses in a pictorial composition. The phrase, "picture of relations," after all, might have been used by Kandinsky to describe an experiment in abstract painting. And yet — this is the complexity — "relation" in James's work always names a special, if indefinable, tie, a tie so concrete it resists any further description. "A personal relation," reflects Strether, "was a relation only so long as people perfectly understood or, better still, didn't care if they didn't" (I, p. 141). It is not something in general; it is something very much in particular, but something that appears persistently, paradoxically, as an instance of a type.

When Strether refuses to name the vulgar commodity manufactured at Woollett and Maria Gostrey begins to "treat the little nameless object as indeed unnameable" (I, p. 61), they perform the movement that James himself had perfected, from the thing (the object) to its kind (unnameable). What makes this gesture so charged is that everything depends on the material specificity of the object: "above all," points out Strether, "it's a thing. The article produced" (I, p. 60). Like a spoil at Poynton it must be a "thing," a determinate object, a concrete article with concrete attributes. If it were amorphous or vague, it could scarcely arouse such uncomfortable emotions: one cannot be embarrassed by a thing in general. But by refusing to identify it — ingeniously, perversely — James places it within that bewildering category on which he so often relies, the abstract class of highly concrete entities. This is the uncanny effect in his use of such terms as "thing" and "relation;" they are those *general* concepts which are made to denote the most *individual* phenomena; they are typical singularities and generic particulars.

Accordingly, to call James's style abstract or general is not yet to state the difficulty. The difficulty is that the style is abstract when the subject is concrete, and it is general when particularity is most in question – as in Strether's description of the economic opportunity awaiting Chad in Woollett.

He'll come in for a particular chance – a chance that any properly constituted young man would jump at. The business has so developed that an opening scarcely apparent three years ago, but which his father's will took account of as in certain conditions possible and which, under that will, attaches to Chad's availing himself of it a large contingent advantage – this opening, the conditions having come about, now simply awaits him . . . That's what I mean by his chance. (I, p. 70)

One fairly wants to scream, "Is *that* what you mean by his *particular* chance? What condition? What opening? What advantage?" – to which James would no doubt respond, "*a* chance, *a* condition, *an* opening." And surely to esteem James's accomplishment is to esteem the merit of that response. It is not a matter of avoiding experience but of choosing a plane on which to describe it. A "condition" is certainly more abstract than a piece of Balzac's grease-stained wallpaper, but it is no less pertinent to the workings of our world.

Earlier an analogy was proposed between Jamesian metaphor and Emerson's Transcendentalism. Here another analogy may be drawn to transcendental philosophy, but this time to its more austere formulation in Kant – specifically to the system of categories described in the so-called "metaphysical deduction." The high Kantian ambition was to determine the underlying concepts of every possible judgment and every possible perception. Whatever empirical variations may occur, these fundamental categories (twelve in the original enumeration) govern the structure of experience: "the categories are conditions of the possibility of experience, and are therefore valid *a priori* for all objects of experience."[28] Jamesian typification can also be seen as an attempt to establish the conditions of possible experience – not within the metaphysical region in which Kant worked but within the confines of distinctly social experience. It is an attempt to think past the inessential features of a situation in order to discover certain deep social features, such as the opening, the advantage, the condition, and the chance that lie behind the idea of any economic opportunity *quelconque*. "Thing," "relation," "difference," "case," "type" — such terms (among many others) reflect a desire to escape the accidents of social life and to identify basic concepts that underlie the diversity of manners and morals. It is not that James aspired to a system of fundamental categories; he owed no allegiance to any ultimate metaphysical generality; he pursued types without a fixed typology. But this fact should not obscure the ambition in James's project that is as rigorous in its way as Kant's: the endeavor to assume a standpoint abstract enough to avoid contingency and general enough to organize the world's variety.

The will to typify, to classify and to categorize obviously places great strain on the autonomy of the individual, a strain that becomes most visible when it involves those characters who interest James alternately as embodiments of a type and as thoroughly atypical individuals. It is often unclear in James — as it is, indeed, in the long novelistic tradition — whether it is a higher value to be the luminous representative of a general possibility or to be a possibility wholly *sui generis*. To choose the former is to risk losing the individual within the class, and to choose the latter is to risk making the individual merely prodigious or merely curious. In *The Ambassadors* the issue is harshly defined during Strether's final conversation with Madame de Vionnet, when he at last understands her passion for Chad. As she breaks into tears, he realizes that his own commitment to her is irrevocable, "quite as if what he thought of her had nothing to do with it."

It was actually moreover as if he didn't think of her at all, as if he could think of nothing but the passion, mature, abysmal, pitiful, she represented, and the possibilities she betrayed. She was older for him to-night, visibly less exempt from the touch of time; but she was as much as ever the finest and subtlest creature, the happiest apparition, it had been given him, in all his years, to meet; and yet he could see her there as vulgarly troubled, in very truth, as a maidservant crying for her young man. The only thing was that she judged herself as the maid-servant wouldn't; the weakness of which wisdom too, the dishonour of which judgment, seemed but to sink her lower. (II, p. 286)

Anticipating his scene, James had written that Madame de Vionnet's "passion simplifies and abases her; ranges her in a category,"[29] and thus in the first sentence of the passage Strether ceases to "think of her at all," noticing only the "passion . . . she represented and the possibilities she betrayed." This is perhaps the gravest instance of the stylistic habit we have been considering: the oddly intimate link between the collective noun and the singular emotional term. At a moment of intensely private feeling Madame de Vionnet is "ranged in a category" according to that severe Jamesian logic which sees irreducibly personal emotion as just what individuals have in common.

And yet, of course, it is not true that Strether has ceased to think of her, nor that James is indifferent to what distinguishes her from others of her type. If she is ranged in a category — the category of creatures and apparitions — she recovers her individuality by excelling in her class, as "the finest and subtlest," the "happiest." The use of the superlative is characteristic and, in the present context, noteworthy; it allows James simultaneously to classify and to particularize at once. The self is placed firmly among its sort, but in the same stroke it is distinguished as the supreme instance of its kind. Nevertheless, if we suppose that Madame de Vionnet's individuality has been secured, we shall be disappointed by the time the sentence concludes: "and yet he could see her there as vulgarly troubled, in very truth, as a maidservant crying for her young man." She is returned to the common category — that is, until the next sentence begins: "The only thing was that she judged herself as the maidservant wouldn't." The sequence epitomizes the movement we have been considering. It alternates restlessly, almost compulsively, between the type and the superlative instance, the general comparison and the incomparable object, between Madame de Vionnet's commonness and her distinction.

James ascends to as high a level of generality as fiction can bear, and from that lofty verbal perspective he depicts the vivid instance. The negotiation between types and particulars, the abstract and the concrete, gives one strong version of our broad preliminary problem and it stands in provocative analogy to the negotiation between social forms and individual lives. It obliges us to consider the terms of description in which modern fiction is to be cast; and it leads ultimately to the question that fixes the ideological attention of James and Conrad: How can an individual human being preserve moral autonomy within the collective forms of social life?

The contrast between Woollett and Paris in *The Ambassadors* is conspicuous but impalpable. The distinction between Puritan duty and Parisian beauty, between the depths of conscience and the sensory surface, is obvious and inescapable, but in themselves these commitments are only scantily described, and any attempt to specify the *tenets* of Woollett's morality or the *sensations* of Parisian aesthetics can do little more than reiterate the initial terms of the distinction: Duty, Beauty. Moreover, what seems to be a contrast between art and morals is so only superficially; conscience has its own aesthetics, and art has a conscience. When a shocked Sarah Pocock asks whether one could possibly owe "duty" to a woman like Marie de Vionnet, Strether returns, "Of course they're totally different kinds of duty" (II, p. 200). The relevant opposition is between two moralities and two aesthetics, "different kinds" of each.

When he greets the second wave of ambassadors, Strether mentions how "complex" the situation has become – to which Jim Pocock jauntily replies, "Oh well, it looks bad enough from Woollett!" (II, p. 86) The shift from "complex" to "bad" sets out the problem of different kinds. Woollett reduces complexity to a moral dualism, and its limitation lies in the poverty of its distinctions, rather than in the distinctions themselves. Strether, who confronts a "prodigy of type" (I, p. 196) in Paris, reflects sadly that Woollett has only male and female types, "two exactly" (I, p. 53), and only "three or four" (I, p. 173) subjects of opinion. Moreover, he arrives in Paris with just one moral contrast, the contrast between good and bad, and although Maria Gostrey gently suggests that the new Chad is "not so good as you think," Strether feels "as if he couldn't *but* be as good from the moment he wasn't as bad" (I, p. 171). Woollett, in other words, is guilty of stubborn abstraction and unrelenting generalization. It is the

33

cultural embodiment, the thematic realization, of James's own inclination to disregard the "particular local case." The formal problem, the strain between the abstract class and the concrete particular, thus enters the novel in the aspect of a community which suppresses nuance and assimilates individuality within an unyielding moral typology. Woollett remains, like Jim Pocock, with all its "categories in hand" (II, p. 89).

Our two leading problems intersect at just this point. The first is the stylistic problem, the elusiveness of concrete subjectivity, which can be seen as a consequence of the technical devices so far considered separately: typification and metaphor. These are the most distinctive features of James's later style, and much of the difficulty in approaching the late novels derives from the rapid alternation of these two verbal resources. No sooner is a character, an event, or a place introduced than it is submitted to the eager machinery of comparison and classification. The effect of typification is to construe experience in increasingly broad terms until at the limit it seems merely a play of forms: "different" "things" in "relation." The effect of metaphor is to aliment experience with new content, with concrete possibilities drawn from distant places. Typification ascends toward the stability of immaterial forms – Chad is a "case" and a "phenomenon" – while metaphor works precisely by transgressing against fixed categories: Chad is a "Pagan," a "boy," "an aged and hoary sinner." The one seeks to establish the austere patterns that underlie manners and morals, while the other seeks to reinvest that domain with emotional density.

Nevertheless, despite the fundamental differences between them, metaphor and typification share one significant feature: a distrust of the isolated individual and a refusal to leave it uninterpreted. Both formal principles look beyond the particular local case; metaphor seeks a resemblance; typification seeks a category. Both disregard the quiddity of the ego, and whether sorted in a category or entangled in a conceit, the "I" risks losing a determinate identity. To be a "phenomenon" and a "Pagan" is a worthy attainment, but it is not yet to be an embodied personality.

The second problem concerns the independence of character

within the constraints of culture. How may a self establish its own beliefs, desires and values when set against the pressures of its community? How may Strether achieve autonomous moral perceptions given the rigidities of Woollett and the evasions of Paris? Much as typification and metaphor challenge descriptive particularity, so Woollett and Paris deflect individual judgment, and, though here one must step gingerly, the conflict of the two cultures in large measure coincides with the conflict of the two stylistic principles.

For if James's will to generality receives thematic realization in the ethics of Woollett, so Jamesian metaphor becomes the characteristic mode of the Parisian sensibility. Early in the novel Strether reflects that "wherever one paused in Paris the imagination reacted before one could stop it" (I, p. 96), and Miss Barrace defines the form that reaction takes: "in the light of Paris one sees what things resemble" (I, p. 207). When Bilham describes Chad's attachments as "virtuous," he is telling "but a technical lie" (II, p. 299), a phrase that might almost serve as a definition of metaphor − as might another phrase applied to Madame de Vionnet, who is said to know how to "make deception right" (II, p. 277). Whereas Woollett abstracts from experience in order to apply its fixed generalizations and to freeze judgment, Paris resorts to technical lies, right deceptions, and illuminated resemblances, that is, the apparatus of metaphor, which melts judgment and frustrates the attempt to sort reality into a stable moral taxonomy.

Although Strether initially believes that he has passed from Woollett's misapprehension to a confrontation with the "real thing," he will come to realize that he has only discovered what the real thing resembles. Paris offers as great a challenge to individual perception as Woollett had, and Bilham's image of a "virtuous attachment" proves just as misleading as Sarah Pocock's portrait of the "hideous" brother with the "wicked" woman. At the beginning of the novel's concluding movement, when Strether discovers Chad and Madame de Vionnet in the midst of their rural rendezvous, he is wrenched from the consolations of Bilham's metaphor, just as he had been wrenched from the complacency of Mrs Newsome's moral dogma. During the crisis of recognition he confronts "the central fact," "the final fact," and "the too evident fact" (II, pp. 263–5), too evident, that is, for Strether's singular theory that "the facts were specifically none of his business, and were, over and above, so far as one had to do with them, intrinsically beautiful" (II, p. 261).

But this violent resurgence of fact occurs within a revealing context that reminds us again how difficult it is to disengage subjectivity from the forms that surround it. Before chancing upon his embarrassed friends Strether roams all day in the countryside which becomes for him a distillation of his experience in France. More even than Madame de Vionnet's salon, it connotes *"the thing"* (II, p. 253), the essence of the culture, the true antithesis to Woollett. The landscape is as if painted by Lambinet; the course of events is as though scripted by Maupassant. Thus, in its one significant appearance in the novel, nature exists only as an expression of culture, with every person Strether meets possessing a "kind of inevitability" and every observation falling into place as "a syllable of the text" (II, p. 253). At the instant of his climactic perception he sees "exactly the right thing," a boat with a lady carrying a parasol and a man holding the paddles, an image that "had been wanted in the picture" all day (II, p. 256). Then, just as he thinks he has found the types to complete his painting and to culminate his drama, he recognizes that these types are disconcertingly particular. James, that is, identifies Strether's recognition of Chad and Madame de Vionnet not as mere coincidence but as a deep "inevitability," a requirement of the composition, a fated emanation from the French countryside.

Accordingly, when Strether understands the truth of the romance, the understanding is inseparable from his appreciation of the integrity of French culture. At the moment he encounters France, he also confronts the personal secret he has fastidiously avoided, and in this light there is a telling detail during the crisis on the riverside. In the first moments of mutual consternation, a nervously garrulous Madame de Vionnet lapses "wholly into French," which she seems to speak "with an unprecedented command of idiomatic turns." Until now, we are told, she has spoken only English to Strether, a "charming slightly strange English" that seemed to give her a "language quite to herself." But when in the first rush of astonishment she returns to French, Strether finds that the language veils "her identity, shifting her back into a mere voluble class or race" (II, p. 261).

If, in the initial perception, Strether sees his imagined rural types resolve into real particulars, there next occurs the contrary movement, in which these two individuals whom he has kept free from any common standard reveal themselves as actors in an ageless convention. Here begins the process James had described as Madame de Vionnet's passion "rang[ing] her in a category," and Strether soon finds himself entangled in "the typical tale of Paris" (II, p. 271). He had assumed that in abandoning the morality of Woollett he could hover in an airy expanse beyond the limits of a merely regional ethic. But when the *terre* itself seems to deliver up the "expert, familiar, frequent" lovers (II, p. 256), when Marie de Vionnet speaks the country's language and surrenders her identity to her "class" and "race," when these three human subjects become actors in a typical tale, Strether confronts the intractability of collective forms and communal representations.

V

Reculer pour mieux sauter — this must be the motto for the next turn of argument. Here I step back to *Heart of Darkness*, back indeed to the origins of that work, with the thought that such a return will not only give a more expansive description of the problems posed by James, but will also begin to suggest some solutions. The life of character inside complex literary forms, the life of subjectivity within social restrictions, the place of living values beneath dying ideologies — these fundamental themes of the present study are Conrad's meat as they were James's milk.

Although the fact has been strangely neglected, it is clear that Conrad markedly altered his conception of *Heart of Darkness* during the brief period of its composition. This issue possesses independent interest, but it will be pursued here as a way to approach a problem in the interpretation of the tale that is also a problem for modern fiction in general. In one of its aspects the issue concerns the terms of definition for fictional character, in particular the alternation among social, psychological and moral categories of description. In a second and related aspect it concerns the peculiar vicissitudes of value within a world in which neither convention nor instinct can provide a secure basis for the ethical sense. As will become evident, Conrad did not begin his tale with a determinate attitude towards these questions, and the act of writing was at the same time a discovery of his subject and a formulation of his response. *Heart of Darkness* does not simply record the unfolding of an action; it unfolds its own mode of understanding action; and by the time it reaches its conclusion it has redrawn its portrait of society, redefined a notion of subjectivity, posited a new basis for morality, and created another foundation upon which this study can build.

In a letter to William Blackwood dated 31 December 1898, Conrad refers to a new story that he is preparing for *Blackwood's Magazine*, "a narrative after the manner of *Youth*" that is already "far advanced." He discloses his working title (*The Heart of Darkness*) but quickly adds that "the narrative is not gloomy. The criminality of inefficiency and pure selfishness when tackling the civilizing work in Africa is a justifiable idea." He remarks that the subject is "of our time distinctly," comparing it to "An Outpost of Progress," while noting however that the new work is "a little wider − is less concentrated upon individuals."[30]

Three days later he tells David Meldrum, Blackwood's representative, that the story would have been finished the day before if his son had not fallen ill, and anticipates that the finished work will be under 20,000 words. During the following week he completes the portion of the story that will ultimately become the first installment of the published work and that conforms well to the initial outline offered to Blackwood. The bitter evocation of imperialism merits the description "of our time," and the rapidly shifting attention among characters and incidents explains why Conrad thought of his story as somewhat diffuse. This early section, as carefully managed as it is, nevertheless remains within the relatively humble boundaries that Conrad had mentioned, a kind of

"Youth"–cum–"An Outpost of Progress" in which the agency of Marlow is brought to bear upon the Social Question.

The early proposal contains no mention of Kurtz and no reference to the motif of atavism. If Conrad could write at the end of December that his tale was almost finished, that it would expose criminality, inefficiency and selfishness, and that it would not focus upon particular characters, then he was doubtless envisioning a story in which the preponderant stress would continue to fall upon the abuses of imperialism. *Heart of Darkness*, in other words, was conceived in distinctly social and political terms, and well into its composition Conrad thought of it in this way. A work which has become perhaps the leading example of modern psychological fiction began with an expressed disregard for the fate of individuals.

Part one not only emphasizes the political question; it stays close to the historical facts. Conrad draws heavily on events he had witnessed, and given the initial statements to Blackwood it is highly likely that he first projected the tale as a reasonably faithful rendering of the European entanglement in Africa, a series of sordid misadventures culminating in the pointless death of a European trader. Conrad's own experience with the trader Klein remains obscure; we know that Klein was brought aboard the *Roi des Belges* at Stanley Falls and that he died during the trip downriver; but we have no reason to suppose that Conrad's encounter with him bore any significant resemblance to Marlow's uncanny confrontation with Kurtz. Indeed the dissimilarity gives us a way to understand why Conrad thought that he would finish the story so quickly and why he assumed, even when it was well advanced, that it would not go much beyond the present end of part one. For if he had continued to trace the pattern of his own unpleasant ordeal in the Congo, the meeting with Kurtz would doubtless have been rendered in far more modest terms and would have served more as a pendant to the angry social critique, a final senseless misfortune in a long sequence of unnecessary blunders. In fact, it is difficult to see how Conrad could have achieved much else within the boundaries he had first planned. Certainly he could not have anticipated the force of Kurtz's provocation when he claimed on January 2, having not yet finished what would become part one, that his account of European criminality in Africa was almost complete.

Because the manuscript remained almost entirely free of revision, *Heart of Darkness* stands not only as a narrative of Marlow's adventure in the Congo but as a record of Conrad's adventure in the English countryside, his own struggle to define his conception while hurrying to meet a deadline with *Blackwood's*.[31] In its present form it therefore retains traces of the changing design. The first mention of Kurtz, and almost certainly first in order of composition, simply identifies him as "the poor chap" (p. 11). Surely it is not as a poor chap that any of us remembers him, and by the end of the tale Marlow will describe his dark career in far more lurid terms. This at least raises the possibility that Kurtz was envisioned more as a victim than as a monster and thus closer to that unfortunate Klein whose last days Conrad had witnessed. Indeed in the manuscript Conrad had originally written "Klein" on the first four occasions that he referred to Kurtz by name.

Halfway through part one Marlow roundly denounces the European presence in Africa.

I've seen the devil of violence, and the devil of greed, and the devil of hot desire; but by all the stars these were strong, lusty, red-eyed devils, that swayed and drove men — men, I tell you. But as I stood on this hillside, I foresaw that in the blinding sunshine of that land I would become acquainted with a flabby, pretending, weak-eyed devil of a rapacious and pitiless folly. How insidious he could be too I was only to find out several months later and a thousand miles farther. (pp. 19–20)

The last comment furnishes a second reference to Kurtz's fall, but careful attention should be paid to the context. Speaking from his retrospective standpoint on the *Nellie*, Marlow invokes Kurtz as the most "insidious" manifestation of the "flabby, pretending, weak-eyed devil." And yet "flabby," "pretending" and "weak-eyed" are perhaps the last attributes one would bestow upon Kurtz, whose unseemly practices will far exceed the connotations of "folly." Furthermore, in this early passage Marlow *opposes* the corruption he will meet upriver to the "manly" devils of violence, greed, desire and lust. But Kurtz, let us recall, will appear precisely as a man who "lacked restraint in the gratification of his various lusts" (p. 57), who indulged

40

"forgotten and brutal instincts," "gratified and monstrous passions" (p. 65).

In other words, this early reference suggests that Kurtz's afflictions will be thoroughly continuous with the criminality of imperialism, that there will be no "choice of nightmares" (p. 63), only one increasingly appalling phantasm. Within this conception Kurtz would pose no distinctly psychological problem; he would represent merely the most extreme, the most "insidious" example of the general corruption. At this point it even remains unclear whether Conrad had anticipated the celebrated motif of voluntary reversion to the primitive. No doubt he intended Kurtz to succumb to the "fascination of the abomination" (p. 10), but there is as yet no hint — in a tale which persistently offers hints — that this will go any further than the miserable plight of Kayerts and Carlier in "An Outpost of Progress," no further, that is, than a flabby, pretending, weak-eyed descent into criminal folly. The crucial transformation occurs when Conrad wrenches Kurtz free from the prevailing folly and recognizes in him an independent problem of monstrous proportions.

On January 9, 1899 Conrad sent off everything that he had written up to the day before, the body of material that would become part one of the story. It is possible then to discern a second stage in the process of composition whose beginning coincides with the beginning of part two. Apparently Conrad found himself at something of an impasse as he tried to continue beyond this point. On January 13 he wrote in frustration to Garnett, referring to the "rotten stuff" he was preparing for *Blackwood's*: "Ah if I could only write! If I could write, write, write! But I cannot."[32] Three days later, however, his tone has changed. He tells Meldrum that he doesn't "think [the tale] will be bad," remarking that "the thing has grown on me."[33]

What has grown evidently is Kurtz. Part two begins with Marlow half-asleep on the deck of his steamer, overhearing a conversation between the Manager and his uncle. The former bitterly describes how Kurtz had travelled hundreds of miles downriver with his ivory and then had abruptly decided to paddle a small dugout back into the wilderness. "As for me," says Marlow, "I seemed to see Kurtz for the first time" (p. 34). In the light of Conrad's own struggles with the story, it is tempting to suppose that the "I" has a double reference, that the author like his character feels that he is seeing Kurtz for the first time, and that in the image of the "lone white man turning his back suddenly on the headquarters" (p. 34), Conrad experienced a turn in his conception of the tale.

This last supposition must of course remain speculative, but the general point should now be evident: that as the tale of "20,000 words" grew to almost twice that length, Conrad found himself far exceeding both the boundaries of his initial conception and the limits of historical event. The concluding sections, precisely those parts which evolved during the two months of writing, are increasingly remote from Conrad's actual and unglamorous African experience. He would later recall his disappointment upon arrival at Stanley Falls, seeing the moment as "an end to the idealized realities of a boy's daydreams."[34] In one respect the invention of Kurtz might be seen as the imaginative heightening of a depressingly banal memory. And it is both instructive and moving to picture Conrad in hard-pressed circumstances in England, rushing to complete a story based closely on his experiences a decade earlier, and then, in a creative parturition that began one of the most fertile periods in modern fiction, discovering a way to surpass the facts, reinterpret the facts, correct the facts.

By the time we arrive at the further reaches of Kurtz's degradation, "poor chap" and "flabby devil" have long since ceased to apply; the tale is no longer "of our time distinctly"; and once Kurtz has uttered his final words and Marlow has lied to the Intended, no one would dream of saying that the subject of the work is "inefficiency." Here we may usefully oppose two phrases. In the letter to Blackwood, it will be recalled, Conrad described his story as "less concentrated upon individuals" than "An Outpost of Progress," but late in *Heart of Darkness* Marlow will report that Kurtz's intelligence was "concentrated . . . upon himself with horrible intensity" (p. 65). The difference suggests the great change in the status of the subject from the beginning to the end of this brief tale. *Heart of Darkness*, we might say, discovers how to concentrate upon individuals, and since that is our task as well, we must follow the turnings of the narrative as it gradually secures a principle of individuality which endures its own fragility, suffers its own vicissitudes, and carries the work far from its original design. Indeed Conrad himself came to acknowledge a transformation in the tale. After Cunninghame Graham read part one in *Blackwood's* he sent Conrad his enthusiastic praise. Conrad was delighted, but he cautioned the socialist Graham that the next two installments might not please him as well. "So far," he wrote, "the note struck chimes in with your convictions, — *mais après?* There is an *après.*"[35] This remark establishes the problem that we must now pursue. How does a tale of imperialist exploitation generate an *après?* And why such an *après* as this?

Criticism of *Heart of Darkness* has always focused upon the conclusion, that *après* which is the fiction's crux. The jungle, the horror, the return, the lie — these no doubt pose the most absorbing problems of the work. But part of our purpose is to see how the opening of the tale engenders its culmination, and if we rush too quickly to the conclusion we miss its motivation and diminish its force. We miss, for one thing, the extent to which *Heart of Darkness* is a drama of officialdom. Imperialism presents itself to Conrad as an affair of inefficient clerks, disaffected functionaries, envious subordinates, and defensive superiors — all arrayed within a strict hierarchy whose local peak is the General Manager and whose summit is the vague "Council in Europe." The Company gives identities, establishes purposes, assigns destinies, and, with its bizarre configuration of Central and Inner Stations, constructs geography. The accumulation of ivory is the material goal, but it interests Conrad less than its social consequence, the scramble for position within the institution, which creates its own flabby passions and even its own flabby pentameter: "Am I the Manager — or am I not?" (p. 33).

Conrad, that is, begins *Heart of Darkness* by defining character in firmly institutional terms, asking in effect what happens to the self when it has been thoroughly assimilated into a social form. His answer is that identity becomes indistinguishable from role and that the individual becomes merely a situs within a system of official ties. Names give way to titles. When a curious Marlow asks the brickmaker, "who is this Mr Kurtz?," he is told simply that Kurtz is the "chief of the Inner Station." "Much obliged," laughs Marlow, "And you are the brickmaker of the Central Station. Every one knows that" (p. 79). The problem of character is thus posed as the problem of the institutional self, and this represents the formulation of an issue that James has formulated in equally charged terms: the extension of the collective will into the intimacies of an individual life. It will be worth remembering throughout that while the self strikes many odd poses in our century, these are no more extravagant than the forms of communal domination which enclose them.

In *Heart of Darkness* this relation endures many changes, but it initially presents itself as a contrast between the values of an institutionalized society and the facts of individual lives. As characters become caught in the formalism of the community, these values and facts grow increasingly remote, and part of my task is to follow the violent course of their *rapprochement*. The absurdist aspect of the story's opening movement emerges in the empty assertion of the social ceremonies in the face of irreducibly personal experience. The moral formalism of James's Americans has its counterpart in the bureaucratic formalism of the European imperialists. The Company scrupulously pays brass wire to its nearly starving native employees, and the accountant makes "correct entries of perfectly correct transactions" fifty feet from "the still tree-tops of the grove of death" (p. 22). The incongruity between the living Company and the dying self is a vivid instance of that more general Conradian incongruity between value and fact, between the system of meanings that we collectively devise and the experience that we privately endure.

Here we may invoke Max Weber − not in order to provide a Weberian reading of *Heart of Darkness*, if such a thing is even conceivable, but to generate a distinction that may clarify Conrad's notion of personality. Weber and Conrad were close contemporaries and from the unlikely points of Germany, Protestantism and sociology, Weber came to an intellectual bearing and a moral demeanor close to Conrad's own. In particular, his theory of social organization contains implications for a theory of modern character which should help to illuminate Conrad, but no more than Conrad should help to illuminate it.

Certainly among Weber's most important contributions to sociological thought was his analysis of bureaucracy as one of three fundamental types of social authority, and the one under which he had the misfortune to live.[36] From Weber's mature standpoint bureaucracy is to be regarded not merely as a specific form of organization found in various public and private agencies but as the fundamental mode of modern authority which informs every aspect of social arrangement. Its characteristic features — rationality, hierarchy, secrecy, conformity, anonymity — extend throughout the community and have begun to transform the individual into "a small cog in a ceaselessly moving mechanism which prescribes to him an essentially fixed rank of march."[37] At its limit the bureaucratic sensibility represents the triumph of method and "the exclusion of love, hatred, and every purely personal, especially irrational and incalculable, feeling from the execution of official tasks."[38]

Hence from Weber's own historical standpoint the bureaucrat ceases to be one type among others and becomes the representative figure of the modern age. Lacking both reverence for tradition and hope of revolutionary change, content to sustain the prevailing hierarchy, committed to discipline and routine — the bureaucrat has history on his side and can wait patiently while his dominion extends into every corner of contemporary life. From the perspective of a "value-free" sociology Weber dispassionately charts the rise of the bureaucratic temperament, but a detectable bitterness enters his tone, and outside his formal studies it erupts into derision and contempt.

It is horrible to think that the world could one day be filled with nothing but these little cogs, little men clinging to little jobs and striving towards bigger ones . . . This passion for bureaucracy . . . is enough to drive one to despair. . . That the world should know no men but these: it is in such an evolution that we are already caught up, and the great question is therefore not how we can promote and hasten it, but what we can oppose to this machinery in order to keep a portion of mankind free from this parcelling-out of the soul, from this supreme mastery of the bureaucratic way of life.[39]

Under the same historical pressures Conrad came to much the same perception, and we need to recall a point too often neglected, namely that after Kafka, Conrad is our most searching critic of bureaucracy. Like Weber he consistently sought a principle of opposition to the institutional self, and in the view offered here it is a Weberian rather than a Freudian insight that lies at the origin of *Heart of Darkness* – at its origin, not at its end.

Within this set of concerns the Manager is the exemplary figure, and we greatly distort the work if we neglect the importance of this character who typifies the vulgar sensibility of petty officialdom and who incarnates the criminality, inefficiency and selfishness which Conrad first set out to expose. A man with "no learning and no intelligence," "neither civil nor uncivil" (p. 25), the Manager jealously guards "trade secrets" (p. 57), deprecates "unsound method" (p. 67), and coldly submits human welfare to institutional requirements. The epitome of the bureaucrat, he "originated nothing, he could keep the routine going – that's all" (p. 25). In important respects the Manager is the displaced center of *Heart of Darkness* who would probably have held pride of place in the shorter work that Conrad had first conceived. Conrad's own most bitter experiences in Africa involved his conflict with Camille Delcommune, upon whom the Manager is based, and we need only set off part one from the rest of the story in order to recognize that Conrad's lingering antipathy towards Delcommune and his contempt for European inefficiency would have provided sufficient motive for the story that he originally forecast to Blackwood.

Not only the origins of the tale but its structure must be understood in the context of Conrad's revulsion from the bureaucratic sensibility. Kurtz enters the work, and perhaps entered Conrad's imagination, as an antithesis to the Manager, as though he were summoned into being through the strength of Conrad's repugnance. Marlow first hears his name from the chief accountant who describes him as "a first-class agent" and then, noting Marlow's disappointment, adds that Mr Kurtz "is a very remarkable person" (p. 22). The distinction between "agent" and "person" is fundamental. For in its initial

movement the tale dramatizes the attempt to recover personality from a world of impersonal functionaries, an activity that
begins within a strictly institutional context. Kurtz initially
represents that distinctly bureaucratic figure, the organizational
wunderkind who rapidly ascends the corporate ladder, destined
to "be a somebody in the Administration before long" (p. 22).
Furthermore, he has "moral ideas" (p. 33), and when he is
still "just a word" (p. 29) Marlow posits him as the ethical
alternative to economic piracy. *Heart of Darkness* begins, that
is, by identifying the problem of character as a bureaucratic
conflict, a struggle between the good and the bad official, and
by implication a struggle between moral and immoral forms
of social organization.

These, of course, are not the struggles that we ultimately
witness. But the transformation in the narrative must be
understood against the background of this original problem
— the need to find a perspective from which to oppose institutionalized depravity. Kurtz's turn to the wilderness,
whatever else it becomes, is first of all a gesture of social
rebellion. The Tribe is a rejoinder to the Company. Under
Kurtz's domination it possesses a seamless unity that avoids
the endless articulations of bureaucracy; it knows no legal
formalism, no reliance on a vague "They, above" (p. 22) whose
lofty intentions dissipate in the long descent through hierarchy. For Conrad the inefficiency of imperialism is not one
defect among many: it is a measure of the awful distance between intention and action so inimical to coherent social
purpose. Within the Tribe authority exists not as a remote
official dispatching instructions through the mail, but as a
visible body and a living voice — a "real presence" (p. 48).
The distance between the will and its realization is overcome;
inefficiency disappears as a problem; Kurtz makes the canoes
run on time.

In Weberian sociology the antonym to the rule of bureaucracy is the rule of *charisma*, the "gift," invested in a leader
whose authority depends on neither tradition nor law,
who indeed overturns every traditional and legal norm in
the name of a personal calling acknowledged by an
entire society. Other forms of authority, argues Weber,

accommodate themselves to history; they exist to satisfy quotidian needs and to permit stability in communal life. Charismatic leadership is "alien to all regulation and tradition"; it is "not a continuous institution, but in its pure type the very opposite."

In radical contrast to bureaucratic organization, charisma knows no formal and regulated appointment or dismissal, no career, advancement or salary, no supervisory or appeals body, no local or purely technical jurisdiction, and no permanent institutions in the manner of bureaucratic agencies, which are independent of the incumbents and their personal charisma. Charisma is self-determined and sets its own limits. Its bearer seizes the task for which he is destined and demands that others obey and follow him by virtue of his mission.[40]

Because it violates all custom and tradition and because it offers no justification but itself, charisma always appears supernatural, and its edicts have divine warrant. All value emanates from the bearer of the "gift," and all social activity originates in the will of the leader. A community under charismatic domination necessarily breaks with its past, and for this reason Weber calls charisma "the specifically creative revolutionary force in history."[41]

It will have become obvious that this notion of "the gift" bears closely on Marlow's portrayal of "the gifted Kurtz" (p. 48): "The point was in his being a gifted creature . . . I laid the ghost of his gifts at last with a lie" (pp. 48, 49). What Weber hypothesized, Conrad imagined: a social order dependent on one center, one value, one will.[42] The Russian reports that the natives "would not stir until Mr Kurtz gave the word. His ascendancy was extraordinary . . . The chiefs came every day to see him. They would crawl" (p. 58). There is no need to accumulate examples; it is already clear that this is not like being "a somebody in the Administration." The point, which Weber lets us see clearly, is that the movement between social orders generates a distinction between paradigms of character epitomized by the Manager and Kurtz. Indeed all through our century the Civil Servant and the Atavist have served as cautionary instances, competing extremes for the modern temperament. The one surrenders character, the other accumulates too much. Following Weber, we may think of the

48

difference in terms of bureaucratic and charismatic sensibilities. Following Marlow we may recognize it as a choice of nightmares, two besetting temptations for the contemporary world.

The difficulty in the characterization of *Heart of Darkness*, and the difficulty of its form, is that it pursues a mode of experience until it turns into its opposite. The successful civil servant becomes the tribal chieftain; if this were merely a brute reversal, it would be less disquieting. But the narrative suggests what the horror of Nazism confirmed, that carried far enough the bureaucratic sensibility will engender the charismatic leader. Kurtz thus retains a powerful ambiguity within the design of the tale. On the one hand, he is the *reductio* of imperialism. He stands at the point where rational acquisition becomes irrational accumulation, where economic routine becomes primitive ritual, where a commodity becomes a fetish, and indirect violence becomes overt barbarism. In this respect, Conrad presents Kurtz as the suppressed truth of European immorality, a point well emphasized in the eagerness of the Company to exploit his sordid achievement. Moreover, from what we know of the composition of the story, this emphasis is thoroughly consistent with Conrad's original design. Insofar as Kurtz discloses the concealed logic of imperialism, then he indeed represents the most "insidious" example of "a rapacious and pitiless folly" (p. 20).

On the other hand, even as Kurtz takes the logic of accumulation to its unthinkable extreme, he discovers another logic altogether; folly reaches the point at which it becomes *folie*; and in presenting European abuses at their grotesque limit, he furnishes a principle of opposition to them. This is the complexity in Conrad's final conception: Kurtz represents both the extreme of the colonial temperament and its antithesis. And it was when Conrad thought past the former possibility, the degradation of a virtuous man ("the poor chap") which reveals the depravity of a social form, when he recognized voluntary atavism as the nightmare from which it was possible to awake, that *Heart of Darkness* took its longest step and disclosed another region of subjectivity.

49

There is a revealing lacuna in Weber's analysis of charisma. Having defined the concept and having named some historical instances, Weber proceeds quickly to the subject that dominates his analysis: the waning of charisma, its inevitable subordination to the forces of law and tradition, and its appropriation by those who seek to legitimize their power. Social life under charismatic domination occupies just one paragraph of that immense tome *Economy and Society*, and a phenomenon which Weber regarded as one of the three fundamental types of authority almost completely escapes description.

It is not difficult to see why this is so. Charismatic leadership, *ex hypothesi*, breaks with rules and norms, and in its pure form, holds Weber, it cannot be understood as a social organization in any customary sense. By definition it is extraordinary, the product of the Gifted One who suspends all those conventions, institutions and traditions which sociology takes as its proper subject. Charisma thus exists at the limit of Weber's sociological understanding. It is where the study of the group must become the study of the exceptional individual who molds the group according to his will. Sociology passes into psychology.

What is a puzzle for the system of academic disciplines — where does society stop and the mind begin? — is an opportunity for the literary imagination. Conrad, too, describes the limitations of bureaucracy; he, too, conceives a charismatic alternative; and to this point the analogy with Weber is extensive and heuristic. But because he is bound neither by theoretical presupposition nor by historical fact, Conrad willingly follows the movement from social to psychological experience. A tale that begins with bureaucratic folly imagines a ghastly alternative in tribal violence, and in carrying through that insight, it imagines where social life passes into the life of the instincts. In *Heart of Darkness* and immediately afterward in *Lord Jim* Conrad built a theatre for the psyche — not in an isolated individual but in a social configuration that gave the mind an expanse on which to play itself out. When the Russian withholds ivory, Kurtz threatens to shoot him, "because he could do so, and had a fancy for it, and there was nothing on earth to prevent him killing whom he jolly well pleased" (p. 56). Conrad, in other words, envisions that form of community in which social organization collapses into psychological expression.

After the Russian tells Marlow that the heads impaled on stakes are the heads of rebels, Marlow laughs disbelievingly: "Rebels! What would be the next definition I was to hear? There had been enemies, criminals, workers – and these were rebels" (p. 58). But the next definition, the psychological definition, will indeed be telling. The story in effect offers a succession of concepts under which to sort human character, a series of definitions which unfold from one another and which lead Marlow himself to change his very categories of description. Through its own strenuous logic *Heart of Darkness* pursues the representation of bureaucracy until it becomes the representation of a monstrous passion, and fully to appreciate the tale as a psychological fiction is to appreciate the way it must excavate a place for the mind. Here is Conrad's promised *après*; the psyche is a sequel to society. In accordance with the daunting imaginative logic that conjoins center and edge, what is inner and prior (the anarchic realm of instinct) only discloses itself as outer and subsequent – much as Kurtz's darkest impulses only reveal themselves in his *postscriptum* ("Exterminate all the brutes") (p. 51).

The standard interpretive response to *Heart of Darkness* has been to approach it as a tale of many levels. In a characteristic opinion Lillian Feder called it "fairly obvious" that " 'Heart of Darkness' has three levels of meaning: on the one level it is the story of a man's adventures; on another, of his discovery of certain political and social injustices; and on a third, it is a study of his initiation into the mysteries of his own mind."[43] One certainly recognizes the motive behind this habit of interpretation. It furnishes a way to accommodate the diversity of Conrad's interests; every topic enjoys a level of its own. But this dogged metaphor achieves harmony at the price of great simplification. It sorts various motifs into distinct fictional regions and avoids asking how they pertain to one another. Imperialism is in the attic, instinct in the cellar, and while they can "reflect" and "recapitulate" one another, they need never have an awkward encounter on the stairs. The customary result is that the political theme drops from serious consideration, habitually regarded as a superficial manifestation of the deep psychological predicament.

Part of my point in attending to the composition of *Heart of Darkness* was to discourage the temptation to bring its beginning and its end into easy harmony — in particular to discourage the idea that social and psychological concerns merely expressed the same experience on two distinct levels. The structure of the fiction, like its origins, suggests a more complex relation. It suggests that society and the psyche are not two levels but two antagonists, and that as *Heart of Darkness* invents for itself a genre of psychological narrative, it discovers a standpoint from which to contest grotesque political abuse. One must not be misled by the novel's most celebrated words. The unredeemable horror in the tale is the duplicity, cruelty and venality of European officialdom. Kurtz himself, in *speaking* horror, immediately renders himself less horrible. He ensures his standing as a "remarkable man," a man who has "summed up" and so achieved "a moral victory paid for by innumerable defeats, by abominable terrors, by abominable satisfactions" (pp. 69, 70).[44]

This last quotation already intimates another change in this continually changing design. Kurtz is not only a figure for the modern psyche; he becomes, improbably, unexpectedly, a figure for modern morality. The end of his lust, his greed, his terror, his satisfaction is a "moral victory," and this curious begetting establishes the final problem that this phase of argument will pursue. To this point I have considered how Conrad's social conception transformed to a psychological conception, how the institutional self metamorphosed to the instinctual self. But here I want to discuss a further and equally consequential transformation, namely, as I have already implied, from mental concepts to moral concepts, from psychology to ethics.

It is clear, first of all, that Kurtz's fall is not merely due to the surge of instinct that routs social values; it is due to a failure of the values themselves. The prelapsarian Kurtz had talked of pity, science, progress, love, justice and the conduct of life — "burning noble words" (p. 50) Marlow calls them. They constitute an ideology of enlightenment, a collective moral inheritance which, plainly enough, arouses virtuous aspiration and then proves unequal to the passion it excites. Kurtz's words fall under the heading of "principles" that "fly off at the first good shake" (p. 38).[45] But the failure of principle does not mark the demise of value in *Heart of Darkness*, only a change in its source. If value cannot descend from social ideals, it must ascend from the psychic abyss.

A perception of the distance between fact and value is, we have seen, fundamental to Conrad's assault on prevailing social conventions. The incongruity between the sound of moral words and the spectacle of sordid deeds excites his contempt and gives urgency to the representation of anarchic instinct. Certainly, a familiar approach to *Heart of Darkness* considers it a rejection of the values of progress and enlightenment in the name of such facts as passion, greed and violence. But we need to acknowledge a third category of Conradian concepts that is distinct from both the class of groundless ideals and the class of amoral instincts.

During Kurtz's final crisis Marlow watches "the inconceivable mystery of a soul that knew no restraint, no faith, and no fear, yet struggling blindly with itself" (p. 66). Here is Conrad's improbable image for the foundation of morality, an image which locates the moral source not in social convention but in an inconceivably mysterious gesture of the individual mind. Kurtz, a man without restraint, struggles to restrain himself. It is a primitive psychological movement, the self confronting the self, an act of will originating *ex nihilo*. The importance of restraint in *Heart of Darkness* is thoroughly obvious, but perhaps not thoroughly perspicuous. Restraint, after all, is a psychological concept that in itself implies no ethical norm; it presupposes no moral code and commits one to no opinions about love, progress, or the conduct of life. How, then, are we to understand its prominence?

When Marlow encounters the unlikely self-control of the hungry cannibals aboard his ship, he stands amazed: "Restraint! I would just as soon have expected restraint from a hyena prowling amongst the corpses of a battlefield" (p. 43). Then he immediately adds, "But there was the fact facing me — the fact dazzling to be seen, like the foam on the depths of the sea" (p. 43). "Restraint" thus possesses a strategic ambiguity. It belongs to the domain of objective description ("the fact facing me"), but it is already imbued with value ("dazzling to be seen"). It names a concrete perceptible datum and at the same time a basic virtue. Along with other subtle devices to be considered in a moment, "restraint" gives Marlow a way to overcome the distance between description and evaluation. He need not struggle any longer to apply transcendent ethical concepts to refractory experience; now he can locate moral value *within* individual experience. A notion such as restraint suggests the possibility of a natural basis for ethics, a non-moral ground for morality, a reconciliation between fact and value.

As he watches the natives who howl and dance on the banks of the river, Marlow wonders what motives and impulses sway them. And what is most notable about the possibilities he considers — "Joy, fear, sorrow, devotion, valour, rage" (p. 38) — is the casual compounding of emotions and virtues. States of mind (joy, rage) are not clearly distinguished from moral states (devotion, valour). Similarly, in his reflections on Kurtz's final words Marlow sees them as the expression of "belief," "candour," "revolt," "truth," "desire" and "hate," the sum of which, as we know, is a "moral victory." Perhaps as deep as any urge in Conrad is the desire to let evaluation emerge spontaneously out of description, in accordance with his high aesthetic conviction that when he has described the world faithfully he will also have described his faith. Much like restraint, terms such as "devotion," "belief" and "candour" suggest to Conrad both mental facts and moral values, and they suggest too that in the right circumstances the psychic life can lead naturally, almost imperceptibly, into ethical life.

In this way *Heart of Darkness* again transcends its own principles of structure. Having begun with a distinction between the good and the bad bureaucrat, and having rudely supplanted it with a nightmarish choice between social venality and passionate license, it ends by offering the individual moral psyche as a slim third term between these weighty alternatives. Marlow, it is plain, is the one who seeks to cultivate this vulnerable site, and to consider the fate of individuality in *Heart of Darkness* is finally to consider Marlow's fate. To conclude, then, we must ask how his fragile autonomy can be sustained. After the bureaucrat, after the atavist, how can he find a character of his own? How can Marlow by himself secure values for himself?

In an early expression of disgust at the feckless plotting of the Company agents, Marlow observes that "there is something after all in the world allowing one man to steal a horse while another must not look at a halter" (p. 27). In its context the judgment seems unexceptionable, but it represents a precept difficult to sustain. What is this "something" that distinguishes the worthy horse thief from the wicked obeyer of laws? Marlow does not elaborate, but he persistently relies on this form of reasoning. He misleads the brickmaker merely in the hope that it might "somehow" help Kurtz. And in explaining his aversion to lies, he invokes no general canon but a personal response, even an eccentricity: lying "makes me miserable and sick, like biting something rotten would do. Temperament, I suppose" (p. 29). Marlow never shrinks from judgment, but he judges without abstract ideals, without general principles, indeed without consistency.

Kurtz had spoken to the Russian of love "in general," and later when he appears in the jungle surrounded by a thousand armed natives, Marlow comments bitterly, "Let us hope that the man who can talk so well of love in general will find some particular reason to spare us this time" (p. 59). This is the foundation of Marlow's moral sense: a contempt for ethics "in general" and a demand for the "particular reason." He derides moral absolutes and willingly suspends universals in favor of concrete discriminations. We know that he abominates lies and that he recognizes justice as Kurtz's due, but when he meets the Intended he complies with neither the maxim of honesty nor the claim of justice. Instead he acts as the practical moralist who overturns general ethical conceptions without overturning ethics.

When Marlow describes his "particular reason" for lying to Kurtz's Intended, he makes no appeal to those tainted ideas: progress, pity, conduct of life. He says simply that the truth "would have been too dark − too dark altogether" (p. 76). But what kind of moral concept is "darkness"? Clearly it is no concept at all; it is, if you will, a moral *sensation* — like the "flavour of mortality" Marlow finds in lies. In offering an image for the human predicament, Marlow describes the world as a place where one must "breathe dead hippo, so to speak and not be contaminated" (p. 50). When he discovers that Kurtz has left his cabin in the middle of the night, he experiences a "moral shock" (p. 63), and when he makes his choice of nightmares, he turns to Kurtz "for relief — positively for relief" (p. 61). Shock, relief and the smell of dead hippo are further instances of moralized sensations that take the place of abstract principle. And the climactic example is Kurtz's own valediction. "Horror" is the culminating instance of these almost punning Conradian concepts which engender an unmistakable moral assessment out of an intuitive psychic spasm. In each of these cases the act of judgment appears more as a reflex than a verdict — thus Kurtz's summing-up is not a deliberation but a "cry." Morality becomes an immediate turning of the individual sensibility that exists not beyond but beneath good and evil.

Just here the notion of the "beyond within" recovers its pertinence, because it is precisely the aim of Marlow's moral reflection to insist on the radical immanence of value. The thought that moral life is not superimposed on experience, that the authority of the moral beyond already lies securely within the domain of fact, and that in order to pursue value we need only perceive with acuity — this thought is central to the workings of the tale. It is what allows Conrad to measure the degradations of bourgeois morality even as he retrieves an aboriginal individualist ideal: the integral self as the sufficient register of moral meanings.

"Darkness" is thus the perfect moral term, a term that at once suggests a perception and a value, and hence satisfies the impulse to merge description and appraisal. The transitions from the literal gloom of the African jungle to Kurtz's gloomy horror, from the obscurity of the Intended's drawing room to Marlow's obscure dread, from the black bank of clouds above the Thames to the heart of darkness, appear almost seamless. They do so, of course, only because darkness is a metaphor in which a descriptive property connotes a moral attribute.[46] It is, we should immediately note, almost a dead metaphor. Its ethical associations are so highly conventional and Marlow repeats them so often that it scarcely seems a figure of speech at all. And yet it is just to Conrad's purpose that darkness be a dying metaphor. The more hackneyed the figure, the more secure is the association between literal and moral obscurity, and the more inevitable seems the link between perception and evaluation. By the end of the tale an event as natural as the darkening sky stands as a somber moral warning. Facts are inlaid with value until judgment has become a task for the senses.

Conradian Impressionism is habitually regarded as an epistemological event, an attempt to restore the priority of the sensory apparatus in the literary representation of knowledge. But we do not need to disregard Conrad's epistemology in order to recognize that his Impressionism is at least as significant a moral event. As *Heart of Darkness* moves from an institutional to an instinctual domain, it implicitly asks what lies between these warring regions, and it responds by offering the Impressionist temperament as itself a basis for moral autonomy. The ascent from Kurtzian horror is an ascent to a region of experience in which virtue and vice disclose themselves in sight and sound, taste and smell. Between fragile social conventions and blind passions morality finds a place in the educated impressions of the practical moralist. The world shimmers with value, as it shimmers with color, and there is no need to rely on independent (and dubious) acts of the ethical mind once one has learned to trust intelligent sensations.

Thus the practical moralist makes a curious approach to the working artist — "too dark," after all, is something that a painter might observe of an unfinished canvas. To say this is not to imply that there is anything frivolous in Marlow's convictions, only to suggest that a final consequence of the attempt to embed value in fact is that one comes to rely on intuitive perceptions of consonance and dissonance. "Somehow" and "something," "relief," "shock," "flavour" and "horror" — all reflect the desire to locate the moral sense so firmly within subjective experience that no skein of ethical reflections need ever distract judgment. One simply inspects the world and arranges a balance in the shades of contrast. Darkness becomes the raw material of this aestheticized morality, an almost palpable substance that can be kneaded into form and then disposed of according to intuitions of ethical fitness. Marlow takes it from Kurtz, flourishes it before the Manager, withholds it from the Intended, confers it upon his shipmates. Each of these acts has a reason, but they are all "particular reasons," so particular, indeed, so securely lodged in concrete circumstance, that they reveal Marlow as no moral metaphysician, only perhaps as a sculptor in darkness.

VI

"Call it then life." (I, p. 168)

"To 'save' you, as you called it?"
 – "I call it still." (I, p. 274)

". . . such a complexity of relations – unless indeed we call it a simplicity."
(I, p. 36)

"He scratched his chin as he asked himself by what name, when challenged – as he was sure he would be – he could call it for her."
(II, p. 66)

One of the chief intentions of this first chapter is to argue that the individualist stress of James and Conrad is no evasion of social reality; to suggest, on the contrary, that it is a critique of social failure. Without granting any sustained sympathy to revolutionary political movements, Conrad and James nevertheless engage in attacks, at once precise and relentless, on dominant forms of sociality. Precisely in the attempt to disengage some relic of integral subjectivity from the dislocations of collective life, they expose the specific cruelties of particular communities. And the very attempt to extricate moral character from these cruelties shows how the ego is composed by the social body, and how much flesh must be torn if it is to stand alone.

In the late work of James, language is both the source of communal solidarity and the occasion for what remains of the subject's freedom. Jamesian experience is necessarily verbal experience, because only within a system of concepts can experience appear at all; only through the assignment of words does it receive contours, achieve structure, attain value. Other figures in this study will dream of prising language apart from the world in order to see reality at last without a veil of words. But for James the only way to see the world is through its verbal veil. Put simply, one must live within a language; there is nowhere else to live.

The difficulty (and the opportunity) is that while the world must inevitably assume verbal form, no particular form has a claim to sovereignty. In Paris Strether comes to appreciate both the necessity of language and the relativity of words. Having applied the phrase "sacred rage" to Waymarsh, Strether, we are told, must "find names for many other matters" (I, pp. 46, 48); he must find names because the old ones fail to apply and new ones are not given.[47] As the quotations above suggest, the novel abounds with baptismal utterances, requests for definition, stipulations of meaning. Strether puzzles over Chad's extraordinary appearance until he finds that it has "taken on a name — a name on which Strether seized" (I, p. 156): Chad is a pagan. When he learns of Chad's tie to the Vionnets, he goes "in search of the 'word' as the French called it" of that relationship, settling fatefully on Bilham's phrase, "a virtuous attachment" (I, pp. 180, 182). Clearly, these are not idle acts of denomination. They express the attempt to give form to increasingly elusive experience; and, as James teaches so carefully, to decide what something should be called is a deep and consequential engagement of a self with its world. Perhaps the most vivid instance is Sarah Pocock's offer of a name for the change in her brother, "I call it hideous" (II, p. 205).

This last example, like the others before it, suggests that naming is an act of individual will, a bestowal upon the world of a personal valuation. Characters indeed seek a congruence between a verbal form and a private resolve, but Jamesian language has resolves of its own — "a certain inherent dignity, value, and independence," as James put it in the review of *Azarian*. The problem occurs when one's own dignity clashes with the dignity of the common language, a condition which Strether frequently endures, nowhere more awkwardly than in an early exchange with Chad. When Chad reveals that he enjoys "good relations" with Madame de Vionnet, Strether asks,

"I mean *how* good are they?"

"Oh awfully good."

Again Strether had faltered, but it was brief. It was all very well, but there was nothing now he wouldn't risk. "Excuse me, but I must really — as I began by telling you — know where I am. Is she bad?"

" 'Bad'?" — Chad echoed it, but without a shock. "Is that what's implied — ?"

"When relations are good?" Strether felt a little silly, and was even conscious of a foolish laugh, at having it imposed on him to have appeared to speak so. What indeed was he talking about? (I, p. 239)

He is virtually talking gibberish, and this is because he clings to concepts not supple enough to capture the heterogeneity of moral life. In his simple ethical typology "good" and "bad" divide the universe, and there is no commerce between them. What confuses Strether and what gives the book its moral impetus is the variety of things that can be called good. One can be a "good American" or a "good woman" (I, pp. 131, 170); one can have a "good name" and a "good nature" (I, p. 117); one can "make a good thing" of an enterprise or do someone else good (I, p. 66). Waymarsh wants to be "as good as" Strether and Maria (I, p. 45), while Bilham, who proudly insists that he is "good enough," regretfully notes that Jeanne is "too good" (I, p. 277). Strether's initial feeling of paradox stems from his assumption that these instances must cohere, and he is bewildered at the thought of having "good relations" with a "bad woman." Later, when he and Maria discuss the "awful," the "impossible," Jim Pocock, she asks whether Sarah and Mrs Newsome know "how bad he is." Strether notes that they do not, but then adds, "Well, he *is* good, too, in his way. It depends on what you want him for" (II, p. 141).

The recognition that people and events can be good in their way, that the good depends on what one needs and wants, that badness and goodness do not divide the world — it is such a perception that initiates the activity James had projected in ambitious terms. In his outline of the novel he had written that Strether "revises and imaginatively reconstructs, morally reconsiders, so to speak, civilization."[48] He does so, in great measure, by reconsidering the language, the "stamped and authorized coinage," in which the values of civilization inhere. Having freed himself from moral simplicity, Strether reinvents his language of value. He learns to make distinctions finer than good and bad, coming to delight in Madame de Vionnet, not so much because she has moved from one side of Woollett's dualism to the other as because she has engendered a new terminology of value: "beautiful," of course, but also, "subtle," "fine," "harmonious," "sublime." Strether refines his terms of appraisal, and the task of reconstructing, reconsidering, revising civilization becomes a quest for more precise evaluative adjectives.

In the painful scene that closes *The Ambassadors* Strether tells Maria Gostrey that he must return to Woollett in order "To be right," explaining that his "only logic" is "not, out of the whole affair, to have got anything for myself" (II, p. 326). Maria asks why he must be "so dreadfully right" and then adds a sad protest, "It isn't so much your *being* 'right' — it's your horrible sharp eye for what makes you so" (II, p. 337). All through the novel moral discussion has emphasized the nature of the "good": the good woman, the good American, good relations. But in these final moments Strether wants to be not good but right and even admits that he is "bad" in wanting such.[49] This change is not fortuitous. "Right" often has a peculiar significance in James that we can address by way of an elusive comment from his criticism. In an essay on Edmund Scherer he praises the author because,

besides the distinction of beauty and ugliness, the aesthetic distinction of right and wrong, there constantly occurs in his pages the moral distinction between good and evil.[50]

The thought here could no doubt have been more perspicuously expressed. It is clear (at least) that beauty and ugliness stand on one side and good and evil on another; the difficulty involves the expression that stands between them, "the aesthetic distinction of right and wrong." A possible reading, though not finally a persuasive one, would place the phrase in parallel to the one that precedes it. Right and wrong would then indicate a specifically aesthetic domain, narrower than the wide realm of beauty and ugliness, which can include, for instance, people and landscapes. But neither the context nor the syntax encourages this interpretation. A more natural reading would take the second phrase in apposition to the first, construing it, roughly, as "the aesthetic *manifestation* of right and wrong" – so that James, in effect, would be implying that beauty and ugliness are the forms that right and wrong assume when they enter the region of art. Applying this thought to the rest of the sentence, one can deduce that just as right and wrong take the aspect of beauty and ugliness in the aesthetic realm, so in the realm of ethics they appear in the "moral distinction between good and evil." There is no need to anchor the meaning of an unsteady sentence, but it is important to see that for James "right" is, perhaps, a movable concept which pertains to the aesthetic as well as the moral sphere.

Strether, we should notice, does not say that he wants to *do* right; he says that he wants to *be* right. This is not a common moral locution: "right" in the moral sense usually applies to actions rather than to people.[51] Moreover, it ordinarily implies the fulfillment of a duty or an obligation. But Strether is not using the term in this sense; the issue is not how he can act rightly but how an action can make him right. In his speech at Gloriani's party he speaks of the need to act "at the right time" (I, p. 218) – not, that is, the morally scrupulous time, but the apt or felicitous time. Examining the relics which Madame de Vionnet displays in her home, Strether surmises that she has "a deep suspicion of the vulgar and a personal view of the right" (I, p. 245). And when he first sees the still unidentified couple boating on the river, Strether, we recall, considers the image "exactly the right thing," just what "had been wanted in the picture" (II, p. 256).

His final declaration, "To be right," has important links to these uses of the term. Strether is not raising a general point about moral rules or ethical principles or even norms of etiquette. He appeals instead to his own rigorous perception, "my only logic," and asks what – given his history, his circumstances, his values and his temptations – will allow him to be right, as a line in a drawing or a phrase in a sonata is right. He is once more placing himself within a composition, and in this respect he is making a distinctly aesthetic decision, expressed in terms of "harmony" (II, p. 320), rather than duty.

This is not to say that "right" loses its moral connotations. On the contrary, as the cryptic sentence from the Scherer essay suggests, the force of "right," as opposed to "good" or "beautiful," is that it stands at the place where moral and aesthetic judgments meet, and in this respect it works much like Marlow's "darkness," which depends, too, less on analytic reflection than on a "horrible sharp eye." Like Marlow's judgment "too dark," Strether's aspiration "to be right" involves a formal as well as an ethical judgment; it requires a sharp act of perception that can identify the necessities for this man at this moment in these circumstances. A judgment so private cannot be sorted according to any moral code, and having freed himself from chimerical notions of the good, Strether can at last be right for himself.

The lot of both Marlow and Strether is to wrest themselves from the oppressive demands of others only to find themselves confronted with moral solitude. The independent judgment, the private logic, the sensory response, the personal word, the self-generated value, the self-assigned destiny – these are achievements which immediately raise new doubts. Free at last from the more crippling distortions of social life, Marlow and Strether must ask whether sociality as such is a hollow ideal.

Marlow's lie to the Intended may indeed be an attempt to sustain the necessary illusions on which communal life is based, the fictions that make life together supportable, but it is at the same time a violent repudiation of communal ties. What makes the lie so ghastly and so compelling is that it preserves a social ideal by creating opacity between individuals; it founds community on the basis of estrangement. But this fateful verbal act must be set against the verbal act which follows after some unspecified lapse of time, namely Marlow's narrative itself, which tells what had been suppressed (Kurtz's last words) and which can be seen as an act of reparation, a reparation after the lie. Where the lie divides, the narrative means to join. The question is whether it can do so, whether it can successfully atone for Marlow's verbal sin or whether it is only another, more prolonged, form of failure. The problem is especially acute in light of the highly distrustful attitude towards language that manifests itself in *Heart of Darkness* — as, for instance, in the following passage.

He was silent for a while.
". . . No, it is impossible; it is impossible to convey the life-sensation of any given epoch of one's existence — that which makes its truth, its meaning — its subtle and penetrating essence. It is impossible. We live, as we dream — alone. . ."
He paused again as if reflecting, then added:
"Of course in this you fellows see more than I could then. You see me, whom you know. . . ."
It had become so pitch dark that we listeners could hardly see one another. For a long time already he, sitting apart, had been no more to us than a voice. There was not a word from anybody. The others might have been asleep, but I was awake. I listened, I listened on the watch for the sentence, for the word, that would give me the clue to the faint uneasiness inspired by this narrative that seemed to shape itself without human lips in the heavy night-air of the river. (p. 30)

In the sceptical readings of the tale that have become common this passage is often cited as evidence of the inevitably solipsistic fate of the Conradian ego. Marlow concedes his own failure to communicate, and the narrator then intensifies the point through an irony which takes away the little Marlow had given. Marlow, it seems, cannot express what he knows and cannot know what he expresses.

Admittedly, language in *Heart of Darkness* is a clumsy instrument for establishing intimacy, for exchanging meanings, for winning assent, for achieving agreement, for securing mutual understanding. Nevertheless, it is well to remember one blunt point: even the solipsist can dream of perfect intimacy with another. Marlow can never step outside the boundaries around the self to discover if he has communicated to another, but from within these boundaries he can record the tale of another communicating to *him*. In voicing his reactions to Kurtz he suggests how a listener might respond to elusive speech — as much to imply that if, improbably, his hearers are to comprehend him, they must stand towards him as he stood towards Kurtz. Although Marlow must remain locked within his cage, he can speak (perhaps to no one) of hearing (or perhaps imagining) a cry from another cage, and he thus creates an image of how understanding would occur, if only understanding *could* occur.

It is presumably evident that in the passage above Marlow, "no more . . . than a voice," has become identified with Kurtz whose "gift of expression" he will deeply ponder and whom he will call "A voice! A voice!" It is perhaps less evident, although no less important, that through the "uneasiness inspired by [Marlow's] narrative," he is identified with Kurtz's antithesis, the Manager, whose authority depends precisely on the fact that "he inspired uneasiness."

This curious double identification has arresting implications for the novel's structure of values, suggesting as it does that Marlow occupies the place where Kurtz and the Manager meet. More immediately, it bears on the problem of communication. For even as Marlow despairs of his ability to represent the events of his narrative, he takes on the attributes of the two principal figures within it. He *embodies* those whom he vainly attempts to describe. What he cannot depict, he can perhaps be.

The telling of the story becomes a reenactment of its central relationships, an acting out of the problem it describes, a performance which reaches its goal not when the actors understand the meaning of the drama but merely when they are able to assume their roles. When the frame narrator listens to Marlow, to a man who is no more than a voice; when he endures the uneasiness that this man inspires; and finally, climactically, when he looks at the Thames waterway and sees a heart of darkness; then he plays Marlow to Marlow's Kurtz, and, more subtly, Marlow to Marlow's Manager. A transaction has occurred, a gift has been given. Marlow cannot know that this has happened, and this is the true pathos of Conradian language: even its successes are unknown. But standing outside this world, *we* can know them; we know that a man rattling his cage has rattled the cage of another.

We cannot say that language has communicated meaning, but it has perhaps transmitted an experience, something that cannot be described in words but that may be aroused through words. Language may miss the mark; it may fail to articulate the sensation; but in missing the mark, it may create the sensation. Not in what language says but in what it does lies its power, or, as Marlow puts it in *Lord Jim*, "The power of sentences has nothing to do with their sense or the logic of their construction."[52] Speech is not an exchange of shared meanings; it is an attempt to point at something beyond its reach; it is indeed a bodily activity, a performance, an impersonation of the ineffable – as in the Russian's narrative, "this amazing tale that was not so much told as suggested to me in desolate exclamations, completed by shrugs, in interrupted phrases, in hints ending in deep sighs" (p. 56). Of Marlow's tale, too, we can say that it suggests rather than tells, that it relies on the method of shrugs and hints, interruptions, exclamations and sighs. If Marlow can never represent the individual life-sensation in words, he may nevertheless engender that sensation in another, never knowing that he has done so, never believing that it is possible.

Whether Marlow's listener has grasped the "subtle and penetrating essence" we cannot know. All one can say with certainty is that he has taken over Marlow's metaphor: he looks towards the end of the world and sees a heart of darkness. Metaphor, indeed, is the most important resource in the hinting, shrugging, sighing pursuit of a state beyond the reach of words. And part of the further cunning of an image such as "darkness" is that it flourishes in just those unfavorable conditions that surround Conradian speech. As an image of absence it can succeed where other images fail; one might even say that it succeeds through failure. If Marlow fades into a dark void, if the sky grows black, if meaning becomes obscure and value murky, this only confirms the force of the metaphor. The narrator's very difficulty in comprehending Marlow's tale becomes an argument for its central figure: darkness is the one thing that can be seen with poor eyes.

The narrator makes no answer to Marlow's monologue. What could he possibly say? Within the asymmetry of Conradian speech, some must speak while some must listen, and only when the precarious verbal transaction is finished can the hearer enjoy the privileges of speech. "You don't talk to [Kurtz]," says the Russian, "you listen to him" (p. 53). Marlow, having listened, now talks at length, much as his taciturn auditor on the *Nellie* goes ashore and becomes an author. There is no moment of mutual recognition in which individual minds meet in the transparency of conversation; there is only a series of urgent monologues which make no claim to disclose a truth, which dramatize the limits of language, which affirm the privacy of experience, and which nevertheless create a tight chain of solitaries, each of whom believes that he has learned but doubts whether he can teach. No one subjectivity can tell what another knows and feels, but as an image moves from the wilderness to Kurtz, to Marlow, to the narrator, to the reader, the gift of darkness is blindly exchanged.

If *Heart of Darkness* alternates between garrulous speakers and silent listeners, in *The Ambassadors* there is garrulous speech on both sides, and in general what the monologue is to Conrad's method, the dialogue is to the method of James. Instead of attempting to reach beyond language to some complex nonverbal state, Strether attempts to get *into* language, to enter a circuit of verbal exchange where one might undertake that imaginative revision of civilization which is the novel's most ambitious goal. To Marlow's celebrated aphorism, "We live, as we dream – alone," Strether implicitly responds, "We live as we speak – together."

When Maria Gostrey first meets Bilham, she quickly passes a favorable judgment, "he's one of *us!*" and we learn that "Strether knew that he knew almost immediately what she meant" (I, p. 125). Knowing that one knows what the other means is precisely what Marlow had considered impossible. In *The Ambassadors* it is not easy but it can occur, and it is what gives the Jamesian dialogue its distinctive form, the subject of conversation so often becoming the conversation itself. The dialogues regularly turn inward, twisting back upon themselves through requests for clarification, definitions of terms, specifications of reference, elaborations of meaning. A process of mutual adjustment occurs, in which characters learn one another's language – they learn what things are called – and what seems to be only a preparatory act, finding words that each can understand, is frequently the culmination. The odd *contentlessness* of Jamesian conversation is due to the fact that its real aim is often not to say anything in particular but to establish shared terms of exchange.

During a late conversation Strether and Chad cautiously allude to Sarah Pocock's loathing of Madame de Vionnet. "She hates me in Paris," says Chad, and Strether continues:

"She hates in other words — "

"Yes, *that's* it!" — Chad had quickly understood this understanding; which formed on the part of each as near an approach as they had yet made to naming Madame de Vionnet. . .

Strether knew as immediately whom he meant. . . (II, p. 222)

The phrase "understood this understanding" tersely states the aim of these conversationalists, a perfect mutual consciousness that arises only within the dialogic encounter, a reflexive knowledge, the understanding of an understanding — a condition scarcely imaginable in the work of Conrad.

The disturbance of social experience, either in its American or its European forms, lies in the way it impedes such understood understandings, particularly in the way that language obscures the intentions of its speakers. The risk is that merely by speaking a language one will, like Madame de Vionnet, have one's identity veiled by "class" or "race." A useful way to regard the Jamesian dialogue is as an internal response to the estrangements of language, whose ambiguities and opacities reproduce the ambiguities and opacities of communal life.

The dialogue, with its pursuit of linguistic transparency, with its attempt to sift multiple meanings and to fix unstable references, with its fussy attention to nuance and suggestion, aims to clarify the obscurities of language through the act of speech. After Strether has refused to name the object produced at Woollett, Maria Gostrey wonders whether it is "bad": "And she explained that she meant improper or ridiculous or wrong." No, responds Strether, it is simply "small, trivial, rather ridiculous" and lacking in "dignity." "It's a false note?" asks Maria. "Sadly," answers Strether, "It's vulgar" (I, p. 60). The exchange plays out in miniature an activity which Strether will pursue throughout the novel and which has been described here as an attempt to refine the language of appraisal, a quest for the precise adjective. Strether must multiply distinctions

within his language, never leaving its boundaries, never free
from its constraints, but mobile enough to set its terms against
one another, until the language of the tribe is, for the
moment, adequate to the needs of the speaking subject.

At this point a capstone may be gingerly placed on the structure of the argument. This discussion has proposed that the
question of subjectivity in *The Ambassadors* is at once
ethical/political and tonal/formal, that it involves a social
negotiation between two importunate communities, Paris and
Woollett, and a stylistic negotiation between two much-
exploited devices, metaphor and typification. Furthermore it
has proposed that these distinctions run parallel to one another:
typological generality is the chief resource of Woollett and
metaphor the leading device of Paris. We have already considered Strether's attempt to establish a third moral attitude
distinct from the attitudes of Paris and Woollett, an attitude
epitomized in the movement from the "good" and the
"beautiful" to the "right," and now, to conclude, a third
stylistic term must be acknowledged, a formal alternative to
typification and metaphor.

One of the most distinctive mannerisms in James's dialogues
is the short almost tautological utterance, composed of personal pronouns, the verb 'to be' and a demonstrative adverb:
"there he is"; "you're not where you were"; "here I am";
"then there we are."[53] The generous use of verbal emphasis
is notable in the late style, and by far the greatest number of
such emphases occur in these simple expressions: "It isn't *you*";
"I've done *this*"; "you're better than *that*" (II, pp. 29, 67, 120).
These phrases regularly punctuate Strether's conversations and
often serve to culminate complex discussions, without it being immediately clear why these expressions have the force
which characters attach to them. " 'That,' Strether gave it to
her more vividly, 'is where I am' " (II, p. 41). Such an assertion predicates nothing, advances no argument, imparts no
information. It merely affirms what no one would care to
doubt.

These phrases are composed entirely (or almost entirely) of
what have come to be called "indexicals," namely those expressions – pronouns, tensed verbs, and demonstrative

adverbs — which change their designata according to changes in time, place and speaker. Such terms as "this," "now," "here," "there," "I" and "you" may preserve their meaning from sentence to sentence — "I" will always indicate the speaker, "now" the moment of speech — but since speakers change and moments pass, these words continually change their reference. As Baker and Hacker put it, "to understand a sentence with an indexical is to know such things as who uttered it, what he was pointing to, when and where he was when he spoke"[54] — with the result, for instance, that Strether and Sarah Pocock struggle over the fate of Madame de Vionnet, while identifying her merely as "this person here." The attempt to offer a neutral or impersonal description of the world has often foundered upon these constructions which irresistibly impose what Benveniste has called "subjectivity in language."[55] Indexicals, to put the matter in more familiar terms, describe the world from a point of view, and one can only understand the description after locating the point of view.

The provocation of language in *The Ambassadors* is precisely that it unsettles, even estranges, point of view. Language itself has its own internal demands that can obstruct expression and distort judgment, and any attempt to apply it with precision, especially to apply evaluative terms with precision, must confront ambiguities that inhere in the structure of concepts and reflect essential ambiguities in culture. The short indexical sentence might be seen as an effort to escape the entanglements of this seductive system. Next to such terms as "beauty," "goodness" and "freedom," expressions such as "here I am" or "there we are" say very little within the system of collective representation. Indeed they say very little at all. But if they communicate few facts, they serve a subtler purpose.

Early in the novel Strether tells Bilham that Chad is someone "he should have enjoyed being 'like' " (I, p. 220). And later, during the long vigil after his discovery in the countryside, he reflects obsessively that intimacy "was *like* that — and what in the world else would one have wished it to be like" (II, p. 266). It is a complex idiom — "being like that" — but it is tied to James's deepest commitments. To recognize something as "like that" is not to know its causes or its consequences, but to acknowledge it as an irreducibly singular phenomenon which must be understood on its own terms. This is neither theoretical nor figural knowledge; the recognition depends on a direct encounter, a felt acquaintance, and often manifests itself in definitive judgment — as in Kate Croy's verdict upon Milly Theale, "She's *like* that."[56] If intimacy is *like* that and Milly is *like* that, then there can be no further appeal. We have arrived at a crux, an integrity, a final truth that cannot be paraphrased, only reasserted. Hence, speaking on behalf of her mother, a high-minded Sarah Pocock demands of Strether, "What is your conduct but an outrage to women like *us*?" (II, p. 199) The peculiarity of the phrase is that it purports to name an essence, just by affirming the thing itself — like her, like that, like us.

In a strict sense the best late-Jamesian answer to the question, "What is your experience like?" is an impatient wave of the hand, "Like this!" Thus at the climactic moment when Madame de Vionnet no longer tries to conceal her love for Chad, she begins to weep "giving up all attempt at a manner," and then sobs out, " 'It's how you see me, it's how you see me' — she caught her breath with it — 'and it's as I *am*, and as I must take myself, and of course it's no matter' " (II, p. 285). She utters little more than a string of uninformative identities announcing that he sees her as she appears and that she is as she is. Madame de Vionnet's encounter with suffering, like Strether's encounter with intimacy, can only be identified with a demonstrative grunt, "this" or "that" or "it."

Subjectivity for James cannot be captured in a mark on the body, in a mental scar, in the "lumpish past," in the literal event, in a verbal tic, in an emotional obsession; it cannot be captured, that is, in any "particular local case." Indeed the notion of "being like that" may be seen as an alternative to Balzac's exhaustive pursuit of local particulars. Jamesian individuality does not come in pithy particulars; it comes enwrapped in all the types that include it and all the metaphors that illuminate it; it cannot be isolated; it is a seamless totality, the sum of its relations. We miss the force of *The Ambassadors* if we tear Strether from the dense web which locates him and whose many strands make him an artist, a critic, a debtor, an apostate, a youth, a critic, a mirror, a mind, an ambassador, and many other things.

James describes his aim as "thickened motive and accumulated character" (I, p. viii), and what allows motive to thicken and character to accumulate are just those acts of typification and those flights of metaphor which transform Strether's limited adventures into his limitless imaginative experience. But the provocation of these two rhetorical instruments, much like the two communities with which I have associated them, is that they define the subject from without, fixing its identity from an external public standpoint with its own names and values. Against this threat of self-abandonment James does not offer an integral personality, wrenched from its context, proudly displaying its own self-sufficiency. Instead he offers moments of rare perception in which the "I" surveys the web that holds it, recognizes the coherence of the pattern, understands what it is "like," and knows it as its own.

In the third stylistic moment, the indexical moment, the speaker bypasses the nuances of diction, neglects the subtleties of rhetoric, in order to make an immediate gesture from a specific point of view: "it's as I *am*," "she's *like* that," "I've done *this*." Such a verbal reflex stands in sharp contrast to the desire to find names for things, classes for particulars, metaphors for facts. It is a simple act of ostension, conscious subjectivity pointing at the world, gesturing at a state too complex to describe. The "I" does not escape the entanglements of its relations, but it sees them from the inside and affirms what it might merely have endured.

"I want to know where I am," says a helpless Strether at one point (I, p. 235), and not long afterward we learn that "he had simply stood fast on the spot on which he had then planted his feet" (II, p. 23). The difficulty is that the spot moves beneath him. One way to formulate Strether's endeavor is as an attempt to find moral poise in an endlessly changing world. His early rigid adherence to the good and the true proves inadequate to the nuances of moral experience, and, as we have seen, his wanting to be "right" at the end of the novel suggests the attempt to adapt morality to the highly particularized requirements usually associated with aesthetic judgment. "Here I am" cannot be counted as a moral gesture, but it can be seen as an effort to establish a standpoint from which such a gesture might be made; even more fundamentally, it can be seen as Strether's reminder (to himself) that he *has* a standpoint. It is not fixed in the way he once thought goodness and truth were fixed; Strether cannot help floating in such a fluid world. But he can maintain a perspective that changes with the changing scene and that allows him to have, not a fixed view, but a constant angle of vision. This is the power of "here" and "there"; they adjust to the scenery.

"Then there we are" (II, p. 327), declares Strether, and the novel ends on as colorless a remark as one could imagine. But its colorlessness is its peculiar virtue. Among all the subtleties and duplicities, the ironies, the ambiguities, such an expression achieves a kind of linguistic purity almost invulnerable to the dangers of interpretation. With his intransitive unilluminating final comment Strether affirms what is already, what is necessarily, the case. He declares that he and Maria are, well, where they are. If this seems a trivial recognition, we should remember that Strether was the one who always considered "something else; something else, I mean, than the thing of the moment" (I, p. 19), and whose reason for being somewhere was simply "the desire not to be, for the hour, in certain other places" (II, p. 4). Clearly, one cannot construct a very articulate description of the world on the basis of "you" and "I," "is" and "were," "this" and "that." But the reliance on such terms allows subjectivity, at this moment, in this place, to be its own point of vantage without enduring the dislocations of common speech. Strether, we recall, had once imagined that Marie de Vionnet possessed "a language quite to herself," but in his own use of these pronouns, these demonstratives, these verbal emphases, he takes steps towards securing a language to himself – not in the sense that his words are unavailable to others but in the sense that their significance depends essentially on the speaker at the moment of speech.[57]

During his walk in the countryside Strether comes to a significant realization that in other circumstances, in another novel, would seem wholly banal, namely "that in *these* places such things were, and that if it was in them one elected to move about one had to make one's account with what one lighted on" (II, p. 254). Two paragraphs later he will light on Chad and Madame de Vionnet, but he has made himself ready. The work of the mind is so important to our appreciation of James's accomplishment, and to his appreciation of his own accomplishment, that it has obscured the extent to which the agitations, gropings, hesitations and decisions of the mind yield ultimately to the acceptance of a condition external to itself. The restlessness of the fine conscience ends in a fine stillness: "there we are." After all the estrangements of language and culture, Strether retains nothing more, but nothing less, than a point of view. His recognition, "in these places such things were," is little more than a tautology, but a tautology that was unavailable to him before, and within the context of the novel, to see *this such there now* is an achievement of significant scale. Strether has learned he is "here" exactly wherever he happens to be.

Strether and Marlow must live through a crisis in social history and a crisis of expressive forms. A new rigidity in the common culture, quickened by the consolidation of capital and the new imperium, and an imprecision in the common language, especially the language of judgment, inhibit the expression of moral identity and precipitate the imaginative and stylistic responses traced here. Furthermore, the peculiar configuration that I have called the "beyond within" – in which the voice from beyond the threshold whispers at the heart's core and in which extravagant metaphors become the truth of common experience – makes psychological flight as unavailing as physical flight. The two maxims that have served as epitomes, the Conradian judgment that everything is in the "mind of man" and the Jamesian perception that the history of emotion resides in language, dramatize the entanglement of the one in the many, the private eye in the public body.

Both works demonstrate the awful collusion between inner promptings and outer pressures, and in response both contemplate a barely conceivable point between the inside and

the outside of the "I," a place between desire and convention.
In Conrad this is the region of moral sensations, the ethics
of the surface of the skin, which make a claim distinct from
the claims of passion and principle, and in James it is the site
of self-consciousness as such, subjectivity as a bare but sub-
sistent point of view. These rarefied forms of individuality are
not just metaphysical curiosities; they are attempts to purify
the subject so that, in times of cultural crisis, it can still be
a worthy bearer of moral value. Strether and Marlow must
pass through a prolonged ascesis until they have mastered the
delicate balance between private will and public constraint.

Not to demand anything for oneself and not to submit to
the demands of others − this is the difficult equipoise which
these two protagonists seek. In *Heart of Darkness* it manifests
itself in the image of Marlow as "a Buddha preaching in European clothes" (p. 10), while in *The Ambassadors* it appears in
the "pure flame of the disinterested" (II, p. 132) which Strether
carefully tends: "He wished not to do anything because he
had missed something else, because he was sore or sorry or
impoverished, because he was maltreated or desperate; he
wished to do everything because he was lucid and quiet. . .
It would have sickened him to feel vindictive" (II, p. 295).
Caught between the rival claims of others, Strether and Marlow
forge positions whose strength, in James's phrase, is that there
is "nothing in it" for themselves (II, p. 60).

Indeed the ideal of disinterestedness, whether it displays itself
in Marlow's Buddhist concentration or Strether's quiet lucidity,
suggests a way to understand the longer narrative rhythms of
these two works. For disinterestedness is not detachment; it
is the product of a deep engagement with the world that ends
by suspending the ego among the various appeals it meets. The
very disinterestedness that gives Marlow and Strether a measure
of freedom from the interested parties around them depends
on those interested parties for its existence. It is a negative virtue
that exists only as a principle of balance among contending
rivals; it is a third term that needs to locate itself between two
others.

Heart of Darkness and *The Ambassadors* are in their broadest
movements novels in three acts. Each begins with a movement

75

of disaffiliation, the gradual withdrawal of an individual from his native culture until its norms and values have lost their moral necessity. The estrangement of Marlow from European rationality and the alienation of Strether from American ethical dogma culminate when each acknowledges alternative values promising a release from the cramped quarters of inherited beliefs. The second movement involves the embrace of this inadequately understood alternative: Kurtz's enlightened Africa, Chad's beautiful Paris. By imagining the virtues of these novelties, Marlow and Strether establish a standpoint from which to challenge a rigid cultural form. But when Marlow, standing on his boat, looks to the shore and sees the barbaric signs of Kurtz's fall, and when Strether, standing on the shore, sees Chad and Madame de Vionnet in a boat and recognizes the civilized lie of their romance, each confronts the impossibility of escaping moral limitation.

Such a perception has led others to relativism. Both works disclose the terrifying *integrity* of culture, its self-sufficiency, its self-enclosure, its indifference to those outside its walls. What Strether says of Mrs Newsome − "she hangs together with a perfection of her own . . . that does suggest a wrong in *any* change in her composition" (II, p. 239) − might be said of the community she epitomizes and indeed of every community in *The Ambassadors* and *Heart of Darkness*. Each has its perfections, necessities, sympathies and cruelties, its own "typical tale" and its own moral narrowness. And if, as James himself wrote, there "comes a time when one set of customs, wherever it may be found, grows to seem to you about as provincial as another," then the temptation is strong to value all customs equally.[58] But in the third act Marlow and Strether refuse the relativist abstention and decide between two provincialisms. Marlow makes his "choice of nightmares," and Strether's resolve appears in only slightly milder terms, when he places himself on the side of "the fierce, the sinister, the acute" (II, p. 271). Yet, what is most remarkable is that in each case the fateful choice coincides with a withdrawal from the chosen object. As Strether moves to bring his peculiar drama to its dénouement, he reflects that: "He must do both things; he must see Chad, but he must go" (II, p. 304). He must see

Chad in order to affirm the value of Paris and Madame de Vionnet, and he must go in order to protect the unity of the self from the unity of its community. Strether, notes James, has changed so profoundly that to stay in Paris with Maria Gostrey "would be almost of the old order."[59] The radical gesture is to return home, because home is precisely where one can never be *at home*. The same is evidently true of Marlow; he must *hear* Kurtz but he must go. Like Strether, he goes home in order to go into exile.

In *The Ambassadors* and *Heart of Darkness* it requires two cultures to construct an individual. There can be no self-definition through retreat to a strictly private region; there *is* no such region; as Kurtz shows, even madness makes its own society. When Strether at one point refers to "you ladies," Miss Barrace offers a trenchant response, "As one of us, you know, I don't pretend I'm crazy about us" (II, p. 174). No comment could express the issue more exactly, the simultaneous recognition and refusal of a common lot. The elaborate final maneuverings of Strether and Marlow represent, among many other things, the attempt to establish an "I" from within, necessarily within, the sphere of "us." Faced with contending values they choose one and then decide to live with the other. Only in this way can they preserve the *friction* that sustains the "I" against the "us" and allows subjectivity to live on within the snares of social life.

CHAPTER TWO

Liberalism and symbolism in *Howards End*

Liberalism and symbolism, both unwieldy terms, become more unwieldy when brought together. They seem to belong to such different orders of description and such different strains of modernity that it provokes a small mental shudder to recall that John Stuart Mill and Charles Baudelaire were near contemporaries. Although no one would mistake E. M. Forster for either Mill or Baudelaire, liberalism and symbolism are prominent in his ancestry, and *Howards End* (1910), which occupies a place in both lineages, marks a striking point of connection between political hopes and literary tropes. The only thing more vivid than Forster's perception of social constraint was his perception of imaginative escape. Looking at the world from the standpoint of historical necessity and the standpoint of visionary possibility, he saw depth in modern experience but also incongruity, because he saw with one liberal and one symbolist eye. It is necessary to correct for the parallax. In following the competition but also the cooperation of these perspectives, this chapter gives the issues raised in the first chapter a turn towards politics and a turn towards mysticism. It asks what happens to the experience of the self when its own modes of understanding come into conflict and when it is unsure whether it has sustained a symbolic victory or a political defeat.

In the work of Forster it is possible to glimpse what the development of the novel might have been if at the turn of our century it had endured an evolutionary, rather than a revolutionary, change. Forster belongs neither with the stout Edwardians, Wells, Bennett and Galsworthy, nor with the lean modernists, Joyce, Woolf, Ford and Lewis. He shared with the latter the sense of an irrevocable historical transformation

78

that necessarily alters the methods of art, but he could never muster the conviction for a programmatic assault on traditional forms. For this reason he continues to occupy an ambiguous position in the history of modern fiction. His own formal experiments, which are by no means negligible, often appear as involuntary expressions of his own sense of loss, and much of their inspiration, as I hope to show, lies in the attempt to revive a dying tradition.

I

"Oh, to acquire culture!" thinks Leonard Bast, "Oh, to pronounce foreign names correctly."[1] He is walking alongside Margaret Schlegel, who has just pronounced Wagner's name (correctly, one must assume) and who has promised to recover Bast's umbrella, thoughtlessly taken by her sister during a concert at Queen's Hall. Bast stammers, falls silent takes his umbrella, refuses an invitation to tea, bolts home, reads Ruskin. Then, reminded of the disparity between the flat of an insurance clerk and the stones of Venice, he lays Ruskin aside with this unhappy thought: "Oh, it was no good, this continual aspiration. Some are born cultured; the rest had better go in for whatever comes easy. To see life steadily and to see it whole was not for the likes of him" (p. 52).

Arnold's formulation was a touchstone for Forster who came back to it repeatedly in *Howards End* — its progressive restatements marking the development of the novel's argument. On this first occasion it broaches the problem of modern character, which for Forster (certainly not uniquely) is a problem of lost unity, lost because of related historical pressures: urbanism, imperialism, cosmopolitanism, bureaucracy, the estrangement of social classes. But there is another implication in Arnold's phrase that has particular bearing on Forsterian characterization: the attention to a form of response (seeing) rather than a form of action.

The initial and decisive characterization of Margaret Schlegel identifies her leading quality as "a profound vivacity, a continual and sincere response to all that she encountered in her path through life" (p. 7). Forster thus endows her not with a desire but with a *disposition*; he is concerned less with her will to act than with her "sincere response" to what she encounters. Of the boorish Charles Wilcox we are told that "Want was to him the only cause of action" (p. 93). Forster mentions such an opinion only as a way of dismissing it; he himself is primarily interested in neither wants, nor causes, nor indeed actions in their conventional sense. *Howards End*, like so much of Forster's work, suggests that the incidents which determine the broad course of life, both the intimate movements of the soul and the rude spasms of history, exceed the reach of individual will. One is accountable neither for one's desires nor one's epoch. Both exist as ungovernable forces that change particular lives but resist the workings of human agency, and therefore Forster declines to describe them with precision. He prefers to maintain strict attention upon the subject that interests him most; the region of individual experience that lies between the insurgence of the feelings and the oppressions of history. Part of the reason that Forster has come to seem outdated is that the space between history and the emotions has progressively narrowed in our time, but in *Howards End* there is still room to maneuver. Nevertheless, in the face of such powerful antagonists, what is to be done?

One cannot change one's desires; one cannot alter the movement of history. But it is possible to change the form and style of one's response, and here we come to a telling aspect of the novel's method of characterization: its tendency to describe individuals in terms that refer equally to the English literary tradition. Tibby derives from the Wildean nineties; Leonard Bast connects his aspirations to Ruskin, Meredith and Stevenson; the Schlegel sisters (as others have noted) descend from *Sense and Sensibility*; Miss Avery is a late incarnation of a Gothic housekeeper; and the narrator alternately assumes the tones of Thackeray and Trollope. Through a kind of historical ventriloquism Forster displays the novelistic tradition he has inherited. This is more than an exercise in stylistic virtuosity; it serves to underscore an arresting fact, the intimate connection between fictional character and literary mode. Indeed character in *Howards End* is essentially a mode of aesthetic response, where this is understood not as the casual striking of a pose but as the deepest form of one's engagement with experience. That human responses vary so greatly poses perhaps the chief difficulty of the novel: the heterogeneity of modes, the diversity of styles, tones and manners.

Forster, who acknowledged his great debt to Jane Austen, is commonly linked to Austen and James as a novelist of manners. One might better say that he is a novelist of bad manners, who attends less to the shared norms and values which govern a community than to the moral awkwardness that results when incompatible norms and incommensurable values collide. Thus, Helen's "high-handed manner" (p. 177) competes with the "breezy Wilcox manner" (p. 178); Evie develops a "manner more downright" (p. 147) while Tibby remains "affected in manner" (p. 247); and Margaret finds Leonard's class "near enough her own for its manners to vex her" (p. 35). Forster assumes nothing so stable as a coherent system of human conduct; indeed in his most serious purpose, he dramatizes the search for a moral manner, which becomes one with the search for an imaginative mode.

Beethoven's Fifth Symphony provides a comic and anodyne example. It excites a great variety of reactions — Mrs Munt's surreptitious foot-tapping, Helen's reverie of heroes and goblins, Tibby's attention to counterpoint — but the variety is unthreatening because it overlays a fundamental point of agreement, namely that the "Fifth Symphony is the most sublime noise that has ever penetrated into the ear of man. All sorts and conditions are satisfied by it" (p. 29). Beethoven, however, is valuable just insofar as he is an exception. Precisely the problem which the novel poses is the difficulty of such agreement and the incongruity of diverse sorts and sundry conditions. When Mrs Wilcox fails to "blend" with the Schlegel set, when Leonard describes his squalid flat in the style of Ruskin, when Tibby and Charles attempt to converse having "nothing in common but the English language" (p. 396), the painful dissonance establishes an urgent requirement, the need for an appropriate mode with which to confront the facts of contemporary experience. The Arnoldian conception of seeing life steadily and whole represents an ideal mode for the engaged personality but an ideal which seems to have become obsolete. Arnold's phrase, as we will see, has still wider implications, but then so too does the issue of modality.

The agonies of Leonard Bast reflect both the disgregation of the self and the disgregation of its community — the failure of both to advance in the direction which Arnold had so confidently forecast.

Culture looks beyond machinery, culture hates hatred; culture has one great passion, the passion for sweetness and light. It has one even greater! — the passion for making them *prevail*. It is not satisfied till we *all* come to a perfect man; it knows that the sweetness and light of the few must be imperfect until the raw and unkindled masses of humanity are touched with sweetness and light.[2]

Against such a view, *Howards End* places Bast, whose hopes are kindled only at the cost of great pain, and who, when he burns, gives off no sweetness and little light. Bast will come to mistrust the healing power of culture, as will Margaret Schlegel who thinks of him and arrives at this post-Arnoldian conclusion:

Culture had worked in her own case, but during the last few weeks she had doubted whether it humanized the majority, so wide and so widening is the gulf that stretches between the natural and the philosophic man, so many the good chaps who are wrecked in trying to cross it. (p. 113)

Instead of Arnold's widening isthmus Forster sees a widening gulf. Moreover, the problem does not end here; it goes beyond the "unkindled masses" to infect the privileged few. Halfway through the novel, just before Henry Wilcox proposes marriage to Margaret Schlegel, the two discuss the burdens of house-hunting. Wilcox insists that she is not as unpractical as she pretends, and Arnold's celebrated dictum makes a second appearance.

Margaret laughed. But she was — quite as unpractical. She could not concentrate on details. Parliament, the Thames, the irresponsive chauffeur, would flash into the field of house-hunting, and all demand some comment or response. It is impossible to see modern life steadily and see it whole, and she had chosen to see it whole. Mr Wilcox saw steadily. (p. 158)

The disjunction, steadily or whole, sets out the novel's problem, or to put it better, the disjunction is itself the problem. The novel asks: How can disjunction be overcome? How can Arnold's formulation be rescued and a moral unity restored?

The answer, as readers of the novel well remember, is to connect: "Only connect! That was the whole of her sermon. Only connect the prose and the passion, and both will be exalted, and human love will be seen at its highest. Live in fragments no longer. Only connect, and the beast and the monk, robbed of the isolation that is life to each, will die" (pp. 183–4).

At this point we should recall the view of *Howards End* that has dominated the criticism since it was proposed over forty years ago. In an interpretation which first appeared in his book *E. M. Forster* (1943) Lionel Trilling offered a thoroughgoing symbolic reading according to which *Howards End* was to be seen as "a novel about England's fate," "a story of the class war."[3] Under the assumptions of this account the Schlegels exemplify the predicament of the intellectual situated between the victims and beneficiaries of modern capitalism. Their role is to reach downwards towards a depressed clerical class (as represented by Leonard Bast) and upwards towards a thriving business class (as represented by the Wilcoxes). When Helen bears a child fathered by Leonard and when Margaret marries Henry, the Schlegels symbolically fulfill their historical mission, and at the end of the novel, when Henry, Margaret, Helen and Helen's son settle at Howards End ("the symbol for England"), the reconciliation among classes has been achieved. According to Trilling the novel asks the question, "Who shall inherit England?" and it provides its answer in the final image of the child playing in the hay – "a symbol of the classless society."[4]

Trilling, it is evident, offers not merely an interpretation of the novel but an embrace of certain possibilities within it. Placing himself in a line of descent from both Arnold and Forster, he suggests in effect an Arnoldian recovery from Forsterian scepticism. In so doing, he implicitly proposes a solution to a problem that dominated the opening of this study. Both James and Conrad, as we have seen, struggled to find some accommodation between the necessary entanglements of culture and the specific perceptions, reasons and values of the entangled individual. *Heart of Darkness* and *The Ambassadors*, one might say, extend the dominion of culture by showing the extent to which it informs the intimacies of private life, and they preserve a region of individual autonomy only by contracting it severely. Both works create an image of the colossus that is social life and the buzzing gnat that is private moral experience; and both works leave a chasm between the agitation of the central character and the torpor of the community which surrounds him.

Within the terms of Trilling's interpretation *Howards End* successfully overcomes this division of experience. The symbolic equations between characters and classes – and most notably, the allegorical cast of the conclusion – traverse the distance between individual and social life. Through the resources of symbolism the private gesture is at the same time a public gesture. Activities as personal as love and marriage become signs of amorousness among economic groups. The gnat *represents* the colossus; with that one stroke the problem of disproportion is solved. The question is whether it can be solved so easily. There can be no doubt that the symbolic associations which Trilling identifies pertain to the reading of the novel, but the difficulty comes in trying to decide exactly how they pertain. To address that issue is to widen our concerns; it is to acknowledge the problem of the novel's narrator; it is to consider the formal consequences of Forsterian characterization; and it is to ask how symbolic experience bears on the experience of politics.

II

Forster's narrator in *Howards End* retains the formal prerogatives of his Victorian antecedents: the freedom to rove through space and time, the detachment from the affairs he chronicles, the access to the minds of his characters, and the privilege of unqualified ethical assessment. Dolly, we are told, "was a rubbishy little creature, and she knew it" (pp. 89–90). Here is a definitive judgment in the tradition of the Victorian literary moralists, but here also are signs of diminished power. The trenchant dismissal loses some of its force through these colloquialisms – "rubbishy," and "she knew it" – which give it more the tone of a personal crochet than an Olympian edict. Later, faced with the weighty question of whether

Margaret should have been informed of Ruth Wilcox's bequest, the narrator responds with a mild "I think not" (p. 96). Surely someone who knows that Dolly is a rubbishy little creature might be expected to have a stronger opinion on such a momentous question. But Forster gives us a narrator who constructs the fictional universe with all the resources of a narrating divinity, only to halt suddenly, and to gape at what he has made with the incomprehension of any other mortal.

Consistently in *Howards End* the represented world seems to recede from the one who ought to know it best. Consider, for instance, the initial description of Jacky, the woman who shares Leonard's shabby life on "the extreme verge of gentility."

A woman entered, of whom it is simplest to say that she was not respectable. Her appearance was awesome. She seemed all strings and bell-pulls – ribbons, chains, bead necklaces that clinked and caught – and a boa of azure feathers hung round her neck, with the ends uneven. Her throat was bare, wound with a double row of pearls, her arms were bare to the elbows, and might again be detected at the shoulder, through cheap lace. Her hat, which was flowery, resembled those punnets covered with flannel, which we sowed with mustard and cress in our childhood, and which germinated here yes, and there no. She wore it on the back of her head. As for her hair, or rather hairs, they are too complicated to describe, but one system went down her back, lying in a thick pad there, while another, created for a lighter destiny, rippled around her forehead. The face – the face does not signify. (p. 48)

It indicates no disrespect for Forster to say that Jacky disappears within the description. The passage offers too much information and too little; like Jacky herself it depends on effects; it reveals no attachment to detail for its own sake. The ribbons, chains and necklaces represent merely a gloss on the vague epithets "awesome" and "not respectable," as though the accumulation of aphoristic insights might finally amount to a coherent image. Moreover, the narrator keeps withdrawing from the descriptive act, back to the mustard and cress of childhood and, more significantly, back to an intense consciousness of the verbal process itself. We are told what is "simplest to say," what is "too complicated to describe," what "does not signify." This mannerism appears persistently; a circumstance is invoked and then held to exceed the reach of language. Having mentioned the "poetry" of Helen's rash kiss, the narrator can only shrug: "who can describe that?" (p. 22) Repeatedly, the novel tells us what we will not be told — "Young Wilcox was pouring in petrol, starting his engine, and performing other actions with which this story has no concern" (p. 14) — with the result that there seems a vast penumbral field that exists just beyond the compass of representation. This raises a vexing formal problem to which we must return, but the opening paragraph of chapter six reveals that it is more than a formal concern.

We are not concerned with the very poor. They are unthinkable, and only to be approached by the statistician or the poet. This story deals with gentlefolk, or with those who are obliged to pretend that they are gentlefolk.
(p. 43)

Forster mutes the point with irony, but beneath the irony sounds an issue of consequence: the narrowing of fictional domain. What can the novel now include? What has passed beyond its bounds? Indeed *Howards End* does not concern itself with the very poor, nor for that matter with the very rich, who, one must suppose, are just as unthinkable. Thinkable are the middle class or, more precisely, a few representative individuals of that class. *Howards End* makes no attempt to survey social diversity, and for a novel that broods so heavily over urban life, its London is strikingly depopulated.[5] Forster does not aspire to the capaciousness of the great Victorians; he does not seek to convey the mass and density of modern existence; his is a novel, not of three classes, but of three households. In itself, this restriction is not noteworthy or even unusual, but in Forster it becomes pointed because he retains such a sharp feeling for what he excludes, because the question of domain becomes a crux in the novel, and because it is linked so importantly to the question of Forster's liberalism.

Forster frequently remarked upon the obsolescence of the liberal ideal, but he always expressed that opinion from the standpoint of an obsolescent liberal. He placed himself not beyond the tradition of Victorian liberalism but at its deliquescence, once describing himself as "an individualist and a liberal who has found liberalism crumbling beneath him."[6] It is an odd remark. Presumably, he means to suggest that

English individualism remained intact while its liberalism declined. But it is a surprising political perception that can distinguish liberalism so sharply from individualism, and it is worth asking what exactly Forster meant.

In 1911, a year after the appearance of *Howards End*, L. T. Hobhouse published a small book called *Liberalism* which tersely summarized the state of contemporary liberal theory and which has for us the additional, and more immediate, virtue of establishing terms in which to approach *Howards End*. Hobhouse, who betrays none of Forster's waning confidence, sees the progress of liberalism as "a steady stream toward social amelioration and democratic government," a long course within which he distinguishes two major phases. The first, "older liberalism" worked to endow the individual with civil, economic and political freedom. It challenged "authoritarian government in church and state," and so constituted "a movement of liberation, a clearance of obstructions, an opening of channels for the flow of free spontaneous vital activity." The "old" liberalism was thus an essentially negative activity, devoted to the removal of constraints, sure in the belief that once individuals were allowed to develop freely, an "ethical harmony" would ensue.[7]

According to Hobhouse, Bentham initiated a second phase in which the highest value attached not to the individual but to the community and its collective will. The utilitarian calculus ensured that individual rights did not remain the sole political consideration; it required an adjustment of claims in conformity to the greatest happiness principle; and it looked to the state to harmonize competing interests. This commitment has led to the positive aspect of the liberal movement: the regulation of behavior, the intervention in markets, the exercise of legal restraints and "social control" — an emphasis which threatens "the complete subordination of individual to social claims."[8] As Hobhouse acknowledges, the collectivist impulse has led some to see a rending contradiction in liberal thought: a radical individualism on one side and a state paternalism on the other.

For Hobhouse, however, no such contradiction obtains. It is merely a bogey of those who fail to recognize that an individual right "cannot conflict with the common good, nor could any right exist apart from the common good." He denies any "intrinsic and inevitable conflict between liberty and compulsion," and instead brings together the two emphases which modern liberalism inherits, an individualism and a collectivism. He regards these as mutually dependent commitments: "a fulfillment or full development of personality is practically possible not for one man only but for all members of a community," and the highest aim is not personal liberty but "liberty for an entire community."[9] Hobhouse himself did not expect any immediate realization of this "harmonic conception," but he held to a belief in steady progress, a slow course of mutual adjustment in which the self and the state would move gradually towards equilibrium. Such a view gives expression to the best hopes of modern liberalism: a commitment to social reform and an unremitting respect for personal liberty.

The liberalism that Forster sees crumbling around him is clearly that "new liberalism" which Hobhouse outlines, with its plans for continued legislative reform on a large scale. And when Forster holds on to his individualism, he places himself in effect at an earlier stage of liberal ideology when the emphasis had fallen upon the removal of constraints rather than the regulation of behavior. Unlike Hobhouse, Forster retains no confidence in an emerging balance between these two concerns, personal freedom and public obligation, and faced with these alternatives, he unhesitatingly chooses private before public, friend before country, much as Margaret Schlegel makes this choice:

Others had attacked the fabric of society — property, interest, etc; she only fixed her eyes on a few human beings, to see how, under present conditions, they could be made happier. Doing good to humanity was useless: the many-coloured efforts thereto spreading over the vast area like films and resulting in a universal gray. To do good to one, or, as in this case, to a few, was the utmost she dare hope for. (p. 125)

Later Margaret recalls her sister to this Schlegel creed of moral immediacy, refusing to be bound by abstract principles of justice: "Nor am I concerned with duty. I'm concerned with the characters of various people whom we know, and how, things being as they are, things may be made a little better" (p. 225).

This sentiment reflects the novel's much-discussed commitment to "personal relations," which are what Forster clings to when his liberalism crumbles. But it also bears upon some of its recurrent thematic preoccupations, for instance the lively debate over space and size, an issue which like so many others divides Schlegels from Wilcoxes. When Margaret Schlegel first sees Howards End, she overcomes the "phantom of bigness," remembering "that ten square miles are not ten times as wonderful as one square mile, that a thousand square miles are not practically the same as heaven" (p. 198). Only a few pages later Henry Wilcox, soon to be her husband, insists that "the days for small farms are over": "Take it as a rule that nothing pays on a small scale" (p. 203). Scale is of fundamental concern to Forster, who often saw the problem of modernity as a loss of proportion that could only be recovered through a new respect for *genius loci*. Consistently he teaches the virtues of the small scale, the intimacy that is jeopardized in an age of imperialism. While Henry ceaselessly extends his empire of African rubber holding, Margaret willingly surrenders her "cosmopolitanism" for a house that is "old and little."

A variation on this motif occurs in another issue that follows Wilcox/Schlegel lines, the dispute over the logical categories of experience: types and individuals. After the Schlegels have taken an interest in Leonard Bast, Henry Wilcox tries to intervene: "Miss Schlegel, excuse me, but I know the type," to which Margaret rejoins, "he isn't a type" (p. 144). When Miss Avery frightens Margaret and irritates Henry, the latter erupts: "Uneducated classes are so stupid," and Margaret responds by asking, "Is Miss Avery uneducated classes?" (p. 200). In the last phase of the novel, after the revelation of Helen's pregnancy, Margaret loyally reflects that "Not even to herself dare she blame Helen ... Morality can tell us that murder is worse than stealing, and group most sins in order all most approve, but it cannot group Helen" (p. 309). The narrator concurs, observing that "Preachers or scientists may generalize, but we know no generality is possible about those whom we love" (p. 273). The singular instance thus eludes the coarse generalization; the defense of the small space becomes one with defense of the concrete particular; and the farmer joins hands with the nominalist.

At this point it is possible to recognize the congruence between the various features of the novel that have recently been at issue: the weakness of the narrator and the narrowing of fictional domain, the dismissal of large-scale liberal reform in favor of individual relations, the defense of the small space against the imperial cosmopolis, and the commitment to the concrete instance that resists generalization. In all these respects the novel dramatizes a movement from large things to small, in which the surrender of the broad view makes possible a discovery of value in the rich particular. It should be evident that this emphasis poses insuperable difficulties for a view of the novel as a simple parable of class struggle and national reconciliation, as an allegory of the fate of England. On the contrary, categories such as class and nation frequently appear as the chief villains of the piece. Persistently and passionately, Forster distinguishes between the individual and the class, between "a few human beings" and the "universal gray" of humanity.

And yet no one can dispute that *Howards End* retains grand symbolic aspirations. A novel which finds the very poor unthinkable thinks nonetheless about the state of modern England. A novel which narrows its domain still symbolizes the largest questions that face a culture. How can we square the celebration of the individual with the concern for such high generalities? How does the narrow domain of the plot comport with the broadening symbolic reach? How, that is, can a novel which willfully limits its range dramatize a vision of the social whole? And what do these two commitments imply about character and mode?

Such questions can best be met by a turn to the novel's third reference to Arnold's maxim. Shortly after her wedding, Margaret travels alone to Howards End. As she walks towards the house, she wanders through the Hertfordshire countryside and experiences a sudden and decisive recognition:

In these English farms, if anywhere, one might see life steadily and see it whole, group in one vision its transitoriness and its eternal youth, connect – connect without bitterness until all men are brothers. (p. 266)

This third instance serves as a rejoinder to the previous two. It is possible, after all, to see life steadily and whole, possible to unify, possible to connect. Still, before we surrender to a warm sense of imaginative triumph, we must raise another question. For what kind of whole is this, that ignores the city, that neglects modern life, that retreats to the farms which, however lovely, are surely not the whole of England? John Martin raises this difficulty in his bluff dismissal of Trilling's reading of the novel: "Lionel Trilling declares that it concerns England's fate, but it does not, for it leaves too much of England out of account."[10] And yet Margaret's vision at Howards End suggests a way both to answer Martin's charge and to amend the symbolic interpretation, because paradoxically it is insofar as Margaret leaves much of England out of account that she learns to address its fate. Only when she narrows her view from the cosmopolis to the little house does she achieve a wide social vision. Only by retreating to the part does she see the steady whole. She thus discloses the novel's presiding symbolic figure, synecdoche.

The novel, one might say, is a long preparation for synecdoche. It withdraws from a broad canvas; it reduces its scale; its battles are all waged among individuals. But in retreating to the partial view, it asks those parts to stand for wholes. Helen assails Margaret's decision to marry Henry, and Margaret, defending her choice, moves from one man to many: "If Wilcoxes hadn't worked and died in England for thousands of years, you and I couldn't sit here without having our throats cut" (p. 171). Later, Margaret turns to defend Helen and does so in these terms: "The pack was turning on Helen, to deny her human rights, and it seemed to Margaret that all Schlegels were threatened with her" (p. 286). Henry Wilcox signifies all Wilcoxes, Helen Schlegel all Schlegels, and when Margaret must challenge her husband, his son and their doctor, a "new feeling came over her: she was fighting for women against men" (p. 287). This persistent imaginative gesture must be distinguished from that habit of mind which the novel repudiates, the tendency to ignore the individual in favor of the type, or, in the terms of Trilling's reading, to identify a character and a class. Synecdoche, on the contrary, embeds the whole within the part and only achieves its broad amplitude by respecting the concrete instance and by detaching the self from its class.

The history of liberalism is itself a history of negotiations between part and whole, and the "ethical harmony" toward which Hobhouse aims is put in just such terms. His "ideal society" is "a whole which lives and flourishes by the harmonious growth of its parts, each of which in developing on its own lines and in accordance with its own nature tends on the whole to further the development of others."[11] But for Hobhouse, it must be stressed, this relationship between part and whole is real not figural. Individual and community are materially, socially, politically, bound together, making society "a living whole." "National and personal freedom are growths of the same root," writes Hobhouse, "and their historic connection rests on no accident, but on ultimate identity of idea." If in the modern age the "individual voter" feels powerless, then the pressing need is to establish "organizations" which will "link the individual to the whole."[12]

As Margaret approaches Howards End she has a fleeting political insight of her own: "Left to itself . . . this county would vote liberal" (p. 265). Just here the novel reveals both its lingering attachment to a political ideal and its refusal of a political program. As opposed to Hobhouse's constructive program, Forster's aim is not to secure the bonds that tie the few to the many but to cut those bonds, leaving the county to itself, in the conviction that one can best aspire to the whole by retreating to a part. It is not that Forster abandons hope of social unity: he hopes indeed to "connect without bitterness until all men are brothers" (p. 266), but he sees this as possible only through a *withdrawal* from the large social realm. He asks the part not to stand with, but to stand for, the whole.

Kermode has identified several areas of contact between Forster and the Symbolist tradition, but one point which he does not mention and which deserves particular emphasis here is Forster's keen feeling for *correspondance*: that connectedness between things that things themselves have established, an order which we can only disclose, never impose.[13] Without abandoning political value, Forster seeks to mortify the

political will, in the hope that *correspondances* will then reveal
themselves to the intelligent eye. He can abandon a large fictional domain; can prefer local roots to cosmopolitan
rootlessness; can refuse the general category in favor of the
singular instance; and can still address "England's fate," because
for him, unlike Hobhouse, the effort to "link the individual
to the whole" is a matter not of social organization but of
imaginary figuration. Forster avails himself of a visionary
possibility absent in James and Conrad, but while we should
acknowledge that his technical audacity points beyond the
realist norms of early modern fiction, we must also recognize
that in *Howards End* the post-realist method is in service of
a pre-modern past. Synecdoche allows him to retrieve what
he has lost. It gives him a way to retain symbolic connection.
It is the trope of a waning liberalism.

III

Synecdoche, if one may generalize, is a symbolic figure highly
congenial to the modernist temperament, which is often more
comfortable with the detail than with the panorama but which
is typically unwilling to surrender the broad view. The imaginative task, then, is to cultivate the particular so sedulous-
ly that it becomes radiant with meaning, to polish the fragment until it becomes luminous enough to disclose the age.
The image, the impression, the epiphany, were each turned
to this purpose. And yet, this method of resolution remains
hazardous; the risk is that respect for particularity will become
lost in an awe of generality and that the signified whole will
subsume the signifying part. To read *Howards End* only in
terms of its symbolic correspondences, to describe it as essentially a fable of modern England, is to foreclose one of its most
provocative lines of reflection.

When Margaret Schlegel and Henry Wilcox first move
towards one another in shy steps that will lead to their fateful
marriage, they are described as "advancing out of their respective families towards a more intimate acquaintance" (p. 152).
From this point the novel, which had traded so heavily on
the opposition between Schlegels and Wilcoxes, begins to draw

increasingly fine distinctions within the two families. Thus Leonard originally sees "the Miss Schlegels" as "a composite Indian god whose waving arms and contradictory speeches were the product of a single mind" (p. 137), and only gradually comes to realize that "a Miss Schlegel alone was different": "Helen had become 'his' Miss Schlegel" (pp. 232–3).

This differentiating of characters would be unremarkable, were it not that it placed such strain on the novel's symbolic machinery. Schlegels and Wilcoxes, as is perfectly evident, exemplify Forster's chief alternatives for the English temperament; in Leavis's paraphrase: "'The Schlegels represent the humane liberal culture, the fine civilization of cultivated personal intercourse," while the Wilcoxes "have built the Empire; they represent the 'short-haired executive type' – obtuse, egotistic, unscrupulous, cowards spiritually, self-deceivers, successful."[14] As far as it goes, this view is unexceptionable. It happens, however, that the union between the families, so decisive for the theme of connection, can be realized only by figures who "advance out" of those families. Not just any part will serve to conjure the whole. And it is notable that when the novel moves toward its vision of symbolic union at Howards End, it leaves many characters to one side. The exclusions are certainly plausible. Tibby is too effete, Aunt Juley too inflexible, Charles too unimaginative, Evie too severe, Paul too vague. But the result is that the image of a general synthesis is strikingly particularized. The reader must surely pause over a vision of reconciliation that leaves so much unreconciled.

It is no doubt true, as Trilling says, that Howards End is a symbol for England, but this symbol has a homely material existence; it is "old and little"; and if it suggests the possibility of a transhistorical synthesis, it does so from within the confines of historical exigency. Forster took great pains to establish the immediate social pressures of Edwardianism: the headlong expansion of imperialism, the homogenization of culture, the increasing sordidness of London, and the expansion of its suburbs. Within such a context the farm at Howards End appears as an archaism. Indeed, at the novel's conclusion, at the moment of greatest symbolic promise, the forces of history rudely interrupt. Helen hopes that their stay at

Howards End will be permanent; Margaret says she thinks that it will be: "All the same," remarks Helen, "London's creeping," and she points to a line of red rust beyond the meadow.

"You see that in Surrey and even Hampshire now," she continued. "I can see it from the Purbeck Downs. And London is only part of something else, I'm afraid. Life's going to be melted down, all over the world."
Margaret knew that her sister spoke truly. (p. 337)

Here suddenly is our symbol for the whole challenged like any other part. Howards End, which is to signify England, is contained and threatened by England; the symbolic vehicle sputters; the house is now, again, merely a house, jeopardized by the appetite of suburbs and the smoke of cities.

Howards End, I have said, self-consciously narrows its domain in the spirit of a disillusioned liberalism that withdraws from "the fabric of society" to a "few human beings." I have also suggested that synecdoche offers a figure for imaginative retrieval; it will be possible to restore symbolically what has been lost politically. Now it becomes clear that symbolism has its own fragility, created by the exigencies of history. The signifying talisman can fail to signify, and then one is left with an absurd material object, heavy in one's hands, whose aura has fled. Where, then, does the novel leave us? with the vision of a renewed England, classless, harmonious and whole? or with the harrowing presence of an urban civilization macadamizing the only values which might save it?

In an early essay on the novel, Leavis introduced a line of argument that has become familiar, even standard, in assessments of *Howards End*. He distinguished "comic" and "poetic" emphases in Forster and suggested that often in his early work these two manners were imperfectly amalgamated, leading to a "discrepancy or clash of modes or tones."[15] Alan Wilde has since spoken of the novel's "defective articulation of the symbolic and realistic levels."[16] Indeed, the clash of tones is inescapable, and any reading of *Howards End* must confront its rapidly shifting registers. Between the reverential vision of Mrs Wilcox, "assuredly she cared about her ancestors, and let them help her" (p. 19), and the aphoristic dismissal of Tibby, "dyspeptic and difficile" (p. 28), there yawns a chasm into which less agile sensibilities would surely fall. The ambiguity at the end of *Howards End* — a real house or a symbolic England? — displays the terms of the difficulty, and it is fair for us to demand an explanation.

Here is where Forster's conception of character must affect a reading of the novel as a whole. Character in *Howards End*, as we have seen, is not defined by impulsions from within or compulsions from without; it is conceived in terms of styles, manners and dispositions. Personalities and personal relationships are habitually interpreted in modal terms, and the very categories which critics use to describe the novel *already* apply to its characters: sincerity and irony, romance and sentimentality. Margaret tells Helen that "there is the widest gulf between my love-making and yours. Yours was romance; mine will be prose." Henry, she immediately adds, "lacks poetry" (p. 171). Surely, then, it serves little point to object that the novel contains conflicting modes, since Forster conceives human diversity as precisely a diversity in mode.

Early in the novel, Margaret and Helen discuss whether Leonard Bast is "capable of tragedy" (p. 112). Margaret thinks that he may be, but Helen has doubts, and not long afterwards the narrator seems to settle the question in Helen's favor: "His had scarcely been a tragic marriage. Where there is no money and no inclination to violence tragedy cannot be generated" (p. 120). But in the closing movement of the novel, after Leonards's death, Margaret has the final word. "let Squalor be turned into Tragedy, whose eyes are the stars, and whose hands hold the sunset and the dawn" (p. 328). Margaret, in effect, is seeking to change not an event but a mode, and here is an answer to Leavis. What he regarded as a defect in Forster's sensibility — the "clash of modes or tones" — may perhaps have been a defect, but it was certainly the subject of *Howards End*.

This chapter began by considering the Arnoldian ideal of seeing life steadily and whole, and it can move towards conclusion by recalling a more recent discussion of seeing, Wittgenstein's treatment of "seeing-as" in the second part of the *Philosophical Investigations*. Within the context of a broad consideration of the problem of meaning Wittgenstein reminds us of a certain distinctive visual experience: the abrupt change in perceptual content that can occur through the dawning of a new aspect, the identification of a different principle of coherence, or the sudden recognition of a figure within the ground. Thus we can see the arrangement of lines as convex and then suddenly concave; we can see Jastrow's celebrated design now as a duck, now as a rabbit; we can see a triangle as "a triangular hole, as a solid, as a geometrical drawing, as standing on its base, as hanging from its apex; as a mountain, as a wedge, as an arrow or pointer, as an overturned object . . . and as various other things."[17]

What is distinctive about such cases, observes Wittgenstein, is that the visual object remains unchanged while the visual experience may alter radically: "I *see* that it has not changed and yet I see it differently." It is "quite as if the object had altered before my eyes," as if it "had ended by *becoming* this or that." The connection of this phenomenon to imaginative life should be evident, and Wittgenstein notes in passing that we characteristically attempt to persuade one another of aesthetic judgments by saying, for instance, "You have to see it like *this*."[18]

Here we might profitably recall Margaret's late outburst when her husband refuses to let Helen spend the night at Howards End: "You shall see the connection if it kills you, Henry! You have had a mistress — I forgave you. My sister has a lover — you drive her from the house. Do you see the connection?" Henry lamely responds that the "two cases are different" (p. 305). The dispute, that is, turns on the ability to see not objects or events but "the connection" which exists nowhere in the world but which, once recognized, alters how the world appears. "When the aspect changes," notes Wittgenstein, "parts of the picture go together which before did not."[19] The essential activity in *Howards End* is the changing of aspects and the attempt to communicate such changes — not, of course, for narrowly aesthetic reasons but as a part of the novel's most serious moral purpose. The demand which Wittgenstein records, "You have to see it like *this*," becomes an urgent ethical injunction.

These concerns bear closely on the issue of mode, in

particular the issue of changing modes. For when we suddenly change, say, from regarding a passage as awkwardly sentimental to seeing it as delightfully parodic, our response has
that peculiar character which Wittgenstein describes. We
recognize that nothing in the work has altered and yet we experience a different work. We have the uncanny feeling of "a
new perception and at the same time of the perception's being unchanged."[20] Such considerations should remind us that
the experience of mode is not simply the passive acquiescence
in conventions. To recognize parody, for instance, may require a great imaginative effort, and in moments of interpretive
confusion we often find ourselves changing our ascriptions
of mode as rapidly as we shift between duck and rabbit in examining Jastrow's drawing. Moreover, we can enjoin others
to change their visual perceptions and their emotional experience. When Margaret urges, "Let Squalor be turned into
Tragedy" (p. 328), her imperative suggests that mode is not
fixed and that through an act of heightened perception we may
change what we see.

This last phrase, "change what we see," equivocates between
perceiver and world, but in so doing it locates Forster's hope
for cultural transformation. He wants us to change *what* we
see (the world) by changing what we *see* (the image). To see
Leonard as tragic, to see a house as England, to see a marriage
as the union of poetry and prose — these are imaginative acts
with practical consequences. Learning to live within a different
mode is a way to alter one's style of response, one's manner
of thought, one's habit of feeling. And to persuade others to
share one's mode is to change the life of a community. Forster's
political quietism must be set against this literary activism that
restlessly alters its bearings in the conviction that it will
be a new mode, not a new fact, that will begin to change
England.

The ambiguity between the real and the symbolic must then
be recognized for what it is: not as a confusion of the author
but as a challenge to his characters.[21] After her first visit to
Howards End, Margaret, in other words, engages in her own

recaptured the sense of space, which is the basis of all earthly beauty, and,
starting from Howards End, she attempted to realize England. She failed

– visions do not come when we try, though they may come through trying. (p. 202)

synecdoche. On the basis of Howards End she attempts to realize England; from a symbolically resonant part she wants to attain the whole; and if she fails here she will be more successful later. But the passage makes clear that the symbolic correspondence on which the novel depends is not given; it must be achieved. After the death of Mrs Wilcox, her family puzzles over her wish to leave the house to Margaret: "To them Howards End was a house; they could not know that to her it had been a spirit, for which she sought a spiritual heir" (p. 96). Not all characters, that is, have the gift of symbolic vision, and to Trilling's assertion that the house is a symbol for England, one must agree and then quickly add that it is a symbol only to those who live within the symbolic mode. Parts in the novel do not simply and reassuringly signify wholes. Howards End is no counter standing securely for England. It is an invitation to symbolic activity.

One of the general claims put forward in this study has been that the crisis of subjectivity in modern society often shares illuminating features with the crisis of character in modern fictional form. In *Howards End* this homology is graphically displayed. The failure of the liberal ideal leaves a party of embattled individuals to assume the task of reconstructing a humane community. At the same time, and no doubt for many of the same reasons, the weakness of the narrator leaves central literary tasks in the hands of the characters. Can one start from a house and realize a nation? We might have expected the narrator to adjudicate such a delicate question, but as the novel moves to its crisis the narrator remains a liberal sceptic, and it falls to the characters, especially to Margaret, to raise finer, wider possibilities. This abdication of the narrator, the virtual muting of his voice in the final pages, indicates the refusal of the novel to tell its readers how to take it. The decisive question of how to construe its final events – whether we are to read them tragically, ironically, poetically, prosaically – is posed by the characters themselves who exemplify these diverse possibilities. From within its own boundaries *Howards*

End suggests competing ways in which it might be read. The conflict between the characters is in its broadest implication a dispute over the mode appropriate to the events of the novel, a dispute over the competing claims of realism and symbolism, irony and tragedy.

The instability of the symbol places a special burden on the reader, who by tradition and convention assumes that a symbolic correspondence holds or it does not. Indeed it is hard to see the point of an *intermittent* symbol. *Howards End* has suffered from this plausible assumption, for if it is read in terms of a figural calculus and if its historical perceptions are ignored, then it will seem merely to embody a mechanical optimism. But the strength of the novel is that it offers the symbolic relation not as a fact but as an opportunity: if Margaret's individual perception were shared by enough others, then it would cease to be merely figural and would become a powerful literal truth. Thus the refusal to settle the interpretive question is due neither to Forster's loss of nerve nor to his love of paradox; it reflects the necessary ambiguity between what is real and what is possible. Historical probability insists on the obsolescence of the small farm and consigns it to the gaping suburban maw, while symbolic possibility suggests that on the basis of the farm England might be restored.

It has been said that, strictly speaking, there can be only one *mood* in fictional narrative, the indicative, because "the function of narrative is not to give an order, express a wish, state a condition, etc., but simply to tell a story and therefore to 'report' facts (real or fictive)."[22] But *Howards End* in its undemonstrative manner presents a serious challenge to this assumption. By constructing a coherent historical portrait and a coherent symbolic alternative, it suggests that fiction may escape the confines of the indicative; and there is no better way to describe its fragile visionary prospect than as a reconciliation in the subjunctive mood, the expression of a wish from within the boundaries of fact. The novel concludes with an indicative assertion of social crisis and a conditional hypothesis of cultural renewal; it tells us what is true and what might be true. Logically, thinks Margaret, "they had no right to be alive," and therefore "one's hope was in the weakness of logic" (p. 337) — and, one might add, in the uncertain strength of the symbol.

Howards End concludes by locating the modern individual in the space where history and symbolism meet, each laying claim to supremacy. In its literal narrative it ends with the triumph of history and provides another instance of that distinctive form of internal exile which we encountered in *The Ambassadors* and *Heart of Darkness*. Like Strether and Marlow, the Schlegel sisters make no attempt to escape the larger community; they simply withdraw to a neglected spot within it, where they tend values that keep them at odds with the complacent citizens of the contemporary world. But *Howards End*, goaded by its memories of political aspiration, imagines how the relation of exiles and citizens might be reversed. Within its conditional symbolism, its subjunctive allegory, the individual grows larger than the society, and those outside Howards End become the exiles, who have misplaced the center of their culture and have mistaken a passing phase for a permanent truth. If, as Margaret hopes, the house belongs to "the future as well as the past" (p. 337), then the present age becomes an aberration instead of an inevitability; contemporary history is reduced to a parenthesis, Howards End containing it instead of it containing Howards End. Such is the *elasticity* of experience in this novel, contracting and expanding according to changes in mood and mode, offering visionary historical prospects to those who recede from history, exiling the individual and then placing high responsibility upon that exile who might at any moment be asked to signify the community and symbolize its future.

CHAPTER THREE

Justification, passion, freedom: character in *The Good Soldier*

The Good Soldier repeatedly asks, "What is a character?" and to that question it gives more answers than may be tactful. In so doing, it presents with greater urgency a number of problems that we have been pursuing, and it introduces new issues that will occupy us until the end of the study. Ford was a revolutionary with a bad conscience. He was reluctant to discard those traditions which he professed to scorn, and faced with competing alternatives, he habitually preferred both. This makes him a frustration to the literary theorist but a delight to the literary historian who can uncover in his work the strata of earlier methods beneath the radical experiments for which he is known. Ford's interest, of course, is not simply archaeological. *The Good Soldier*, a novel so attentive to the problem of historical transition, itself dramatizes a transition in the notion of character. The ambiguities in that notion become resources of plot, and Ford's refusal, or inability, to employ a single consistent method discloses nuances in the concept of individuality which should not only satisfy the historian but may yet provide some consolation for the theorist.

I

Ford upheld the extreme realist proposition that the success of prose fiction depends on its power to create "an illusion of reality," and in explaining how that illusion might be achieved, he placed special emphasis on what he called "justification," by which he meant the granting of perspicuous motives to behavior that might otherwise appear obscure.[1] To justify, then, is not to defend or to excuse; it is to place the self within a lawlike pattern that will make its motions (and emotions) intelligible, if not predictable. For Ford this task involved establishing a wide context, typically a personal past or a social norm, which would furnish individual action with a background of reasons and causes. It is not enough, he insists, to write that "Mr. Jones was a gentleman who had a strong aversion to rabbit-pie." One must "sufficiently *account* for that dislike": "You might do it by giving Mr. Jones a German grandmother, since all Germans have a peculiar loathing for the rabbit and regard its flesh as unclean. You might then find it necessary to account for the dislike the Germans have for these little creatures; you might have to state that [this] dislike is a self-preservative race instinct . . ."[2]

In his insistence upon justification, Ford places himself in continuity with those Victorian realists whom he so often attacked. As vigorously as George Eliot, he demands rational explanations for surprising actions and seeks general laws to assimilate individual cases. He, too, holds that behavior must yield to analysis and that a convincing illusion of reality requires a transparency of motive and cause. Fordian justification is in the service of verisimilitude, and it belongs to that strain of realism which in refusing to endow the isolated particular with any fictional weight sets out to locate its instances within an expansive, and therefore reassuring, context. From this standpoint a verisimilar character is a fictional token of a real type. Ford thus raises again one of the subjects that has recurred several times in this study, the essential connection between individuality and typicality in the creation of literary character. As diligently as James he subsumes the particular case within the ample category, and as insistently as Forster he registers any disharmony between the self and its class. Indeed, as will become evident, in moving between these two concerns, Ford places new burdens on the notion of individuality and new strain on the concept of character.

Although one remembers *The Good Soldier* for its insistent formal dislocations – its inversions, postponements, reversals and repetitions – it is well to notice that it relies in significant measure on highly traditional methods of characterization. At the center of the novel stands a patient and uncluttered exposition of the early history of Edward and Leonora Ashburnham which traces their upbringing and the course

of their married life, contrasting the unhappily opposed effects of Irish Catholicism and English Protestantism. This form
of characterization relies on social estimates of great generality; the emphasis on the typical aspects of the Catholic or Protestant personality might have appeared with scarcely any
modification in a novel by Thackeray or Trollope. Dowell
fills in background of the sort that Ford sketched for Mr Jones,
a set of circumstances that "account" for the individual and
that ultimately engender what one might call the "justified
self" which emanates from its context and embodies the social
will. Leonora, accordingly, appears as "the perfect normal
woman": "She desired children, decorum, an establishment:
she desired to avoid waste, she desired to keep up appearances.
She was utterly and entirely normal even in her utterly
undeniable beauty."[3] Leonora, that is, does not merely yield
to prevailing conventions; she actively desires them; as a strictly
"justified" individual she exists in perfect conformity to the
norms of her culture and thus becomes a living moral tautology
who wants what she is made to be. "Conventions and traditions," notes Dowell, "work blindly but surely for the preser-
vation of the normal type" (p. 238). He might have added what
he clearly implies, that the normal type works just as surely
and just as blindly to preserve conventions and traditions.

The justified self is the *donnée* of *The Good Soldier*. It is accepted as both a standard of behavior and a norm of intelligibility, with the result that characters themselves undertake the
task of justification. They continually invoke abstract laws and
general categories in order both to understand the behavior
of others and to understand themselves. Dowell, of course,
is the outstanding example. In line with Ford's declared precept
he explains individual character by placing it within a wider
class, on the assumption that the best way to know a particular
is to know its kind. The preeminent instance is the rubric
"good people" which appears frequently in the opening pages
of the novel and furnishes a shorthand characterization of the
four principals: "The given proposition was that we were all
'good people'. We took for granted that we all liked beef underdone but not too underdone; that both men preferred a good
liqueur brandy after lunch; that both women drank a very

light Rhine wine qualified with Fachingen water — that sort of thing" (p. 34). To refer to this example, however, is already to suggest the difficulties of Fordian justification. Conspicuously, the description "good people" fails to account for the characters it describes. It does not explain; it conceals; and this obvious incongruity between concept and character initiates far more subtle difficulties in the novel. For it becomes clear that the plot turns on the incongruity which individuals exploit for their own ends.

Characters engage in *characterization* as one of their leading occupations and one of their chief forms of evasion. Notably, Florence confirms her seduction of Ashburnham by misdescribing his character. During the visit to the museum at M—, she descants on Ludwig and Luther the Courageous, and then, gesturing at the "pencil draft of the Protest," tells Ashburnham that "it is because of that piece of paper that you're honest, sober, industrious, provident, and clean-lived. If it weren't for that piece of paper you'd be like the Irish or the Italians or the Poles, but particularly the Irish" (p. 44). Leonora, who recognizes the infidelity to follow, flies into a rage and nearly gives herself away to Dowell. She recovers by resorting to the methods of Florence, easing Dowell's fears with a deceptive characterization: "Don't you know that I'm an Irish Catholic?" Dowell, who writes that these "words give me the greatest relief that I have ever had in my life" (p. 46), admits that "jealousy would have been incurable. But Florence's mere silly gibes at the Irish and at the Catholics could be apologized out of existence" (p. 67). Jealousy, an ineradicably personal emotion, hides beneath the reassuring impersonalities of cultural generalization. Justification no longer serves, as in Ford's critical proposal, to account for an action; it works now to disguise it. Florence identifies Ashburnham as an "honest" and "clean-lived" Protestant while her eyes invite him to adultery. Leonora labors to preserve her status as a type, an "Irish Catholic," when what is at issue is not a general kind but a particular passion.

Much of the drama of *The Good Soldier*, as Hynes has pointed out, turns on a struggle between convention and passion, which present the characters with conflicting and irreconcilable demands: passion, as Hynes puts it, "reveals the secrets of the heart which convention exists to conceal and repress."⁴ One may extend the point. For it is not only a question of competing values or a struggle between expression and repression, it becomes a matter of the stability of character as such and our capacity to interpret behavior at all. Passion is not simply one mode of experience among others; it is an affront to intelligibility. It not only violates the "rules" which convention lays down; it challenges the very possibility of rules, norms and laws that govern human behavior. And it is not simply that characters must choose between passion and convention; it is that character begins to lose integrity as a concept.

For who in this world can give anyone a character? Who in this world knows anything of any other heart – or of his own? I don't mean to say that one cannot form an average estimate of the way a person will behave. But one cannot be certain of the way any man will behave in every case – and until one can do that a "character" is of no use to anyone.
(pp. 155–6)

The notion of justification, as Ford had developed it in his criticism, depends precisely on the notion of establishing "average estimates": Mr Jones as a German, Germans as averse to rabbits, and so on. *The Good Soldier*, however, relies on the procedure only to press it to its limits where justifications can no longer justify, where average estimates must hesitate before uncommon passions. By the end of the novel Dowell has tested the limits of rational explanation. He has interpreted character by religion, by nationality, by gender and by the calendar, and then in a weary moment he concedes:

I don't attach any particular importance to these generalizations of mine. They may be right, they may be wrong; I am only an ageing American with very little knowledge of life. You may take my generalizations or leave them. But I am pretty certain that I am right in the case of Nancy Rufford – that she had loved Edward Ashburnham very deeply and tenderly.
(p. 244)

Dowell's disillusionment follows one bold arc of the modernist sensibility. He begins with the presuppositions typical of much Victorian characterization: the individual conditioned by circumstance, composed of intelligible motives, susceptible to moral analysis – the justified self. Then, confronted with the singularity of desire, his "generalizations" totter and fall. He moves to a conception of character that will become predominant in modernist narrative: the individual estranged from circumstance and no longer comprehensible in its terms, confounding familiar motives, beyond the reach of social explanation. When Leonora, that "perfectly normal woman," finds herself in a "perfectly abnormal situation" (p. 240), then "for the first time in her life, she acted along the lines of her instinctive desires" (p. 203). Dowell immediately wonders whether this means that "she was no longer herself; or that, having let loose the bonds of her standards, her conventions, and her traditions, she was being, for the first time, her own natural self" (p. 203). How should he know? His confusion is that of one caught in the midst of an epochal transition, when it is unclear whether convention and tradition or instinct and desire constitute the ground of human behavior — well might he repeat, "I don't know." The passionate instant has overturned an entire history of familiarity. It defies standards of intelligibility, resists the generalities of social explanation and rests its claim to our attention on one incontrovertible fact: it exists.

And yet, as Dowell's narrative proceeds, there emerges a surprising implication which might be put this way. Passion, which has frustrated the attempt to justify the individual, becomes finally its own justification. The first time that Ashburnham "falls" into marital infidelity, unsanctioned sexuality can still appear as anomalous, a radical and unintelligible departure from the life of principle which he has been trained to lead. But by the fifth and sixth times, the erotic surge has ceased to be surprising. Ashburnham "falls" at regular intervals. Indeed, he deviates as consistently as he conforms, until passion loses its anomalous aspect. Ford recognized what Freud had begun to stress: not the singularities of the sexual impulse but its repetitions, compulsions and obsessions. Passion, that enemy of norms and conventions, lays down its own norms, even its own conventions: "poor Edward's passions were quite logical in their progression upwards" (p. 58). The "discovery" of sexuality in the modern period really amounts to no more than the recognition that what seemed to be the anarchy of desire is in fact its own civil state.

The first, the simple, irony of *The Good Soldier* depends on the incongruity between our inherited categories and the individual experience they are meant to describe. Social and moral conceptions fail to explain passion; personality eludes the justifications set in motion to account for it. The private individual remains, as it were, hidden beneath the cloak of social categories. But a second and more disquieting irony, at which we have just arrived, reveals that when the deceptive vestments of traditional characterization are removed, one may uncover not a new freedom but a new constraint. Edward violates the duties of his station merely to place himself at the mercy of his loins. What is more confining than social rigidity? – only, perhaps, private desire.

II

Few novels exploit the resources of the first person as thoroughly as *The Good Soldier*. Dowell changes repeatedly, changes distressingly, from a transparent medium to an opaque barrier. He sees and then is seen seeing. He is the one who engages in the persistent attempt to justify the behavior of others, who watches helplessly as "good people" give way to low passions, and who comes to regard the notion of character as "no use to anyone." Yet the difficulties become still more acute and the ambiguities more refractory when Dowell turns from the attempt to understand others and tries to understand himself.

Near the close of the novel he offers this notorious self-description:

In my fainter sort of way I seem to perceive myself following the lines of Edward Ashburnham. I suppose that I should really like to be a polygamist; with Nancy, and with Leonora, and with Maisie Maidan, and possibly even with Florence. I am no doubt like every other man; only, probably because of my American origin, I am fainter. (p. 237)

It is not wounded national pride that leads me to reject that description, only the recognition that Dowell's many idiosyncrasies do not suddenly become coherent when placed under the rubric "American." The remark is an explanation only in form, and it reveals again the extravagant failure of justification in the novel. Since Dowell has not displayed even the mildest tremors of sexual desire, there seems no good reason to credit his extemporized salacity. Faced with such an improbable confession, one is tempted to interpret Dowell in terms of hidden motives or suppressed desires, and, admittedly, it is difficult to confront his inconsistency, his passivity and his sexual abstention and to resist the urge to diagnosis.[5] Indeed Dowell, like his critics, refers to "dual personality" and "unconscious self" (pp. 103–4) as possible lines of explanation. These classifications, however, amount only to new attempts at justification within a novel that reveals this as an especially hazardous activity. "Dual personality" is scarcely more illuminating than "American" in explaining the "queer shifting thing" that is Dowell (p. 248). One might make better sense of him by granting the possibility that he is beyond justification, in a sense that I shall attempt to explain.

A traditional view recently systematized by Seymour Chatman holds that fictional character is a compendium of traits assembled in the course of narrative, traits which gradually concatenate into a represented whole. The fictitious name serves as a bare peg to which qualities are appended, and the qualities *make* the individual who then exists, in Chatman's phrase, as a "paradigm of traits."[6] Undoubtedly such a view describes one norm of fictional characterization. When Trollope introduces Dr Grantly as "proud," "wishful" and "worldly," he prepares the reader to meet a man who exists primarily as an aggregate of attributes, and Grantly's great struggle with Mr Slope is not so much a conflict of characters as a clash of characteristics.[7] But can every fictive individual be understood as a sequence of relevant adjectives? *The Good Soldier* obliges us to confront such a question. When Florence describes Edward as "honest, sober, industrious, prudent and clean-lived," she describes a norm which extravagantly fails to obtain. The novel will reveal other traits – guilt, sentimentality, lubricity – that more accurately describe Edward and that belong to another order of description, personal and affective rather than moral or religious. But this change in "paradigm" does not in itself threaten the notion of character as the sum-total of characteristics. That more revolutionary task falls to Dowell.

No matter how generous our standards of behavior, as long as they are standards, they will not contain John Dowell, who defies norms of consistency and purpose, who credits the most implausible lies, whose moral valuations shift from sentence to sentence, whose memory leaks like an old man's, and whose attention wanders like a child's. He fails to experience emotion appropriate to the circumstance and fails to distinguish the essential from the trivial.[8] As Schorer delicately puts it, his is a "mind not quite in balance";[9] John Meixner, less delicate, calls him a "psychic cripple," "a severely neurotic personality."[10] Still, Dowell would be less puzzling if he were only more so. If he passed thoroughly beyond the bounds of reason and ethics, then we could assign him to that comfortable rubric, Madness in Literature. The difficulty is that although Dowell continually violates our expectations of rational behavior, he performs no act that would place him beyond the moral pale. He commits no physical violence, yields to no repugnant impulses, violates no taboos, causes no suffering. On the contrary, as Hynes has stressed, he seems the one character in the novel capable of selflessness.[11] He also manages to write a novel. If he does not obey familiar norms, neither does he conform to our notions of lunacy. He occupies a strangely lit zone between tact and catatonia and is no more intelligible as a madman than as a gentleman.

As a way of approaching Dowell, it will be useful to recall some well-known aspects of Fordian Impressionism, and to remember that the reality whose illusion Ford sought to create was found in the instantaneous apprehension of experience – not in the "rounded annotated record" but in the "impression of the moment," "the impression not the corrected chronicle."[12] Since the world appears to us only in "various unordered pictures," the first obligation of the literary artist is a meticulous attention to that variety and disorder, to "the sort of odd vibration that scenes in real life really have."[13] Ford never denied that we ascend from perception to knowledge and from sensation to understanding, but he regarded these as distinctly secondary activities. The world of solid objects and coherent events is subsequent and often spurious, and never to be mistaken for the patches of color, the fields of light, the noise, dust and confusion out of which it arose. Not the concept but the impression, the sensation and the emotion constitute the foundation of experience. What is more, they constitute its essence. This, indeed, is a fundamental Fordian assumption with far-reaching consequences for the representation of individuality: that in the beginning of experience lies its essence.

"The whole world for me," writes Dowell, "is like spots of colour in an immense canvas" (p. 14). This statement should do two things. It should connect Dowell himself to the Impressionist temperament, and it should remind us of his insufficiencies as a knowing intelligence. Moreover it should suggest a connection between these two aspects of his situation. Dowell, it is plain, is more than a character and more than a narrator in *The Good Soldier*; he is an instance, and to an extent a theorist, of literary Impressionist doctrine. He not only conforms to Ford's principles of narrative; he defends those principles in Fordian terms, offering the familiar argument that, because neither lives nor "real stories" follow an orderly sequence, a narrator who wants his stories to "seem most real" must proceed in "a very rambling way" (p. 183). Dowell meets the terms of his covenant. He disregards fact in favor of impression, follows the wanderings of memory, ignores chronology, allows unlikely juxtapositions, digresses freely. These formal dislocations have often been remarked, not least by Ford himself. What has gone unremarked, however, is the way that these aspects of form become aspects of personality. The connection between narrative structure and fictive character has been a paramount concern in this study, and here as elsewhere it is necessary to ask what general relation obtains between the formal innovations of the modernist novel and the norms of characterization on which it continued to draw. In the case of Dowell, one can begin by saying that his narrative strategy is one with his psychological provocation. The refusal to provide structure, the passive acquiescence in confusion, the divagations of memory — these are not merely technical commitments, they are distinctive and disturbing elements of character. Having described the world as spots of color on a canvas — a remark that might seem merely a pictorial observation in the vein of Pissarro — Dowell passes immediately to a confession of personal weakness: "Perhaps if it weren't so I should have something to catch hold of now" (p. 14). His literary method becomes a measure of his bewilderment, and in one important respect, as I now hope to show, to the question "What ails Dowell?" it is instructive to answer: he is suffering from Impressionism.

In response to his early critics, Monet made the celebrated rejoinder, "Poor blind idiots. They want to see everything clearly, even through the fog."[14] It is a forceful reply, but it should not divert us from a blunt question: Why do fog and dusk, twilight and movement, appear so prominently in work of the Impressionist school? These paintings frequently involve difficult perceptual circumstances: a cathedral seen through the mist, a haystack disappearing in the fading light, a chaotic street scene glimpsed from a window. Similarly in literature (one thinks of Conrad and Faulkner as well as Ford) the most vivid instances of Impressionist method are associated with conditions of emotional fragility, mental unsteadiness, and even madness. Why should this be so?

As an historical movement the rise of Impressionism is quite evidently connected with certain assumptions of philosophic empiricism, in particular the belief that we never directly perceive objects, only discrete sensory stimuli or — in the jargon of more recent epistemology — *sense-data* out of which we subsequently construct our images of material things.[15] As long as this seemed a self-evident truth, it made good aesthetic sense to probe beneath the specious image of solid objects with sharp outlines and constant color. However, now that this philosophic view has lost its inevitability, it becomes possible to see that, at least in the arts, the doctrine of sensation was often a theory masquerading as an experience. Whether or not we agree that J. L. Austin "has refuted sense-data," most of us cheerfully acknowledge that the common language of description is adequate to our usual purposes and that in our ordinary encounters with the world it would be unnatural, even grotesque, to invoke the terminology of sense-data in order to describe what we see.[16] In his memoir of Austin, Isaiah Berlin made a remark that has special pertinence to our concerns here. According to Austin, wrote Berlin:

> The sense-datum language was a sub-language, used for specific purposes to describe the works of impressionist painters, or called for by physicians who asked their patients to describe their symptoms – an artificial usage carved out of ordinary language . . . which was sufficient for most everyday purposes and did not itself tend to mislead.[17]

Berlin made nothing of his particular examples; he was merely concerned to show the awkwardness of characterizing ordinary experience in the language of the epistemologists. But it is indeed notable that the description of a patient might resemble the description of symptoms of illness and that the Impressionist boast to see only patches of color and fields of light might serve as the unhappy complaint of a suffering patient. Clearly, this is not to imply that Impressionism is itself a pathology, only to suggest that the rather bland defense of its methods as faithful to ordinary perception conceals the extent of the provocation.

In its most significant manifestation Impressionist painting is a critique of normal perception, just as literary Impressionism is a critique of conventional narration. Both aim at the "real" by violating the "normal," and this fact begins to explain why their formal principles are so often realized in unusual circumstances. The momentary impression, after all, no matter how fundamental it may be to the process of perception, displays itself only in rare conditions; generally speaking, it is only at times of perceptual or psychological stress that familiar images decompose into the sensations of which they are made. Ford presents Dowell, and Dowell presents himself, as an example of the scrupulously realist narrator, but given the theoretical presuppositions of Impressionism – the commitment to sensations and perceptions in all their heterogeneity and disorder – it is not difficult to understand why the realist narrator passes so inexorably into the aberrant character.

Indeed, this is the paradox of Impressionism. In pursuing the foundation of normal experience, it dismantled the structures on which we normally rely. Monet used to say that he would have liked to have been born blind and then suddenly to have gained his sight, "so that he could have begun to paint . . . without knowing what the objects were that he saw before him," and it is certainly noteworthy that a perceptual norm should take the aspect of such a rigorous and unlikely condition.[18] We no longer find critics who describe Impressionist painters as "lunatics" presenting the "frightful spectacle of human vanity working itself up to the point of dementia."[19] But the hasty Impressionist rejoinder to their hasty critics — "this is how things appear" — cannot be a final answer, for it does not explain why realist principles should lead so naturally to the margins of experience, and why situations of strain and confusion should assist "real perception." A movement, which in its literary and pictorial manifestations claimed to offer a general theory of human perception, comes quite often to describe human perception *in extremis*, and the most significant contribution of Impressionism to the history of sensibility may lie not in what it has taught us about the normal instance but what it has revealed about the marginal case. Ford's Dowell is in this respect an exemplary figure in the Impressionist tradition, for carried to its imaginative extreme the representation of "unordered pictures" always risks ending in the representation of the disordered self.

III

Here, a point which has been submerged must be raised into plain view. For it should already begin to be evident that the demand for "justification" rests awkwardly alongside the cult of the "momentary impression." In effect, two realisms meet in *The Good Soldier*. On the one hand, as we have seen, Ford follows his Victorian antecedents in thinking of the real as the rationally known. The insistence upon justification is first of all a demand for intelligibility, guided by the conviction that literature can account for the apparent mysteries of character, that it can provide a background and a context which will furnish perspicuous explanation, and that in so doing it will achieve a successful "illusion of reality." Ford, however, displays a second, more characteristically Impressionist

114

emphasis in which the real is identified, not with the known and understood, but with the perceived and lived. The insistence on the "impression of the moment," the "odd vibration," the "queer effect," belongs to the attempt to reproduce experience as it first strikes the perceiving consciousness, before it assumes the shape of intelligibility. Within this emphasis, attention falls not on the rational pattern but on the immediate sensation.

In his criticism Ford suggested that these two realisms were complementary: "Your Impressionist can only get his strongest effects by using beforehand a great deal of what one may call non-Impressionism. He will make, that is to say, an enormous impression on his reader's mind by the use of three words. But very likely each one of those three words will be prepared by ten thousand other words."[20] He thus implies that the known past leads naturally to the lived present and that an intelligible history can "justify" a momentary impression. But Ford, like many others, imagines more finely than he methodizes. *The Good Soldier* reveals an incommensurability between experience as known and experience as lived, and perhaps the most compelling aspect of its characterization is the flight of individuality from the rational categories adduced to explain it.

Which is passion – known or lived? Certainly passion would appear to be the decisive instance of lived experience refusing the canons of rationality. Indeed, it first appears that way in *The Good Soldier*. But in the further course of the novel, as this chapter has argued, desire becomes routine and predictable, as much a matter of knowledge as of sensation. Far from an exuberant denial of all restriction, it becomes finally a constraint as severe as the moral conventions which oppose it. Passion comes to indicate, not so much originally lived, as obsessively reenacted experience.

And yet, part of the trenchancy of *The Good Soldier* is that it imagines experience more immediate than passion. It imagines a phase of subjectivity that is not only prior to knowledge but also prior to desire; and it does so, of course, through the figure of Dowell. Schorer sees the book's "controlling irony" in the fact that "passionate situations are related by a narrator who is himself incapable of passion."[21] But the irony runs even deeper than Schorer suggests, because Dowell's lack of passion appears not simply as a deprivation but as an opportunity. Much as his great wealth frees him from material need, so his *accidia*, to use Schorer's term, frees him from the tyranny of desire. He is divested of all want. And if someone should argue that this makes Dowell a mere nullity, I readily concur, disputing only the qualifier "mere."

Dowell describes himself as having "no occupation," "no business affairs" (p. 78), "no attachments, no accumulations" (p. 21) and "nothing in the world to do" (p. 22): "I suppose I ought to have done something, but I didn't see any call to do it. Why does one do things?" (p. 15). Doing nothing, he feels nothing, and feeling nothing, he knows nothing: "You ask how it feels to be a deceived husband. Just heavens, I do not know. It feels just nothing at all" (p. 70). In important respects, let us recognize, Dowell *is* nothing. No "paradigm of traits" can describe him, because there is nothing substantial to describe: no determining past, no consistency of opinion, no deep belief, no stable memory. He cannot be "justified." There is no accounting for Dowell.

This chapter has suggested that the problem of character in *The Good Soldier* is one with the method of Impressionism, and now greater force can be given to that claim. For Dowell's "nullity" is simply the final consequence of the Impressionist pursuit of immediate experience, the attempt to render a first stratum of personality that exists before doing, feeling and knowing take place. At the instant of experience one is neither humble, nor kind, nor greedy, nor wise. The notion of a trait, as an enduring attribute of character, cannot yet apply. Character exists only after the fact, and it is Ford's boldest stroke to imagine a personality virtually without characteristics – individuality before it has assumed the articulations of character. This scarcely conceivable state attracts but eludes psychological interpretation; it can never be adequately explained; the great challenge is to imagine it. In Dowell, Ford gestures at a nothing that precedes something in human personality, a formless, contentless, traitless self which does nothing, feels nothing, knows nothing, and which exists as a pure consciousness behind every one of its manifestations.

Such a state, of course, must remain a bare ideal. Even if it can exist (which one has reason to doubt) it certainly cannot persist. Dowell collides painfully with the world, not once but continually. The novel begins with his fall into consciousness, and falling into consciousness becomes his vocation. At every moment, he confronts experience as though for the first time, and up to the very last he remains *rudimentary*. In *Heart of Darkness*, I have argued, Impressionism offered Marlow a way to overcome the yawning gulf between fact and value and to create an individual ethic on the basis of moralized sensations: relief, shock, horror, etc. But Ford's Impressionism, more extreme in almost every respect, severs this natural connection between the realm of value and the realm of sensation, leaving Dowell to confront his ethical dilemmas with a persistent "I don't know." The certainty of Marlow's moral intuition depends on the settled angularities of his temperament, but Dowell has nothing so precise as a settled temperament. He appears throughout as one who has just emerged from an absolute detachment and who must now begin to take up the attitudes and values that constitute human character.

In his most provocative remark, Dowell writes at the end of the novel that:

I guess that I myself, in my fainter way, come into the category of the passionate, of the headstrong, and the too-truthful. For I can't conceal from myself the fact that I loved Edward Ashburnham — and that I loved him because he was just myself. If I had the courage and the virility and possibly also the physique of Edward Ashburnham I should, I fancy, have done much what he did. He seems to me like a large elder brother who took me out on several excursions and did many dashing things whilst I just watched him robbing the orchards, from a distance. (pp. 253–4)

Wiley considers this "the ultimate in self-deception," and Schorer calls it Dowell's "weirdest absurdity, the final, total blindness of infatuation and self-infatuation . . . for observe the impossible exceptions: courage, virility, physique! What sane man could except them?"[22] But is the question one of sanity? Or is it perhaps that still more difficult issue, the question of character as such? Dowell refuses here, refuses with a supreme negligence, to define himself in terms of traits. He regards courage, virility and physique as secondary qualities, mere contingencies which scarcely bear on the problem of identity. He speaks of watching Ashburnham "from a distance," but it is himself he sees from a distance, examining his endowments as though they had only accidental relation to the being that possessed them.

One certainly recognizes the force of the opinions of Wiley and Schorer. If, all evidence to the contrary, Dowell can say that he is Ashburnham, then it would seem that he can say anything. Indeed he can, for in an utterly improbable way Dowell becomes a compelling image of the free man. His very incapacities, his lack of physical and moral passion, his hesitations and confusions, his insouciance in grave circumstances, his self-avowed "faintness," release him from the definitions that circumscribe others. He is finally and frankly indeterminate, neither a creature of convention nor a slave of passion. If this unsuits him for the task of living, it prepares him for the act of writing. Being nothing, he can call himself anything. His deprivation coincides with his freedom; Dowell, the true man without qualities, can choose any qualities. If few readers can accept his assertion that Ashburnham was "just myself," no reader can prevent the claim. Dowell cannot *be* Ashburnham, but he is extravagantly free to say so.

As a man, Dowell is weak and led by the nose, but as an author he is a free agent who can utter any opinion, no matter how unlikely, with no fear of contradiction beyond self-contradiction. All else about Dowell may be doubtful, but one thing is certain — he writes; and part of the force of Fordian Impressionism lies in the recognition that character in narrative may be a late and clumsy reconstruction but the act of writing is prior and irreducible. The passivity of the cuckold gives way to the restless activity of the writer, who asserts and retracts, confesses and denies, soliloquizes and apostrophizes, changes his story, changes his mind, and arrives finally at the point of exhaustion: "It is so difficult to keep all these people going" (p. 222). Within a novel that so frequently refers to the power of convention and circumstance, the composition of a narrative becomes a way to recover autonomy. This is not the freedom of an heroic agent gloriously ascendant who tramples barriers in pursuit of noble ends. Dowell's is free action in its most primitive aspect, an unformed ego taking its first steps towards articulation, surprised by the world but more surprised by itself.

The moral agony of *The Good Soldier*, and its difficulty, depend in large measure upon the way in which this single fiction contains incommensurable principles of individuality. The novel which asks: "What is a character?" makes drama out of its competing answers. The justified self, which personifies its cultural context and embodies its values, struggles against the passional self which personifies and justifies only itself. This contrast would seem sufficiently grave, but *The Good Soldier*, as I have been suggesting, imagines a further refinement and a new provocation in Dowell, who is less a character than a voice only faintly and incidentally attached to a body, a culture, a religion and a past. Ford looks beyond the exigencies of circumstance and the urgencies of desire, past convention, past consistency, past justification, to subjectivity in its most ineliminable aspect.

In this sense *The Good Soldier* presents one boundary of the expanse that this study is attempting to traverse, a limiting case in which the self is an unreachable quiddity only posing as a personality. The movement towards Dowell is like the movement towards the Cartesian *cogito*, but once Ford arrives at this spare foundation, he, like Descartes, begins the task of reconstruction. The novel thus belongs to an emerging pattern of detachment followed by tentative steps toward sociality, isolation followed by a longing for community. Certainly Ford offers nothing so grand as Forster's hope for a symbolic recovery of the liberal ideal, nor even anything so modest as the evanescent mutual understanding within the Jamesian dialogue. Having withdrawn so far, Dowell can make only a halting return. His community is no wider than his impressions, but in pressing his hesitant way among them, he begins to choose a world.

A novel which opens by dramatizing the collapse of those moral and psychological categories by which we habitually live concludes by dramatizing the awkward and tentative steps by which morality and character might be renewed. Out of "nothing" Dowell invents himself. Choosing to place himself in the "category" of the passionate may not be tantamount to *feeling* passion, but it is to embrace one possibility among others. Dowell's freedom, tenuous though it may be, reanimates the ethical sense that had languished in Edward, petrified in Leonora and died in Florence. Morality, degraded by convention and thwarted by passion, hesitantly reappears in the simple judgments of a mind struggling to weigh its preferences. After the endless repetitions of "I don't know," Dowell says "nay" to Florence and Leonora and "yea" to Nancy and Edward. He may not yet know, but he *decides*, and in so deciding, he gives a picture of morality in its nascent state, founded not on inherited norms but on original judgments of value.

The temptation is great to see Dowell in a state of final disintegration, the coherence of the ego lost in a shower of impressions. But what appears as the disintegration of character might better be regarded as a condition that oddly resembles it, namely the formation of character. Like Monet's blind artist suddenly given sight, Dowell comes confusedly into being. Each new utterance is a fresh collision between the mind and its environs. Assuredly, this is not a familiar condition, but neither is it madness. It is rather an imaginary posture of human character that Impressionism is particularly suited to render: a radical innocence that perpetually rediscovers the world and posits itself in startled speech.

CHAPTER FOUR

Form's body: Lewis's *Tarr*

I

A man, an artist, let us call him T, realizes that his flirtation with B has gone too far, and feeling that he has already been guilty of deception he brings their sentimental dalliance to an end. A second man, K, also an artist, suffers a hopeless passion for a woman, A, who gives no sign of returning his desire. B and K, the one brooding over her former lover, the other absorbed with his futile yearning, are thrown together; through a series of awkward chances, they find themselves romantically entangled. T returns to discover how things now stand. In his maudlin wanderings through Paris, nostalgic for his past with B, he meets A and the two fall in love.

Cast in such formal terms, this situation might have furnished the kernel of a Jamesian novella in which the rigorous geometry of emotions, in particular the symmetric reversal of the original couplings, would have been submitted to the most exacting and delicate refinements. However, when we consider that T (that is, Tarr) indulges his moral weakness and dramatizes his cruelty; that Kreisler binds himself to Bertha by raping her during a portrait session; that he accidentally kills a man whom he meant to kill by design; that he commits suicide; that Tarr marries Bertha when she is pregnant with Kreisler's child; that he visits her punctiliously from four to seven, reserving the rest of the day for his continuing romance with Anastasya — then it is clear how far we are from Jamesian refinement. Still, the point of the opening exercise in abstraction was to indicate that a formal astringency underlies the psychological excess that is so visible in *Tarr*. The subject of this chapter is the place left for individuality between the novel's strenuous formalism and its presentation of human character as something highly *informal*, something disorderly, unruly, even unseemly.

Almost the first thing that Tarr does in this novel that bears his name is to offer a rigorous distinction between two forms of experience, art and life, or more particularly art and sexuality, and to place his own concerns firmly on the side of the former. "Sex," announces Tarr, "is a monstrosity."[1] He expounds a version of the psychoanalytic notion that art is the displacement of libido and gives the idea a sharp unpleasant twist towards misogyny: "The most suspicious fact about any man with pretensions to intelligence is the possession of an intelligent wife" (p. 18). He happily concedes his own sexual vulgarity — "no one could have a coarser, more foolish, slovenly taste than I have in women" (p. 21) — and presents this as a symptom of genius.

With most people, who are not artists, all the finer part of their vitality goes into sex if it goes anywhere: during their courtship they become third-rate poets, all their instincts of drama come out freshly with their wives. The artist is he in whom this emotionality normally absorbed by sex is so strong that it claims a newer and more exclusive field of deployment... All that delicate psychology another man naturally seeks in a woman, the curiosity of form, windows on other lives, love and passion, I seek in my work and not elsewhere. (pp. 20–1).

This is an immoderate statement of the autonomy of art, and its severity suggests a preliminary distinction between the two characters who dominate the novel, Tarr and Kreisler. For, unlike Tarr, Kreisler is incapable of the aesthetic sublimation. He is a failed painter whose "emotionality" cannot discharge itself in form: "When the events of his life became too unwieldy or overwhelming, he converted them into love; as he might otherwise have done, had he possessed a specialized talent, into some art or other" (p. 101). The result is the series of catastrophes which mark the descending arc of his life: the estrangement from his father, the unrequited passion for Anastasya, the rape of Bertha, the duel with Soltyk, his flight and his suicide. After his death, Tarr offers this appraisal of his grim career: "I believe that all the fuss he made was an attempt to get out of Art back into Life again. He was like a fish floundering about who had got into the wrong tank. *Back into sex* I think would describe where he wanted to get to: he was doing his best to get back into sex again out of a little puddle of art where he felt he was gradually expiring" (p. 314).

On its face the relationship between Tarr and Kreisler conforms to a principle of structure with which we are now familiar, a form in which two protagonists of the same sex control the plot and divide fundamental attributes between them. Among many other instances, Marlow and Kurtz, Dowell and Ashburnham, Strether and Chad Newsome, Nick Carraway and Gatsby, Lily Briscoe and Mrs Ramsay, all provide variants on this form. In place of a conventional romantic tie, these characters are bound through relations of identification and opposition that place them at a remove from other figures in the work and make their association dramatically central. No doubt these emotionally charged pairings derive from conventions of romance that had dominated so much Victorian fiction, but in making the protagonists of the same sex and in removing romantic love as the basis of connection, these narratives open the way for a new and distinctive configuration. Typically, the two figures divide between passivity and activity, asceticism and sensuousness, contemplation and will, restraint and license; and, also typically, the dramatic emphasis comes to fall upon the passive, ascetic, contemplative and restrained individual who becomes the center of moral discrimination and frequently serves as a figure for the artist. The opposition often assumes the form of an international confrontation, in which the collision between the protagonists summarizes deep moral, psychological and ideological differences.

The introduction of the principals in *Tarr* certainly invites a host of such antitheses, and it is in the context of a firmly antithetic structure that the novel has consistently been read. Munton provides a representative view when he writes that "*Tarr* is structured around a set of oppositions: Tarr and Kreisler, Tarr and Bertha, Bertha and Anastasya, representing two kinds of sex; the true artist and the false; body and mind." According to Parker, Kreisler is "driven by passion as Tarr is dominated by ideas," while Kush sees an opposition between

123

consciousness and will. Jameson offers a more elaborate reading of the novel, but he too describes it in terms of a "binary agon," interpreting the difference between Tarr and Kreisler as the difference between ego and id, the "non-action" of contemplation and the "violent action which is the passive 'suffering' of instinct."[2] Such opinions seem to have much to recommend them. The novel's characters are themselves quick to establish oppositions with one another; they eagerly align themselves within a system of differences. But this very eagerness should make us suspicious and should at least encourage us to look more closely at the novel's structure and to regard its schematism as a first, not a final, step. In order to do this, it will be necessary to pay close attention to the methods of characterization in *Tarr*, and from this point we will move quickly between the problem of character and the problem of form until we have discovered that they are so close we need not move at all.

II

The assault which Lewis made on character was at the same time an assault on emerging modernist orthodoxies. To a movement that located the value of personality in the mind, that conceived identity in terms of psychological states, that pursued the intimacies of introspection, and that sought a language for the unconscious – to this movement Lewis responded with the body. In a superficial respect this emphasis suggests a comparison with Lawrence who also broke with certain prevailing modernist habits in order to restore attention to bodily experience. But, unlike Lawrence, Lewis did not regard the body as possessing an inherent dignity, as revealing the mystery of creation, or as offering hope for individual and social renewal.[3] For Lewis the body is not a source of value but a rebuttal to every moral valuation; it confronts luminous morality with opaque matter; it is *absurd*, because "there is nothing that is animal (and we as bodies are animals) that is not absurd."[4] Lewis cites William James in defense of his claim:

One need only shut oneself in a closet and begin to think of the fact of one's being there, of one's queer bodily shape in the darkness (a thing to make children scream at, as Stevenson says), of one's fantastic character and all, to have the wonder steal over the detail as much as over the general fact of being, and to see that it is only familiarity that blunts it. Not only that anything should be, but that *this* very thing should be, is mysterious. Philosophy stares but brings no reasoned solution, for from nothing to being there is no logical bridge.[5]

Following James, Lewis regards the body as an affront to reason, a clumsy obtrusive absurdity that passes itself off as *us*. It is the indelible mark of a material existence that can offer no justification for itself, that can be explained but never understood. Moreover, it perversely refuses to remain dead matter; it has lofty pretensions, it is a "thoughtful body" (p. 286). When Tarr meets Hobson in the scene that opens the novel, he considers it "insanitary to have their bodies shuffling and gesticulating there" (p. 12). Of Kreisler we are told that "on very troubled days his body, like the finger of a weather-glass, would move erratically" (p. 109): "this giant body . . . sat down or stood up with an air of certain proprietorship"; on the street it is "given the freedom of the city by every body within sight at once, heroically installed and almost unnaturally solid" (p. 83).

"Suppose," writes Lewis, "you came upon an orchid or a cabbage reading Flaubert's *Salammbô*, or Plutarch's *Moralia*, you would be very much surprised. But if you found a man or a woman reading it, you would *not* be surprised." But you *ought* to be surprised. "It is just as absurd externally" because it involves "the intelligent behavior of matter." This is the basis of Lewis's theory of comedy: "The root of the Comic is to be sought in the sensations resulting from the observation of a *thing* behaving like a person. But from this point of view all men are necessarily comic: for they are all *things*, or physical bodies, behaving as *persons*."[6] Lewis, one might say, is an inverted Cartesian. He too posits an uncompromising distinction – Descartes's "real distinction" – between mind and body, but whereas Descartes then attempts to prove that the human essence is an immaterial soul only accidentally linked to an embodied form, Lewis sees humanity as essentially (and comically) bound to the body. As Tarr tersely puts it, "The body is the main thing" (p. 33). From an "exterior" perspective — the perspective which Lewis consistently recommends — we confront a world not of minds but of absurdly purposive lumps of matter that behave autonomously and *intelligently*, without any signs of direction from the mind, indeed often in leering opposition to its biddings. The body acts as an independent agent with, as it were, a mind of its own.[7]

The literary picture of individuality, as we have had many occasions to see, is habitually associated with the life of the mind. When James writes of Strether that he enjoys "an amount of experience out of all proportion to his adventures," it is the intervention of vibrant consciousness that transforms Strether's exiguous adventures into his opulent experience. But for Lewis, even more radical in this connection than Lawrence, the adventures of what he calls the "wild body" create possibilities for individual experience which the mind can scarcely understand and of which it highly disapproves. The sensitivity to the world that other moderns locate in the activity of thought Lewis locates in the reflex of a nervous limb, the recoil of the hand, the spasms of the back and shoulders.

It is not that Lewis ignores the existence of an inner world, a mental universe with its own distinctive character. It is simply that the mind is no closer than the body to establishing the ground of personal identity. Thoughts and emotions do not possess that intimate *inwardness* which the realist tradition had ascribed to them. Indeed, they often seem as external as the body. Tarr "gave a hasty glance at his 'indifference' to see whether it were OK" (p. 48); he "met his thoughts with a contemptuous stiff veteran smile" (p. 326); together he and Anastasya "promenaded their sinuous healthy intellects" (p. 240). Ideas, attitudes, faculties, beliefs, emotions — these exist as so many objects in one's mental inventory, to be inspected, serviced and discarded. They do not define, they merely inhabit the personality; and any attempt to pierce to the innermost thought, the central emotion, must expect to find, not an ineliminable sincerity, but more elaborate artifice.

As the earliest Science wondered what was at the core of the world, basing its speculations on what deepest things occasionally emerge, with violence, at its holes, so Bertha often would conjecture what might be at the heart of Tarr. Laughter was the most apparently central substance which, to her knowledge, had uncontrollably appeared: often she had heard grumblings, quite literally, and seen unpleasant lights, belonging, she knew, to other categories of matter: but they never broke cover. (p. 65)

In an even more disquieting image, Tarr recalls Schopenhauer's picturé of boxes within boxes and describes himself as a "mummy-case": "only he contained nothing but innumerable other painted cases inside, smaller and smaller ones. The smallest was . . . a painting like the rest. – His kernel was a painting, in fact: that was as it should be!" (p. 55).

There is no *place* where one can look for the self in *Tarr*; the inside brings one no closer than the outside; identity has lost its usual marks and can no longer be defined in terms of privileged thoughts or intimate emotions. There is no center of experience for individual characters, and perhaps the dominant conceit in Lewis's early work is the image of the self as a possession like any other, a mere appurtenance which gives no definition to the personality, constitutes no essence, fixes 'no identity. Tarr speaks of the "poor heightened self [Bertha] laces herself into" (p. 67), while Kreisler comes to "put himself aside": "always up till then immersed in that self, now for the first time he stood partly outside it" (p. 92).

But who is this Kreisler who stands outside himself? Who is that Bertha who laces herself into herself? An apparent answer is found in one of Tarr's early metaphors which describes imagination as "the commander-in-chief" who "keeps in the rear." Imagination, maintains Tarr, "is the man." Lest, however, we conclude that here is the missing essence of identity, we should quickly recall the proposition that begins Tarr's speech: "Nobody *is* anything or life would be intolerable" (p. 17). The imagination is what lies behind every manifestation of character but it has no content; it does not define the self; it only projects *selves*. "I'm an indifferent landlord," announces Tarr, "I haven't the knack of handling the various personalities gathered beneath my roof" (p. 23). "I am a hundred different things," intones Kreisler, "I am as many people as the different types of people I have lived amongst" (p. 258).

127

Much of the activity of the modern novelistic imagination, and much of its anxiety, was to establish a secure basis for individuality. This we have repeatedly seen. It is a recurrent thematic concern, the struggle to wrest a figure of the self from the snares of its milieu, and it is an urgent formal issue, the need to define the contours of character. But Lewis stands within this study as the rebel's own rebel, who acknowledges the problems of his contemporaries but who would rather aggravate than relieve them. He too identifies the integrity of individual character as a difficulty that any modern fiction must confront, but he is of interest here not because he proposed a solution to the difficulty but because he extended it, deepened it and revealed it as still more fundamental than had been thought.

Characters in *Tarr* casually discard identities, choosing new "personalities," "selves" and most often "roles," a term which emphasizes the obsessively self-dramatizing aspect of behavior in the novel.[8] When Bertha assumes a pose of noble sacrifice and Kreisler contrives his "revolutionary motif" (p. 151), the two meet in their fateful unanticipated kiss: "It was like a stage-kiss: the needs of their respective roles had been satisfied" (p. 145). Personality is a theatre-prop in a drama staged by the imagination, and in this respect Lewis anticipates a perception that has become a sociological commonplace: that identity is a part one plays; one plays at being oneself. Lewis gives that idea a turn towards the macabre. His characters are consistently betrayed by the roles they have chosen; the drama never goes as planned, with the result that characters are left staring blankly at the costumes they have donned.

Imagine a species, highly conscious and self-conscious, which actively formulates intentions only to find them constantly thwarted by the material world, most notably by that very body which was meant to enact them. Imagine further that these creatures expend prodigious mental energies in trying to justify what they have done by accident, constructing "a vast scaffolding of fable and ingenious explanation" (p. 192) to that end. Imagine finally that the justifications prove no sturdier than the original intentions and that they too are overturned by a stubborn and careless world. Such, says Lewis, are we. Our minds do not direct our bodies so much as they pursue them, trying to restore the authority of human intention when the damage has already been done.

After the unexpected scandal of the kiss, Bertha decides to see more of Kreisler because by "deliberately exposing herself to criticism, she would be effacing, in some sense, the extreme *involuntariness* of the Boulevard incident" (p. 179). Lewis compares her to a person who "has made some slip in grammar, say: he makes it again on purpose so that his first involuntary speech may appear deliberate" (p. 180). The attempt is to appropriate blind purposelessness to the service of human will, but it persistently fails, and in the case of Kreisler it fails not only persistently but spectacularly. He means to kill Soltyk in a duel, and then, in the worst of all possible outcomes, kills him accidentally, pulling the trigger as he stumbles. Even his suicide, voluntary by definition, becomes an exercise in self-deception. Kreisler arranges the materials for his hanging "like a boy preparing the accessories of some game":

he recognized what these proceedings meant, but shunned the idea that it was serious. In the way that a person disinclined to write a necessary letter may take up his pen, resolving to begin it merely, but writes more and more until it is in fact completed, so Kreisler proceeded with his unattractive task. (p. 293)

T. S. Eliot called the portrait of Kreisler "a study in humiliation."[9] It is an astute remark that does more than state the novel's theme; it describes a leading technique of characterization. Lewis submits the helpless mind to the exactions of matter, leaving little for consciousness to do but witness its own degradation.

Lewis, I have said, sets himself against his modernist contemporaries, enjoying his contempt for the revolutionary as much as he enjoys his contempt for the conservative. Although he presents himself as an antagonist in general, his work exists in special antagonism to the work of Ford Madox Ford, and they appear together at the middle of this study because they offer such stark alternatives for modern character. In the person of Dowell, Ford detaches subjectivity from its physical manifestations, imagining mental life before it takes on embodied attributes; and in so doing, I have suggested, he creates an unlikely image of the free man. Lewis, on the other hand, immures the ego in its body, never letting it escape the quakes and tremors of its physical form, and exposing its illusion of freedom to the tyranny of automatism. What these antithetic conceptions share is a challenge to individual agency. Dowell exists at such a great remove from the physical world that his mental activity remains without material consequence and his freedom must remain a verbal freedom. Lewis's characters are so deeply embedded in the corporeal world that often when they err, we can only blame the laws of physics.

Hence critics often wonder how seriously we are to take Kreisler's inexorable decline.[10] It is a fair question, but we must recognize that before it is a question for the critic it is a question for the characters and especially for Kreisler himself. The satire, the emotional distance, the farce, the elaborate posturing, the mock-seriousness – these are not merely features of the novel's mode; they are features of Kreisler's mode, and they make it difficult for him to understand the gravity of his own situation. He attitudinizes up to the moment of his death. Certainly one great challenge of the work is the disparity between event and tone; characters perform brutal gestures with broad grins. After he has raped Bertha, Kreisler comes to apologize; working himself into "a more and more urgent dramatic hypocrisy" (pp. 201–2) he promises to avenge the crime he has committed and then smiles "at the conclusion of his mock-eloquence" (p. 202). The risk in such a scene is that it may seem to encourage the thought that no action is immune from comic irreverence. Lewis indeed entertains such a nihilistic thought, and if his sensibility stalled here, as it sometimes threatens to do, then the novel would be merely repellent. But he is aiming at a more worthy and sophisticated idea: not that grave events are susceptible to travesty, but that travesty can itself lead to moral catastrophe – as surely, and perhaps in our time more surely, than passionate sincerity.

During the exchanges leading up to the duel between Kreisler and Soltyk, Tarr becomes "astonished at the rapid tragic trend of these farcical negotiations" (p. 270). Lewis invokes the precedent of tragedy as often as that of comedy, but while his comic methods fall within a recognizable tradition, the tragic emphasis bears only a weak connection to our usual understanding of the mode. Lewis ignores the problem of tragic choice, the relationship of the hero to the community, the theme of recognition; he does not ignore but subverts the tragic emotions of pity and terror. Only one aspect of tragedy successfully holds his attention: the acknowledgment of a dark fatality that derides human purpose. It is the inexorability of the tragic movement that concerns him, the conjunction of forces that yield necessity — the way, as he puts it, that possibilities are "weakened by the nearness of Certainty" (p. 278). And yet, tragedy in this sense is not clearly distinguished from Lewisian comedy with its own emphasis on the involuntary reflex and the mechanical action. Tarr explains that comedy is "always the embryo of Tragedy" (p. 66), and Lewis looks for those moments when there occurs a sudden shift between the modes, brutality emanating from the midst of farce. If the root of the comic is the perception of a thing behaving like a person, one might say that the tragic perception in Lewis is that of a person behaving like a thing, enduring the descent from the voluntary to the involuntary, from the imagination into an unimaginative world. The human body thus stands at the nexus of the two modes; it is the site of the comic upsurge of matter and the tragic fall of the mind.

III

As I indicated at the opening of this chapter, the plot of *Tarr* has a peculiarly abstract quality — peculiar, that is, in light of the grimly concrete actions on which it turns. Characters stand in carefully articulated relations of balance and opposition; and when Tarr informs Anastasya that he continues to see Bertha "for form's sake" (p. 332), Lewis surely means us to understand "form" in its aesthetic as well as its social sense. Individuals possess, as it were, a certain mass and volume that determine possibilities for the dramatic configuration — much as Tarr looking at a photograph discovers that the "set angle" of his head "fitted in with the corresponding peculiarities of [Bertha's] head and bust" (pp. 49–50). Characters consistently treat one another as "material for 'arrangement' " (p. 53),

131

as items within an elaborate spatial design in which each ego is defined by all the others. Two characters cannot occupy the same place: this is the novel's Euclidean axiom, whose corollary is that characters must engage in a constant jostling for position. Lewis exaggerates the systematic aspect of character relations to the point where a change in one character becomes a change for all. In this world, to move is to move someone else.

Displaying the sensibility of that plastic artist who had led English painting towards abstraction, Lewis is even more explicit than James in making the requirements of formal structure dictate the behavior of individuals, with the result that characters begin to formulate their motives in terms of spatial demands. When Bertha chooses the heroic part and decides to set Tarr free (hoping in this way to win him yet), she realizes that she must find "a somebody else" to dislodge him. And when Tarr finds his old role taken, he quickly chooses a new one, the "obstacle," who will attempt to protect Bertha by befriending Kreisler. In this way, "a regulation 'triangle' " (p. 229) is established, and when Tarr thinks that Kreisler has eluded him, he rushes to "get back into position again" (p. 242). Moreover, just as the unstable dyad of Tarr and Bertha had conjured Kreisler, so the triangle now summons Anastasya. In order to satisfy spatial requirements Tarr feels "compelled to requisition" a new player. Flirtation with Anastasya, he reasons, "would be a reply to Kreisler (an Anastasya for your Otto) and restore the balance: at present they were perched upon a sort of three-legged affair. The fourth party would make things solid and less precarious" (p. 233).

Lewis thus takes the motif of romantic rivalry and submits it to a stringent formalism that subordinates emotion to the demands of geometric balance. A pattern of placement and displacement continually repeats itself; the novel is fabricated out of a series of substitutions. Kreisler is branded by the fact that his father supplanted him in the affections of his fiancée. When he arrives in Paris he discovers that he can no longer borrow money from Ernst Vokt because Soltyk has "superseded [him] in the position of influence as regards Vokt's purse" (p. 89). Later Soltyk compounds the indignity by attaching himself to Anastasya, an action which so enrages Kreisler that before the duel he presents "a false picture of the situation in which the heart was substituted for the purse, and Anastasya for Vokt" (p. 258).

This last remark underlines the eerily abstract quality of these relations, in which the terms can change while the rivalries persist: Soltyk supersedes Kreisler, Kreisler replaces Tarr, Tarr supplants Kreisler, and Bertha is "officially presented to her successor" (p. 302). Characters willingly place themselves in stark antitheses; the plot advances through the struggle of contraries. When Tarr and Kreisler clash in the latter's room, it appears that the novel is moving towards the final confrontation of opposing principles; indeed Tarr readies himself for a "bellicose visit . . . launched to a slow blast of Humour, ready, when the time came, to turn into a storm" (p. 249). At this point the novel appears to conform to that dualist structure which its critics have described and which its modernist antecedents had anticipated, but before assimilating *Tarr* to this rigid configuration, we must return to some old concerns and then advance to some new ones.

Until now two emphases have governed the argument of this chapter. First has been the distinctive challenge to the autonomous ego posed by Lewis's methods of characterization: the reification of the mental universe, the careless dismissal of emotional unity, the abasement of voluntary agency, the dispersal of personality into countless roles. Both the "comic" and "tragic" modes of the novel achieve their force by assailing the pretensions of the individual, and the conceit that links these methods and modes is the anarchic independence of the body. However, in a second emphasis, what distinguishes *Tarr* is its rigorous formalism which abstracts from the material world and arranges characters in structures of nearly mathematical austerity. On the face of it, this is a separate, even competing, emphasis, and certainly the experience of reading *Tarr* involves an uneasy alternation between its heavy bodies and its weightless forms. But in calling this chapter "Form's body," I have meant to suggest a relation between these contrary aspects of this provoking novel; in particular I have meant to imply that the novel's form cannot be detached from its matter; and in what follows I intend to show what happens when an antithetic structure meets a monolithic character.

IV

One of the consequences of Lewis's assault on the usual criteria for personal identity — emotion, thought, will, purpose — and his insistent emphasis upon the "wild body" is that character is deprived of any refuge where it can be incontestably itself. There is nowhere for the personality to retreat where it will be immune from the "energy and obstinacy of the rest of the world" (p. 292). Accordingly, characters are no more likely to be guided by inner ideas than by outer objects — rooms, letters, watches — which determine moods, condition thoughts, create roles.[11] Instruments put people to use. The members of the Bonnington Club

changed and metamorphosed themselves with *its* changes. They became athletic or sedentary according to the shifts and exigencies of this building's existence. They turned out in dress clothes or gymnasium get-ups as its destiny prompted, to back it up: one month they would have to prove that it *was* a gymnasium, the next that it *was* a drawing-school, so they stippled and vaulted, played table-tennis and listened to debates. (pp. 147–8)

Then, lest we think that the will has no effect, it turns up in unlikely places: Tarr "seemed to have caused [his height] himself" (p. 30). Multiplying the causal powers that affect the course of events, Lewis presents human agency as neither effective nor coherent. But he shares little with the deterministic conceptions of the late nineteenth century which hypothesized a unified force that remorselessly swept individuals in its consistent path.[12] Lewis sees no such unity or consistency; rather, he sees a noisy competition among many causalities. Nor does he discount the possibility of freedom; he simply prefers to locate it in physical objects rather than in human beings.

The asperity of Lewis's prose style — the rough rhythms, the inversions, the abrupt shifts in attention — is at least partly due to the perception of the heterogeneity of agents and causes. From this standpoint any number of things may qualify as the subjects of action, and Lewis's sentences often seem the bloody relics of a war fought between substantives over the right to the nominative position. In this conflict human beings often end as the victims — direct objects. Indeed one of Lewis's most distinctive stylistic habits is to choose improbable candidates to be the subjects of unlikely transitive constructions. Kreisler's corpse "personally insulted" each member of the French police staff (p. 293). After Tarr has ended a day of painting, "his depression again grasped him, like an immensely gloomy companion who had been idling impatiently while he worked . . . Nausea glared at him from every object met: sex surged up and martyrized him" (p. 206). And in a sentence that only Lewis could have written we read that "The inertia and phlegm, outward sign of depressing everyday Kreisler, had found someone, when he had found Vokt, for whom they were a charm and something to be envied" (p. 92).

One might plausibly call "transitivity" the condition of experience in *Tarr*, transitivity in the strict sense — the passing over of some quality or power — with the result that characters dwell within a universe where anything might suddenly become an agent and anyone might become its object. This condition binds subjectivities to the material world in ways that we have seen, but it also binds them to one another in still more striking ways. In the simplest cases emotions are distributed as though they were so many commodities. Thus Bertha "transferred her hatred from herself to Kreisler" (p. 218), while Tarr finds that "some of his passion for Bertha flowed over on to her fellow countryman" (p. 297). In more extreme formulations the very boundaries of character are obliterated. Tarr reflects upon love and concludes that "the people that love us become part of us; it is a dismemberment to cast them off. Our own blood flows out after them when they go" (p. 70). He explains his tenderness for Bertha as "due to her having purloined some part of himself, and covered herself superficially with it as a shield. Her skin at least was Tarr" (p. 70).

This last example is not only a cunning conceit; it is virtually a statement of method. Lewis entertains an anarchic literary perception that anticipates radical experiments later in the century. Suppose character is not something irreducibly private, something irrevocably *owned*, but rather an agglomeration of properties that others can come to possess. Suppose that a proper name does not simply denote an individual but connotes a set of qualities that can be exchanged, transferred, appropriated. Then, disconcertingly, characters will no longer be distinct. Thus Kreisler regards Soltyk as "an attribute of Vokt" (p. 151) and sees Tarr "as part of Bertha, a sort of masculine extension of her" (p. 230). Character is not a unique configuration of traits, nor a bounded essence; it is a *condition* that can pass beyond the usual boundaries of subjectivity, branding, tainting, contaminating others. Much of the struggle between individuals takes the form of a struggle to impose one character upon another. At the extreme, the proper name passes to the defeated party. Bertha, whose skin had once been Tarr, realizes that she has become a "sort of Kreisler," so much that Kreisler himself shuns her.

"Everybody," concludes Tarr, "all personality was catching: we are all sicknesses for each other" (p. 70). If character is a sickness it can be spread, and one of the novel's controlling images is the contagion of personality. This is not the sort of image that readers can easily accommodate; there are few presuppositions more basic to the experience of narrative than that the unfolding of the story will refine distinctions among its human particulars. But Lewis inverts that principle; by the end of the novel every major character has been described as a variant upon another.

When Bertha finds herself bound to Kreisler, she imagines the reaction of her friends: "Tarr to Kreisler: from bad to worse" (p. 180). Her friends are right in at least this respect: the difference is one of degree, a question of scale, a matter of more or less. Lewis habitually relies on comparative adjectives in describing his characters, a device that emphasizes the similarity within differences. Anastasya's hair is "the same colour as Bertha's only it was darker and coarser" (p. 320); Bertha is big but Anastasya is "even more substantial" (p. 214); and after recording the latter's denunciation of her rival, the narrator coolly observes that her "romanticism, in fact, was of the same order as Bertha's, but much better class" (p. 295).

Deep antagonism only conceals a deeper likeness, as Butcher and his car are said to be opposites "but with some grave essential in common" (p. 37). The novel intimates that identity is not a matter of fundamental difference, only relative intensity, and plainly this threatens the integrity of the several rivalries. Soltyk resembles Kreisler; he is Kreisler's "efficient and more accomplished counterpart" (p. 89); and at the moment of their duel, opposition suddenly turns into *its* opposite; "[Kreisler] *loved* the man" (p. 278).[13]

The result is that as the novel continues, the antitheses which had organized it begin to corrode. Resemblance supersedes opposition; personal identity wavers. After the fiasco of the duel, Kreisler wonders if he, not Soltyk, were the one who has been killed and if his wandering presence were only the movements of a ghost. In the opening pages of the novel, Tarr describes Bertha as probably "the one thing on earth I am not like" (p. 32), but later he will enjoy "being German himself — being Bertha as well" (p. 224). He compares his relationship with Anastasya to "a mother being given a child to bear the same size already as herself" (p. 327), and then, reversing the gender of his conceit, he begins to suspect that Anastasya has crossed an imaginary line between male and female. There remains the most important example of a decaying antithesis, but it will be best to address it within the context of another formal problem, where it will be not only provocative, but downright disruptive.

V

The climactic movement of the novel, which begins when Tarr sets out to stage a final confrontation with Kreisler, opens in a familiar modernist vein. Lewis rigorously narrows the perspective to a single actor, suppresses relevant information and permits only a slow movement towards a surprising recognition. In this respect the sequence belongs to a line that includes Marlow's midnight search for Kurtz or Strether's riverside discovery of Chad and Madame de Vionnet. Here the narrative assumes Tarr's perspective as he wanders through the city in search of Kreisler, finding him at last in a café engaged in obscure reckonings of his own, scarcely mindful of

Tarr's arrival. Suspecting that Kreisler's absorption is a ruse, Tarr settles into a chair and waits for a sign. After a few moments Kreisler abruptly leaps up; Tarr raises a hand to protect himself; but Kreisler moves quickly past on his way to slap the hapless Soltyk sitting at another table. At this point Tarr recognizes "the peculiar miscarriage of his plan" (p. 252) and comes at last to realize (as does the reader) that Soltyk, not he, is the destined participant in Kreisler's drama.

Just at the moment when he had felt that he was going to be one of the principal parties to a violent scene, he had witnessed, not himself at all, but another man snatched up into his role. As he watched the man Kreisler had struck, he seemed to be watching himself. And yet he felt rather on the side of Kreisler. (p. 253)

This is a movement that we know well: the construal of behavior in terms of roles, the substitution of one character for another, and the sudden change in the configuration of relationships. This particular instance, occurring at a decisive moment in the plot, will let us consolidate a range of pertinent issues and should allow us to place the question of character in firm relation to the problem of narrative form.

First, it should be noted that Soltyk, by "snatching up" Tarr's role, unsettles the symmetry which the novel had so teasingly constructed. The choreography of romantic desires had led to an elegant "four-legged" design — Tarr, Kreisler, Anastasya, Bertha — so tidily arranged that Jameson has been able to project it upon the structuralist rectangle derived from Greimas. But Lewis's rectangle is a pliable form, easily redrawn. The presence of Soltyk disturbs the system of oppositions that had led towards the confrontation between Tarr and Kreisler. The immediate result is that Tarr is relieved of the role of enemy: as long as Soltyk plays his part ("he seemed to be watching himself"), Tarr is free to convert opposition into alliance ("he felt rather on the side of Kreisler"). Indeed he is pressed into service as Kreisler's second in the duel that is quickly and improbably arranged. Here, then, is that final moldering antithesis. Tarr and Kreisler cease to be polar terms; the climactic brawl between them is averted; and a novel which seems to trade on opposition proves to trade more heavily on similarity.

This last point has important bearing on a second aspect of this scene. Tarr, as I have said, provides a controlling point of view for the beginning of the dramatic sequence, and his discovery that he will not be a party to the coming violence would only seem to improve his position as a detached but attentive observer who will sift the meanings of events. Tarr, however, declines this role. He agrees to serve as Kreisler's second only until a "substitute" can be found, and as soon as his replacement arrives he withdraws unobtrusively, "leaving Kreisler for ever . . . to his very complicated, mysterious and turbulent existence" (p. 253). Tarr's withdrawal is an exemplary act and a significant divergence from the modernist paradigm that the novel had seemed to invoke. It is difficult to imagine Marlow abandoning Kurtz to pursue business upriver, or Strether ignoring Madame de Vionnet at the moment of crisis. These novels, as is perfectly evident, require an unfailing intimacy between the moral observer and the passionate agent. But Tarr, having bestowed a brief glance on the unhappy scene, cheerfully departs, and with him departs the possibility of a contemplative consciousness which might have weighed the significance of the unfolding events. The thwarted duel, the accidental murder, the suicide – these dramatically central incidents do not receive the independent scrutiny that had seemed likely; they appear without the mediation of a detached consciousness and are presented merely in the dim light of Kreisler's own reflections, such as these are.

Lewis later remarked that his novel ought to have been called *Otto Kreisler*.[14] Although this would not have been a much happier solution (one would then have wondered about the curious Englishman who dominates the beginning and the end), it would have explicitly acknowledged what every reader must feel, that the great weight of the novel lies with Kreisler, with his passion, his suffering and his self-annihilation. It is not necessary to know whether he ran away with Lewis's initial conception – which seems likely – but it is crucial to see that as he moves through the novel he alters the disposition of the whole.

Conrad, James and Forster each attempt to draw a circle of individuality within the wreck of social life, and then each attempts to move from the naked ego toward a reinvented community. The Conradian ship, the Jamesian dialogue, the Forsterian house – each represents a cautious attempt, fraught with uncertainty, to extend intimacy, to transmit perception, to share meanings and in these ways to restore a possible basis for social life. *Tarr*, too, concerns itself with the problem of part and whole, but not in order to pursue an equilibrium between them, nor to create the basis for community, rather to expose what we may call anti-community – the purely external ties that bind individuals within a senseless aggregate.

In *Tarr* the relation of part and whole depends on no subtle verbal or symbolic resources; it is brutally straightforward; the part *infects* the whole. If personality is "catching," if individuals are sicknesses for each other, then, for instance, Forster's elaborate synecdoche can give way to the more direct methods of contagion. Kreisler is a disease; the plot is his epidemic. Lewis would later write that the subject of the novel was "the elaborate and violent form of suicide selected by Herr Kreisler, involving a number of other people."[15] The image of entangling others in one's suicide gives a kind of photographic negative of social experience; the individual no longer struggles to reach accommodation with the community, but simply implicates it in his fate. Of the modern figures of passionate excess – such as Kurtz, Ashburnham, Gerald Crich, Gatsby, Sutpen – Kreisler is perhaps the most daunting because he seeks nothing for himself but the spectacle of his own humiliation. He is a "stormy and concrete nothingness" (p. 153) who envelops others in his nihilism, the enemy of all distinctions who steps past every boundary and thus submits the action of the novel to an emotional heightening. Kreisler achieves nothing more than the death he had erratically pursued, but he leaves "Kreisleriana" (p. 326) for the others.

Once one recognizes that the habitual movement of the novel is toward an overcoming of its own oppositions, then it is possible to see Kreisler's decline not as an aberration but as the extreme of a condition which other characters are made to endure – which Tarr, most notably, endures. In a moment of horror Bertha has imagined Tarr and Kreisler "welded in one" (p. 180), and at the end of the novel we learn that her child, violently fathered by Kreisler, "bore some resemblance to Tarr" (p. 334). This is the final telling irony that confirms the general progress: Tarr, like Bertha before him, has become "a sort of Kreisler." The artist who had declared that "sex is a monstrosity," who had claimed to find in painting what others find in women, leaves the novel as an accomplished sexual athlete. Womankind, "Kreisler's Theatre," is now Tarr's theatre. He marries Bertha, whom he visits daily, but lives with "his illicit and more splendid bride," Anastasya (p. 334).

When, one might ask, does he paint? It is a pertinent question. "Surrender to a woman," Tarr had held, "was a sort of suicide for an artist"; accordingly he had maintained his "artist's asceticism" (p. 213); soon we learn that "as for painting he ceased almost to think of it" (p. 249). It should be evident that the dualisms of mind and body, art and sex, contemplation and action are not sustained. At a respectable English distance Tarr follows Kreisler into moral and instinctual license, and the women whom Kreisler had pursued with violence, Tarr approaches more decorously but no less surely. By the end of the novel the initial distinction between art and sexuality has dissolved and has been replaced by a coy distinction within sexuality itself: Bertha's "bourgeois-bohemianism" and Anastasya's "swagger sex."

It may now be clear why Tarr fails to assume the role of contemplative observer during Kreisler's final crisis. The novel began by inviting that distinction between consciousness and action which is such an important principle of structure in modernist fiction. Tarr then seemed to represent a sovereign arbiter who might impose unity on a varied whole — an artist aloof from life, an imagination distinct from human appetite. But under the pressures of the narrative, Tarr becomes increasingly indifferent to the virtues of contemplation. Kreisler's furious passage through the plot amounts to a thrashing of the contemplative ideal; he brutally eroticizes the novel and makes it impossible for any character to remain merely an observer of life's passions. Tarr is in no position to furnish the values of mind. No longer an effective figure of opposition, he is merely another counterpart with his own

141

erotic ambitions; thoroughly disinclined to devote himself to scrutiny of Kreisler, he is no longer, if he ever was, Jameson's figure of "contemplation" and "non-action." The man who shuffles between women has become a passional figure ill-suited to perform the offices of mediation.

The consequence is that the novel does not achieve that form of totality pursued by Conrad, James and Ford, the totality of a supervening consciousness whose responses are to give form and meaning to events. Here is where the problems of character and structure are most intimately bound in *Tarr*. As characters lose a sovereign identity, so too does the form of the novel lose its sovereignty. When Kreisler finally provokes Soltyk beyond endurance, the latter responds like an engine "over-charged with fuel":

the will was released in a muffled explosion, it tore within at its obstructions, he writhed upright, a statue's bronze softening, suddenly, with blood. His blood, one heavy mass, hurtled about in him, up and down, like a sturgeon in a narrow tank. . . . His hands were electrified: will was at last dashed all over him, an arctic douche and the hands become claws flew at Kreisler's throat. (p. 280)

This is the moment towards which Lewisian characterization tends: the abrupt loss of control and the anarchic expression of the wild body. It is a disintegration of the ego that corresponds to the dissolution of narrative structure. The fiction, like the characters within it, moves towards a release of energy when fixed oppositions melt away leading to a noisy and turbulent dispersal. Kreisler compares himself "to one of those little nursery locomotives that go straight ahead without stopping; that anyone can take up and send puffing away in the opposite direction" (p. 117). When Tarr withdraws during the novel's climactic sequence, he is declining to turn the locomotive in a new direction; accordingly, Kreisler does not swerve in his approach towards murder and suicide. At the end of the novel we learn that "Anastasya and Bertha did not meet" (p. 334), and this is the condition towards which the plot tends: the isolation of its principals from one another. *Tarr* approaches neither peace nor carnage; its characters merely pass beyond opposition, towards similarity, and freed from the burden of confrontation they puff away in separate directions,

each following the uninterrupted course of a private obsession. The novel is by no means formless, but it constructs a
form that continually anticipates a release from form, just as
the dance at the Bonnington Club exists for the moment when
a careening Kreisler throws it into anarchy. "My passion for
art," notes Tarr, "has made me fond of chaos" (p. 241).

In the final lines of the novel the narrator summarizes Tarr's
future with his two women, noting that Bertha will divorce
him to marry an eye-doctor and that he and Anastasya will
never marry and will have no children. The following
paragraph is the novel's last.

> Tarr, however, had three children by a lady of the name of Rose Fawcett,
> who consoled him eventually for the splendours of his 'perfect woman.'
> But yet beyond the dim though solid figure of Rose Fawcett, another rises.
> This one represents the swing back of the pendulum once more to the swag-
> ger side. The cheerless and stodgy absurdity of Rose Fawcett required as
> compensation the painted, fine and enquiring face of Prism Dirkes.
> (p. 334)

This is a sudden dizzying transcendence of the entire plot, the
formal counterpart to Soltyk's over-charged emotional engine.
In a final rude substitution two leading characters are abruptly superseded, and the two who replace them make their en-
trance just in time for the curtain to fall. It is an arbitrary assertion of the novelist's power, an unconstrained expression of
literary will that flouts all norms of psychological development and formal proportion. In a final abstraction from individual experience Lewis condenses a long romantic history
into a short paragraph, as much to suggest that the novel we
have read might have been told just as tersely. Earlier Tarr
had described "the see-saw whose movement and contradiction was life" (p. 246), and at the last the image is still more
austere. Tarr is merely a pendulum which follows the rhythm
of sexual appetite, a pendulum moreover that with each swing
negates a character, a nightmarish literary apparatus that can
generate fictive proper names without end. This is fictional
form in the degenerate case; all that remains of structure is
a mechanical movement between two romantic types that cor-
respond to no real distinction, only to the idiosyncrasies of
Tarr's prurience.

The final swipe of the comic brush is to make the introduction of a character coincide with the last words of the novel. Prism Dirkes stands on the very edge of the fiction, which can scarcely be said to contain her. In this sense she is at the end of the novel what Kreisler is (hugely) at its middle — a literary disturbance that Lewis has no inclination to suppress, indeed that he has every inclination to encourage. The sliver of a character at the conclusion and the monstrous personality at the center both remain unassimilated provocations; they are to the novel what flailing limbs are to the wild body. Tarr is what these characters have in common; indeed Tarr is what all the major characters have in common. But he does not mediate, integrate or unify; like a pendulum he arrives in order to depart, leaving the form of the novel to enjoy the exuberance of its dissolution.

One does not go to Wyndham Lewis to renew a commitment to humane values; often one does not go to him at all. He is a cold anatomist who laughs at the corpse he dissects. But his virtue, and his justification, is that he is so meticulous in his anatomy that we can reconstruct the living body from the bloody trunk and limbs, from the fragments of emotion and the shards of thought, from the stunned features on the dead face. The failure of agency, the failure of love, the failure of community, the failure of art — these are rendered with a violence that can only be understood in relation to feelings of disappointment and loss, even if these are only our own disappointment and loss. To say this is not to sentimentalize Lewis; it is only to suggest why his wild laughter matters. He is perfectly rigorous in his antagonisms, and his willingness to carry the satiric vision to its conclusion is itself a value in an age of mixed emotions. It is impossible not to recoil from *Tarr* and often impossible not to recoil from its author. But this is no reason to ignore the novel — on the contrary. The success of art must be measured by its repulsions as well as its attractions, and a mark of *Tarr*'s power is how strongly and how *coherently* we recoil and how quickly we flee to the land of the living.

CHAPTER FIVE

"The passion of opposition" in *Women in Love*: none, one, two, few, many

I

The value behind values in *Women in Love* is integrity, not in the moral sense of the term, but in a sense that may be taken as a foundation for morality, integrity as a form of completion, perfection and coherence that justifies our strivings but needs no justification itself. An eye that lingers over the self-containment of a flower or a landscape in vast panorama is an eye that delights in integral and uncompromised wholeness. That is Lawrence's eye. But what arouses Lawrentian wrath and ignites this wrathful novel is the perception that wholeness has indeed been compromised, has been streaked, stained and discolored in faint but ominous ways. Here is part of the description of Shortlands, the Crich family home.

Shortlands looked across a sloping meadow that might be a park, because of the large, solitary trees that stood here and there, across the water of the narrow lake, at the wooded hill that successfully hid the colliery valley beyond, but did not quite hide the rising smoke.[1]

The smoke that curls into the meadow makes a fit image for the disruption of integrity, and it also enforces the historical character of the problem. Industry scars the landscape — "No flowers grow upon busy machinery" (p. 262) — but industry is only the proximate historical influence. Machinery is no more the first cause than flowers are the final victims. The collision between them is a sign of our immediate predicament in contemporary social life, but for Lawrence contemporary social life is itself a sign for something far grander, namely the fall into history as such, the imposition of human will upon an unwilling nature. And in a still vaster, almost incomprehensible perspective, within which the machine appears as only a recent symptom of an ancient disease, the entire length of history enacts a struggle for the form of integrity which dominates all others in *Women in Love*, the integrity of the self.[2] Thus Birkin at one point speculates that:

In the old age, before sex was, we were mixed, each one a mixture. The process of singling into individuality resulted in the great polarisation of sex. The womanly drew to one side, the manly to the other. But the separation was imperfect even then. And so our world-cycle passes. There is now to come the new day, when we are beings each of us, fulfilled in difference. (p. 271)

As this passage (like so many others) implies, the plural in Lawrence's title must not conceal the commitment to singularity; the name "woman" should not obscure the broodings of the male; the emotion ought not to distract us from the critique of emotion. Neither women nor love can be securely placed at the center of the work. The novel approaches the dignity of men through the indignity of women; it probes love in order to find its limits, and it imagines an integral self by imagining what precedes and follows it. As the first phrase in my own title means to suggest, the fate of the individual in *Women in Love* unfolds within a series of other fates, other dimensions, other scales and measures.

It will prove useful to begin at the end of that series, with the many, who fill the mines, who crowd the cities, who intrude from the past and who are detestable just because they are many. In Lawrence's work the multitude is abhorrent because it is multitudinous, because it is everywhere, covering the world, making human depravity conspicuous and suppressing extra-human value. The decadence of the modern period, its irreversible decline, its vulgarity, its timidity, its incoherence – these characteristics that arouse Lawrentian wrath are rarely seen as the work of individuals or even social classes. They are the product of the species as such, and wherever the species gathers in large groups, there its moral sores fester. "Humanity," says Birkin, "is a huge aggregate lie" (p. 187), and Ursula grows despondent at "the sordidness of humanity," which encroaches upon the expanse of nature: "The sea they turned into a murderous alley and a soiled road of commerce, disrupted like the dirty land of a city every inch of it. The air they claimed too, shared it up, parcelled it out to certain owners" (pp. 262–3). For Lawrence humanity in the mass is humanity in its essence, imposing itself upon the world it inhabits, obliterating the possibility of renewal, hurtling towards its well-deserved catastrophe.

Accordingly a persistent reflex in the novel is a revulsion from the mass so violent that it creates an urge to annihilation. As a boy Gerald longs to shoot down the striking miners, and as a man he destroys their humanity with his inhuman machine. When Gudrun passes through a group of colliers' wives and a jeering voice accosts her, she suddenly feels "violent and murderous. She would have liked them all annihilated, cleared away" (pp. 59–60). Birkin is the one who draws an extreme conclusion from these sentiments: if the many are abhorrent, there should be none. "Let mankind pass away," says Birkin, "Let humanity disappear as quick as possible" (p. 111).

Lawrence's reflections on sexuality have too often diverted attention from this troubling motif. Yet from early in the work to its final pages, chiefly but not exclusively through Birkin, Lawrence entertains the categorical view that "man is not the criterion," that "man was as nothing compared to the possibilities of the creative mystery" with its "miraculous unborn species" (p. 580). This is not simply an embittered misanthropy, nor a sentimental nature-cult. It is rather a product of Lawrence's absolutism, his demand for an ultimate ground to value, in the context of which human virtue appears a paltry and evanescent thing, especially when set alongside Birkin's "beautiful clean thought, a world empty of people, just uninterrupted grass, and a hare sitting up." If the reader is that hare sitting up, then this picture will not be disturbing but for a human being to celebrate "a clean, lovely, humanless world" (p. 188) is obviously to place the problem of experience in the harshest possible light. Intermittently, *Women in Love* contemplates the end of humanity, and in a scarcely conceivable way it takes this thought as a basis for the construction of character.

It is not, however, a stable basis. When a spasm of hatred seizes Hermione and she strikes Birkin on the head with a piece of lapis lazuli, he runs from the house bleeding and wanders up a hillside among the "leaves and the primroses and the trees." Then he reflects: "Here was his world, he wanted nobody and nothing but the lovely, subtle, responsive vegetation, and himself, his own living self."

What a dread he had of mankind, of other people! It amounted almost to horror, to a sort of dream terror — his horror of being observed by some other people. If he were on an island, like Alexander Selkirk, with only the creatures and the trees, he would be free and glad, there would be none of this heaviness, this misgiving. He could love the vegetation and be quite happy and unquestioned, by himself. (pp. 166–7)

The image of a "world empty of people" has been delicately adjusted; now Birkin longs for a world empty of *other people*. The uncompromising demand, "Let mankind pass away," has been relaxed to allow for his own survival. Here the revulsion from the human multitude takes the form of a radical individualism which locates value in "free-proud singleness" (p. 332) and which sees all desires and duties as self-generated and self-assigned. "Anybody who is anything can just be himself and do as he likes," he tells Gerald. "I should like [people] to like the purely individual thing in themselves, which makes them act in singleness. And they only like to do the collective thing" (p. 82). Or, as he later puts it with characteristic decision, "First person, singular, is enough for me" (p. 107). In itself this is characteristic romantic fare, but within *Women in Love* it becomes particularly charged because it collides with the proposition that humanity must perish for the good of the world. Birkin, that is, offers two stark antitheses, one between human existence and the inhuman creative mystery, and the other between collective and individual experience. In each case he endorses the latter term and hence assumes the awkward position (awkward, that is, for anyone but Birkin) of both asserting the priority of the individual and calling for the end of humanity altogether.

It is scarcely useful to think of this oscillation as a contradiction, a tension or an ambiguity. Neither Birkin nor Lawrence accepts a norm of rational consistency that would require them to bring propositions into a logical coherence. *Women in Love* willingly tolerates contrary principles, representing ideas as crystallizations of the personality, as deeply rooted as emotions and subject to the same vicissitudes. This leads to the characteristic Lawrentian amalgam of dogmatism and doubt, the intemperate assertion of a metaphysical proposition, followed by an offhand retraction. Still, without imputing a coherence that is foreign to Lawrence's habit of thought, we can reasonably attempt to reconstruct the fitful movement of Birkin's mind. That instructive apposition — mankind, other people — which seems an almost willful solecism rests nonetheless on a keenly felt perception. No individual can constitute a kind. A conception of humanity can never emerge from within the self; it can only derive from our participation with others in a common life. To withdraw from that life, to repudiate "the collective thing," to refuse all common norms (if such a thing is possible) is to escape the dreaded rubric "mankind" which then becomes merely the description of "other people." Birkin pursues a state of being so irreducibly his own that it cannot be understood in the terms of his species. Hermione, sensing this, fancies that Birkin is "not a man," "not one of us" (p. 149). To the extent that this condition is intelligible it can be called "non-human," and to that extent Birkin can meaningfully assert, "I loathe myself as a human being" (p. 187).

The point can be put in another way that will consolidate this initial phase of the argument. In his violent recoiling from mass society, Birkin, like Lawrence, experiences two distinct reactions. He wants to rid the world of its human blight, freeing the inhuman mystery from the taint of people. But at other moments, in other moods, the hatred of the multitude leads him to defend "real individuality." He contemplates the spectacle of human extinction and then pursues a proud singleness. These are not so much two opinions as two pressures which alternately dominate and then suddenly, intermittently, achieve a balance. Thus Birkin will appear before Ursula in "his strange non-human singleness" — a phrase that tersely conjoins these two demands. For a moment he has reconciled his contempt for humanity and his defense of "singleness" by locating the inhuman within the individual. What has been a *condition*, a world empty of people, has become an *attribute*, impersonality. This conception clearly derives from Lawrence's well-known formulation (in a 1914 letter to Garnett) of the "non-human, in humanity" as the appropriate basis for characterization.[3] But *Women in Love* allows us to recognize this formulation as no mere programmatic utterance but as a complex imaginative response to competing imperatives.

No approach to the question of experience could be more extreme than Lawrence's doubt as to whether there ought to *be* experience at all. Through Birkin's polemical offices the annihilation of our species becomes a vivid possibility that runs through the novel at its deepest stratum, shuddering at various moments to suggest the futility of human concerns. The notion of non-human singleness can be regarded as Lawrence's attempt to preserve character by submitting it to his own stringent qualifications. Scarcely able to bear the thought of human presence in the world, he imagines an individuality so radical that it no longer falls within the boundaries of humanity. Thus upon the absolute ground of human extinction Lawrence begets the inhuman individual. Grudgingly, paradoxically, none yields one.

II

"Humanity," says Birkin, "is a dead letter" (p. 111). Later he will add that "I," the "old formula of the age," is itself "a dead letter" (p. 459). This difficulty introduces the expressive problem which we must now confront: Birkin wants to utter the revolutionary word, but he has only dead letters with which to spell it. He seeks a clean rupture with the values of his kind, but to describe the new values he must use the language of the kind. It is therefore not surprising that he comes to a bitter skepticism towards the efficacy of language: "What was the good of talking any way? It must happen beyond the sound of words" (p. 327).[4] Needless to say, Birkin does not fall silent. Although there is "always confusion in speech," he insists that "it must be spoken. Whichever way one moved, if one were to move forwards, one must break a way through. And to know, to give utterance, was to break a way through the walls of the prison as the infant in labour strives through the walls of the womb" (pp. 254–5).

150

Lawrence is certainly not the only modern writer to suspect that language obstructs meaning, but that judgment usually identifies specific hindrances — "rhetoric," "journalism," "adjectives," "abstractions" — and suggests that a strenuous effort might purify literary discourse. Lawrence entertains no such hope. He does not pursue *le mot juste*, nor does he expect to find a pattern in words that will mirror a pattern in the world. Instead he uses language to strike at language, and this leads him to a particular stylistic habit that can best be introduced through the example of the Lawrentian paragraph.

And then she realised that his presence was the wall, his presence was destroying her. Unless she could break out, she must die most fearfully, walled up in horror. And he was the wall. She must break down the wall — she must break him down before her, the awful obstruction of him who obstructed her life to the last. It must be done, or she must perish most horribly. (p. 162)

Nearly every word in this paragraph is repeated or replaced with a synonym. A thought is expressed in the opening sentence, and then in every succeeding sentence: His presence was the wall — he was the wall — she was walled up — she must break down the wall — unless she could break — she must break — she must break — fearfully — horribly — awful obstruction of him who obstructed. Lawrence hurls words on to the page, as though he were hoping that they might finally shatter and let the world itself emerge. In his foreword to *Women in Love* he warns the reader of the "continual, slightly modified repetition," and the mannerism has been well described by his critics.[5] For our purposes it becomes important only as it is set against another form of paragraph.

She ran home plunged in thought. She had been very much moved by Hermione, she had really come into contact with her, so that there was a sort of league between the two women. *And yet* she could not bear her. *But* she put the thought away. "She's really good," she said to herself. "She really wants what is right." And she tried to feel at one with Hermione, and to shut off from Birkin. She was strictly hostile to him. *But* she was held to him by some bond, some deep principle. This at once irritated her and saved her. (p. 205)

The second example gives only part of a longer paragraph.

Her voice was always dispassionate and tense, and perfectly confident. *Yet* she shuddered with a sense of nausea, a sort of sea-sickness that always threatened to overwhelm her mind. *But* her mind remained unbroken, her will was still perfect. It almost sent Birkin mad. *But* he would never, never dare to break her will, and let loose the maelstrom of her subconsciousness, and see her in her ultimate madness. *Yet* he was always striking at her. (p. 202)

As the italics indicate, the stylistic mannerism that concerns me is the use of "but" and "yet" to reverse the direction of thought in the middle of a paragraph. Every writer does this occasionally, but in Lawrence it becomes a rhetorical tic that appears persistently, sometimes obsessively, in *Women in Love*. The two passages above are notable only for the frequency of the mannerism. All through the novel, particularly when a given character is under strain, Lawrence constructs paragraphs that depend on the reversals identified by "but" and "yet." Typically one sentence will present an impulse, emotion or desire and then a later sentence will present a contending impulse, a competing emotion or a contrary desire. "But" and "yet" serve as hinges within the paragraph, pivots which allow it to alter its direction abruptly, creating sudden reversals which are themselves frequently reversed.

In one obvious sense reversal is the antithesis of repetition, but they share an important feature which accounts for their prominence in the Lawrentian paragraph. They are both incompatible with consecutive development. Traditionally, the paragraph has been regarded as that verbal unit which makes development possible, which allows the individual sentence to unfold its implications, mingling with other sentences to form a higher unity.[6] That is, for instance, how I have intended the paragraph you are now reading. But the particular examples that we have just met represent an imperious rejection of continuous development.[7] A character is described in a self-contained proposition; the proposition is reformulated; an alternative is offered; and then the alternative is restated. Lawrence makes no attempt to work these elements into a coherent progression; the "but" introduces a distinct thought that does not emerge from, but contends with, the prior thought.

Although it is not a point that we can explore at any length, it is at least worth mentioning that the principles of structure that govern the paragraph reappear in the broadest movements of *Women in Love*. In the succession of chapters within the novel, as in the succession of sentences within a paragraph, Lawrence parts with the notion that a subsequent event must expand a prior one, or unfold from its presuppositions, or stand in causal relation to it. Individual chapters often function as single coherent propositions ("Man to Man," "Threshold," "Snowed Up"), as self-contained as grammatical units, and it is often easy to imagine an implied "furthermore" or "but" at the beginning of new chapters. Indeed the paragraph serves as a useful rudimentary model for both Lawrentian narrative form and Lawrentian characterization; a sequence of definitive assertions that follow no smooth trajectory of meaning, that can be either intensified or challenged, and that hold open the possibility of a radical break with what had appeared to be a definitive judgment.

The thought can be carried a step further. Much of the force of *Women in Love*, it is plain, depends on its articulating a principle of opposition to the social miasma that weighs so heavily on the temper of the book. And yet, it is a worry in the novel, and a worry for Lawrence in relation to his contemporaries, that an oppositional culture already exists, trumpeting its opposition, bleating its hostility. The portrait of Bohemia in the novel serves as a portrait of all those modernizing gestures which claimed to represent an alternative to a dying culture but which failed to fulfil their adversarial role; and the liaison between Gerald and Gudrun, the captain of industry and the experimental artist, may be taken as a measure of the unhealthy entanglement between the ruling powers and the avant-garde. The failure of the cultural revolt, which is heavily underscored in Loerke's willingness to place art in the service of industry, leaves Birkin and Ursula in the demanding roles of those who repudiate dominant cultural values, but also repudiate the culture of opposition.

In a recent appraisal of the novel, Nixon has commented that whereas in *The Rainbow* Ursula stands as a fierce antagonist of established norms, in *Women in Love* she has become the "most traditional major character" in the work.[8] But in what sense is this so? "I'm sick of the beloved past," says Ursula (p. 444), and elsewhere we learn that "She wanted to have no past" (p. 502). Her traditionalism is only a *trompe l'oeil* effect created by her energetic recoiling from the false revolutionaries around her. The difficulty in situating Ursula coincides with our difficulty in following the argumentative rhythm of the book as a whole, a rhythm of reversal reversed, the act of opposition itself opposed. This pattern repeats on a broad scale what the Lawrentian paragraph so often achieves in microcosm, a play of posits and oppositions incompatible with continuous development, a sequence that affirms a belief, invokes a value, expresses a desire; then cancels the affirmation, the invocation, the expression; and then cancels the cancellation without restoring the original positive terms.

In respect to this pattern, as in respect to almost every other, Lawrence and James stand as natural antagonists. The Jamesian paragraph too stands as an emblem for broader structures, but whereas in Lawrence the paragraph repeatedly assails the notion of development, in James it carries the notion of development to a kind of monstrous extreme. Perhaps its chief attribute is its indifference to the boundaries of individual sentences. Through the dilation of an initial idea, especially by means of an extended conceit, sentences become mutually and irrevocably entangled; the elements of the paragraph reflect one another in myriad ways, unfolding into a pilgrimage of fine distinctions, a safari of nuance. And this developmental ideal is at one with a principal ethical task in *The Ambassadors*, the dismantling of dualism in favor of a moral continuum. Lawrence, on the other hand, is willing to break the continuum, often reducing the relations between sentences to that exiguous "but" which connects them, pursuing not fine distinctions but the elements that lie beneath distinctions — in his celebrated metaphor, the undifferentiated carbon that binds its many allotropes. In the chapter "Excurse" Ursula and Birkin rehearse a version of this contrast.

She talked with lively interest, analysing people and their motives — Gudrun, Gerald. He answered vaguely. He was not very much interested any more in personalities and in people — people were all different, but they were all enclosed in a definite limitation he said; there were only about two great ideas, two great streams of activity, with various forms of reaction therefrom. (p. 386)

The disagreement here stands implicitly as a dispute over the methods and values of fiction. Ursula betrays a conventional novelistic concern for the subtlety of motive, while Birkin goes in quest of the simplicity that underlies subtlety. And although Ursula's opinions have force, it is clear that the novel tends toward the moral austerity which Birkin outlines and which Ursula herself has anticipated in the early outburst "I hate subtleties" (p. 89).[9] *Women in Love*, one might say, is a complex pursuit of simplicity, a simplicity achieved only when a superficial diversity resolves into "two great ideas, two great streams of activity."

The dualism in this last conceit must be understood not only as an attempt to bring chaotic multiplicity towards coherence but also as an effort to counter the monism that threatens to dominate the novel. Two is an aggressive repudiation of the chaos of many, but it is also a challenge to the seamless unity of one. Seen from the first side, that is, the conjuring of two great streams reduces an unformed diversity into the clarity of the dyad. Seen from another side, it contests the vision of one truth, one reality, one destiny, which gives Lawrence's moral critique a great deal of its power, specifically the power to bring apparently disparate phenomena – such as London, modern art, modern love, the miners, the aristocrats – into imaginative coherence.

In an early exchange with Ursula Birkin tries to persuade her that "the silver river of life" is only a consoling illusion, that "all our reality" lies with "the black river of corruption," "the dark river of dissolution." This conceit prefigures the later talk of two streams, but here, notably, the emphasis falls on determining the single historical current that constitutes the "real reality" and so directs the course of contemporary history (p. 238). The difficulty is that if Lawrence's critique gains force by digesting new objects into its monism, his utopianism plainly requires some countervailing pressure. In this respect a major task of the novel is to recover dualism from an encroaching monism, to establish two great streams instead of one dark river.

155

III

If, as I began by suggesting, the controlling ideal in *Women in Love* is an ideal of integrity, it must now be acknowledged that the value of integrity relies in complex ways on the method of opposition: wholeness can only be generated through division, disunity or partition.[10] And if Lawrence inclines to think of the primary integer as the self and its highest activity as "paradisal entry into pure, single being" (p. 332), it turns out that it requires two citizens of Eden to make a paradise for one.

All is two, all is not one. That's the point. That's the secret of secrets. You've got to build a new world on that, if you build one at all. All is two, all is not one. In the beginning, all was two. The one is the result. That which is *created* is One. That's the result, the consummation. But the beginning is two, it is not one.[11]

This passage (from the manuscript of the Hardy study) can scarcely be taken as authoritative or final. One of the teachings of Lawrence's career, no doubt a teaching which he himself had first to learn, is that propositions have no greater stability than emotions and that concepts, no less than characters, palpitate with the rhythm of the plot. But though the passage has no authority, it points to another and celebrated phrase in *Woman in Love* and to a new exigency for the individual. "First person singular" (p. 107) remains the consummation of value but not, it appears, the origin.

So much of the book concerns the enigma of marriage and so much of its repute lies in its ambiguous legacy to modern romance that it is easy to miss the extent to which the Lawrentian pair exists in service of its separate parts. Birkin's vision of romantic equilibrium, "two single equal stars balanced in conjunction" (p. 214), aims not merely to *preserve* the self against the threat of "mingling," "merging," and "fusion." It aims to *constitute* the self which until it enters the dyadic bond is only a congeries of incoherent emotions. Properly conceived, insists Birkin, love is "not selfless — it is a maintaining of the self in mystic balance and integrity" (pp. 215–16).

Why should we consider ourselves, men and women, as broken fragments of one whole. It is not true. We are not broken fragments of one whole.

Rather we are the singling away into purity and clear being, of things that were mixed. Rather the sex is that which remains in us of the mixed, the unresolved. And passion is the further separating of this mixture, that which is manly being taken into the being of the man, that which is womanly passing to the woman, till the two are clear and whole as angels, the admixture of sex in the highest sense surpassed, leaving two single beings constellated together like two stars. (p. 271)

None, one, two — what is notable about this sequence is that the later stages mark less an advance from than a peculiar return to the radical lessons of the earlier. The romantic couple confirms, even constructs, the singular self; passion engenders not a higher union but a higher disunion; and what is more, the sexual collision startles the self out of its moribund humanity, restoring it to that "impersonal" state in which it may rejoin the "grass and hares and adders, and the unseen hosts" in a world free of "dirty humanity" (p. 188). Birkin's picture of an "inhuman" bond between a "final me" and a "final you" joins these several commitments in the paradoxical image of a man and a woman, who remain inviolably single, meeting in a world empty of people.

Women in Love, it should be plain, does not progress through a series of phases or stages; it does not transcend or overcome its contradictions but presents contradictions alongside its resolutions. To make matters more difficult, the two cannot always be distinguished. Every movement forward is also a circling back. Thus, up to the last pages of the novel, Birkin continues his flirtation with nihilism, a motif that cannot be regarded as simply the petulant obsession of an unhappy man. It is rather a moral foundation to which Birkin nervously returns, caressing the possibility of human annihilation, as if to remind himself that in the face of modern depravity this consolation remains. But the solace of death itself suggests a form of life. All through the novel he implicitly asks how, short of willed extinction, there can be integrity in human experience. The notion of free proud singleness is, as it were, one step up from "a world empty of people," but it is no more stable a conception. Radical individualism yields to radical romance, the impersonal tie that is the next movement, cautious and exacting, towards repopulating the world. It is as though, having only grudgingly allowed the species to survive, he insists on the most stringent requirements for its propagation.

IV

Furthermore, what makes the movement to the dyad so hesitant and unsure is that perfect success is only the most cunning form of failure — a point that can be approached through two contrasting patterns of dialogue. An example of the first appears in the chapter "Threshold," where Gerald and Gudrun reach the verge of their dangerous intimacy. Winifred Crich demands to know whether her father will die; Gudrun admits that he probably will; Winifred denies it; and at this moment Gerald approaches Gudrun.

> "It is just as well she doesn't choose to believe it," he said.
> Gudrun looked at him. Their eyes met: and they exchanged a sardonic understanding.
> "Just as well," said Gudrun.
> He looked at her again, and a fire flickered up in his eyes.
> "Best to dance while Rome burns, since it must burn, don't you think?" he said.
> She was rather taken aback. But, gathering herself together, she replied:
> "Oh — better dance than wail, certainly."
> "So I think." (p. 367)

They affirm one another's statements and echo one another's words. Their conversation abounds with phrases such as "that's just it," "so do I," "certainly," "exactly," and this compulsive verbal agreement becomes a way of inciting one another to passionate attraction. Immediately after the exchange above, we read that "both felt the subterranean desire to let go, to fling away everything, and lapse into a sheer un-restraint, brutal and licentious." After an initial period of hostility Gerald and Gudrun place themselves in this erotic *congruity* which seals their mutual fate.

It had already sealed the fate of Birkin's corrupt tie to Hermione, a relationship whose decay shows itself in the lust for mutual affirmation — as, for instance, in Hermione's unrelenting "Yes."

"Yes, I think it is always wrong to provoke a spirit of rivalry. It makes bad blood. And bad blood accumulates."

"But you can't do away with the spirit of emulation altogether," said Gerald. "It is one of the necessary incentives to production and improvement."

"Yes," came Hermione's sauntering response. "I think you can do away with it."

"I must say," said Birkin, "I detest the spirit of emulation." Hermione was biting a piece of bread, pulling it from between her teeth with her fingers, in a slow, slightly derisive movement. She turned to Birkin.

"You do hate it, yes," she said, intimate and gratified.

"Detest it," he repeated.

"Yes," she murmured, assured and satisfied. (p. 77)

On the other hand, Birkin and Ursula quarrel — fiercely, noisily, chronically. In "An Island" he introduces her to his hatred of humankind.

"But there *are* good people," protested Ursula.

"Good enough for the life of to-day. But mankind is a dead tree, covered with fine brilliant galls of people."

Ursula could not help stiffening herself against this, it was too picturesque and final. But neither could she help making him go on.

"And if it is so, *why* is it?" she asked, hostile. They were rousing each other to a fine passion of opposition. (p. 186)

In a later quarrel Ursula comments that "we always talk like this" (p. 255), and indeed they almost always do. The chapter "Excurse," in which they achieve their greatest harmony, also includes their most bitter argument on a "memorable battlefield." The last scene of the novel leaves them in an unresolved quarrel.

We have then two patterns of dialogue: a sensuous conformity of opinion and a "passion of opposition." What makes this distinction arresting is that the verbal agreement between Gerald and Gudrun — traditionally a mark of romantic harmony, the cooing of lovers — becomes associated with their destructive eroticism, while the quarrels between Birkin and Ursula accompany their painfully indirect approach towards emotional equilibrium. With the former two, mutual assent will turn violently into its opposite while the continual bickering between the latter serves to protect them from the catastrophe of "fusion."

These competing styles of speech belong to a more general

concern which we might refer to as the problem of mutual knowledge. When Gerald strikes a violent blow in order to quiet Winifred's rabbit, Gudrun looks at him with "underworld knowledge," and they experience a "mutual hellish recognition." Soon this becomes a glance of "mocking white-cruel recognition" and finally a "smile of obscene recognition" (pp. 317–18). Through most of the novels gathered in this study, mutual recognition, far from being mocking, cruel, or obscene, has most often been a great desideratum. Against the threat of self-confinement the prospect of a perfect transparency between individuals, each knowing what the other knows, has been a high though elusive ideal. Indeed in the modern novel such an epistemological achievement frequently takes the place of a marital triumph. Lawrence, however, betrays few of the anxieties over solipsism that so consistently preoccupy Conrad, James, Ford, Woolf and Joyce; for him the great risk is not imprisonment in the self but descent into the knowing Other. Contrast, for instance, the enraptured attainment of mutual consciousness at the end of part one of *To the Lighthouse* – "She had not said it: yet he knew"[12] – to the ominous recognition between Gudrun and Gerald: "I've stayed at Halliday's with Birkin," he said, meeting her slow calm eyes. And she knew that Minette was one of his mistresses – and he knew she knew" (p. 473).

In *Women in Love* knowing what the other knows usually signals a dangerous convergence of two fixed wills which only give the illusion of harmony. Birkin and Ursula avoid this danger by ceaselessly interrupting their mutual understanding; they leaven their intimacy with ignorance. After Birkin reflects that his marriage to Ursula is "his resurrection and his life," we immediately read that "All this she could not know" (p. 459). Soon after we learn that "they were never *quite* together. One was always a little left out" (p. 531). Bersani reads this as a sign of lingering antagonism, and he is right to do so.[13] But in the light of our present concerns we can also recognize it as a way to forestall the threat of fusion, to avert a dangerous synchrony of desires, and thus to preserve a saving distance. Birkin assures Ursula that they are approaching "a perfect and complete relationship": "We've nearly got it – we really have"

(p. 452). In *Women in Love* the paradoxical way to have a perfect relationship is *nearly* to have it: any closer and all is lost.

No talk of star equilibrium can remove the ambiguities in the novel's picture of romance or give structure to the asymmetries of its narrative form. Having so insistently urged a dyadic balance between two single beings, Birkin no sooner sees it in the offing than he asks, "Does it end with just our two selves?" Ursula wonders what more he could want. "I always imagine," he responds, "our being really happy with some few other people" (p. 452). Ursula does not ask, though she might well have, how these others will find a place between two perfectly poised stars. Birkin once held that the only remaining value was a "perfect union with a woman – sort of ultimate marriage – and there isn't anything else" (p. 110). Now he insists that "a permanent relation between a man and a woman isn't the last word," and he warns against a "tacit hunting in couples: the world all in couples, each couple in its own little house, watching its own little interests, and stewing in its own little privacy – it's the most repulsive thing on earth" (p. 439). Here then is our final category, the few – "some few other people" – who will escape the confinements of the couple. From the imaginary extermination of the multitude and the uncompromising vision of the world empty of people, Birkin has taken some tentative steps toward the recovery of social experience, and this formidable course Lawrence has traversed, from none to one to two to few, constitutes nothing less than an attempt to reinvent a community.

In fact, however, when this aspiration is made concrete, it narrows to Birkin's concern with an "additional relationship between man and man – additional to marriage" (p. 345), and narrows further to Gerald alone.[14] He speaks of a bond with Gerald in the same terms he had formerly applied to his tie with Ursula: "a real ultimate relationship," a relationship in the ultimate of me and him (p. 452). This movement to a few other people, then, is no casual broadening of experience; it conforms to the same severe constraints that we have already noted. Just as the free proud individual retains an aura of inhumanity, and just as the star-balanced couple respects "non-human singleness," so now the extension to the few must preserve the rigorous basis of the dyad. Birkin seeks his few by multiplying the pair: first man and woman, now man and man. It should be evident how daunting Lawrence finds this process of building an acceptable world.

Birkin and Gerald, of course, do not achieve this "additional" ultimate relationship. Gerald declines the offer and then dies before Birkin can revive the prospect. Their *Blutbruderschaft* remains an unrealized possibility, but that it is a possibility and that it is unrealized establish its importance within the unfolding configuration.

The ambiguity of shared experience is nowhere more apparent than in the concluding movement of the novel where the alternative to the fatal consonance between Gerald and Gudrun is the living strife between Birkin and Ursula. These latter have resolved some of their greatest difficulties, but it is not too much to say that the resolution of their difficulties is itself their most subtle problem.

It raises the threat of the "diabolic freemasonry" that unites Gerald and Gudrun and carries them from erotic harmony to murderous antipathy, from obscene recognition to the "cold passion of anger."[15] This last phrase stands in illuminating contrast to the "fine passion of opposition" that characterizes the relationship of Birkin and Ursula. I suggested earlier that definition by opposition is essential to Lawrence's method; now it is possible to see that opposition is not only a method but a value. During one of Birkin's early disputes with Ursula we read that "the little conflict into which they had fallen had torn their consciousness and left them like two impersonal forces, there in contact" (p. 192). *Conflict*, then, is the source of *contact*, and the fact that it is a *little* conflict, one in a series of little conflicts, distinguishes it from the struggle to the death between Gerald and Gudrun that follows their equally deathly accord.[16] It simply will not do, then, to read the final argument between Birkin and Ursula as a sign of limitation without first acknowledging that the strength of their tie depends precisely on its limitations.

Birkin's failure with Gerald is thus a condition of his success with Ursula, first because it keeps the lovers together and second because it keeps them apart. Gerald is what lies beyond them and what lies between them. Birkin's idea of an "essential union with a man" is a utopian possibility that sows real discord, and paradoxically we must see this discord as part of its justification. The aspiration beyond marriage acts back upon the marriage itself, creating the passion of opposition on which it depends. But we cannot emit a relieved sigh, concluding that conflict is an unambiguous good and anticipating that Birkin and Ursula will cheerfully tend their disagreeable garden. The contention between them is genuine, deep and disturbing, something that can be neither tolerated nor overcome; it is one thing to see marriage as a union of opposites, but it is another, more formidable, scarcely conceivable thing to see it as a synthesis of unity and opposition themselves.

With Birkin's reach toward Gerald, the novel extends its unsteady grasp as far as it can, and with Gerald's death, a sudden contraction occurs, returning Birkin to the same stony contradictions with which he began. The loss of the visionary prospect sends a shiver through every hope, to the point where the cherished "way out" appears as "only a way in again." Inconsolable, Birkin finds himself facing grim alternatives.

Either the heart would break, or cease to care. Best cease to care. Whatever the mystery which brought forth man and the universe, it is a non-human mystery, it has its own great ends, man is not the criterion. Best leave it all to the vast, creative, non-human mystery. Best strive with oneself only, not with the universe. (p. 508)

The recurrent image of the non-human mystery, appearing again at the novel's close, reminds us that nothing has been resolved, nothing surpassed, no peace between humanity and the universe has been gained. With this thought Birkin returns to the nihilism that sustains him and that serves as the ground he superstitiously touches before every new ascent. Here, too, he immediately ascends. The movement in the paragraph repeats a movement we have already followed, the unacknowledged transition from the inhuman mystery to the mysterious self. "Best strive with oneself" — this is the logically strained consequence of the proposition "man is not the criterion." But though strained, it is habitual. All the elaborate reflections on community, history, women and love, emanate from the self (the striving male self), and they all return there.

The final quarrel between Birkin and Ursula which appears to turn on the problem of marriage in fact turns on the question of self-definition, self-satisfaction, and self-completion, and it submits those activities to a last withering appraisal. When Ursula demands to know why she is not enough for Birkin, he now answers that she suffices in the womanly way, but in order to make his life "complete, really happy," he wants someone in the manly way. Self-completion, that is, requires "two kinds of love" − a conclusion that at once unsettles the marriage tie, as Ursula quickly sees, and also delivers another blow to the dream of pure single being. It is not simply, as it was earlier, that the ego can only find itself within the dyad, it is that the ego is itself inherently dyadic, equipped with two slots, one for each sex.

On the one hand, then, the Lawrentian self must somehow find a place within a non-human world that grants it no privilege, must enter a mating dance not with another human being but with the fruits and berries. On the other hand, the self can only achieve completion by finding a second self and then a second second self. The individual in *Women in Love* − whose only name is Birkin − is compounded of the inhuman world that precedes it and the interpersonal world that it dreams into being.

The injunction "strive with oneself" may be seen as an acknowledgement of the various and incongruous materials of which one is made − the competing desires, the irreconcilable beliefs, the historical ambiguities − and also as a culminating instance of that passion of opposition which informs the book on every level. Gerald reflects on Birkin's "odd mobility and changeableness" (p. 306); the contessa insists that he is "not a man, he is a chameleon, a creature of change" (p. 149); and Hermione complains that he is "so uncertain, so unstable − he wearies and then reacts" (p. 376). His body itself seems indeterminate, "more a presence than a visible object" (p. 347), and like his opinions it takes many forms. This man who loathes himself "as a human being" lives with a metaphysical restlessness, refusing to be what he is, who he is, where he is. As he quarrels with Ursula, so he quarrels

with himself. Towards himself he remains in a passion of opposition, and if it is a mark of the living couple that it sustain
the antagonism, so it is a mark of the living ego that it never
quite coincide with itself, that it remain out of focus, unformed,
"wavering, indistinct, lambent" (p. 229). It hardly needs to
be said that given this inherently oppositional character of experience, the construal of an ego must be a halting and contradictory movement. With human extinction below and
unrealized community above, the mobile uncertain self enters
the tense oppositions of the dyad and pursues the fugitive condition of not-love between not-selves in no-where.

A tremor runs through *Women in Love*, a nervous palsy that
makes it perhaps the most unpleasant important novel in the
language. If Birkin is a "changer," so is the novel he inhabits,
which never loses its radicalism but continually shifts the
radical ground. The oppositions, the reversals, the inconsistency, the misanthropy, the self-loathing and the self-
contradiction, the quarrelling, negating, denying — these
elements of form and aspects of character have a curious
double function. They register the elusiveness of ideal experience, and in this sense they mark the limits of the novel's
largest ambitions. But they also sustain life in the face of cold
irony, fixed will, static machinery. Next to the harmony of
the ideal, the novel's many disharmonies seem a confession
of failure, but they seem far less discouraging when set against
the perfect stability of death.

CHAPTER SIX

From the epic *To the Lighthouse*

I

Woolf enters this book as she entered the lists of the modern novel, as a woman among a crowd of men and as a literary revolutionary writing after the first wave of revolution had passed. These two conditions, her sex and her age, threatened to make her the modernists' unwanted daughter, at once belated and premature – belated because she seemed doomed to repeat the rituals of aesthetic revolt, premature because she was doomed to live before the epoch of the daughters. *To the Lighthouse*, which becomes finally a vindication of the rights and gifts of the daughter, does so by revealing her as neither belated nor premature but as a timely alternative to the conceptions of character that had dominated English modernism.

It is well to remember that early twentieth-century definitions of the new aesthetic favored a sexual metaphor which cast women as major contributors to precipitous cultural decline. One thinks, for instance, of Irving Babbitt's claim that the "predominance of the feminine over the masculine virtues ... has been the main cause of the corruption of literature and the arts during the past century"; of T. E. Hulme's appeal for a new poetry of "virile thought"; or of Joyce's remark that "T. S. Eliot ends [the] idea of poetry for ladies."[1] The modernist attack on Victorian literary gentility was consistently interpreted as an attack on genteel femininity, and this was especially so in that branching of the movement that Wyndham Lewis liked to call the "men of 1914," among whom he counted himself, Eliot, Pound and Joyce. The social environment would have been enough to direct Woolf's attention to the problem of gender, but as will become clear, the presence of the issue in the immediate literary environment gave it special force in Woolf's imaginative life.

In her diary entry for September 26, 1922, Woolf records a conversation with T. S. Eliot on the subject of the recently published *Ulysses*. Eliot, reports Woolf, had called Joyce a "purely literary writer," and "I said," she writes, "that he was virile — a he-goat."[2] Earlier in the month, just after finishing *Ulysses*, she had conjured an image of Joyce that has surprisingly close bearing on *To the Lighthouse*. Reading the novel, she says, gives her the impression of an author "full of wits & powers, but so self-conscious & egotistical that he loses his head, becomes extravagant, mannered, uproarious, ill at ease, makes kindly people feel sorry for him, stern ones merely annoyed."[3]

In its moral concerns, its psychological appraisal, its very choice of epithet, the passage prefigures in striking ways the characterization of Mr Ramsay in *To the Lighthouse*. Egotism, theatricality, a pitch of intellectual self-consciousness that becomes social unconsciousness, an awkwardness with others that is at the same time a craving for sympathy — these qualities that Woolf assigns to Joyce will become Ramsay's leading traits. Ramsay is "petty, selfish, vain, egotistical"; he possesses an "insatiable hunger for sympathy"; asks "you quite openly to flatter him." Lily Briscoe feels that "this great man was dramatizing himself"; James thinks how "he might be shouting out at some fisherman's sports; he might be waving his arms in the air with excitement"; while Bankes thinks that it is "a thousand pities that Ramsay could not behave a little more like other people."[4]

Our point of entry into the novel will then be this notable fact: that the main lineaments of Ramsay's character coincide with those Woolf projects into her picture of Joyce. This perception, however, must be complicated by the biographical connection between Ramsay and Woolf's father, Leslie Stephen, a connection which makes *To the Lighthouse* a direct struggle against the still looming presence of the Victorian patriarch. It is the relationship between these two paradigms for Ramsay, the one neglected, the other acknowledged, that opens a line of approach to be followed here. That Woolf conceives her leading modernist rival in the same terms in which she reconceives her father, that the attempt to bear the burden of male modernism mirrors the attempt to bear the burden of paternal authority, that the problem of family historical identity coincides with the problem of literary historical identity – all this suggests a reading of *To the Lighthouse* against the background of *Ulysses*. If it will require an energetic suppression to keep *Ulysses* from erupting into the foreground, so much the better, since that will merely place us closer to Woolf's own difficult situation.

Ulysses lays claim to being our modern epic, and that claim deserves serious acknowledgment, particularly here where Woolf's antagonism to Joyce may be understood not only as antagonism toward a "virile" sensibility but also as suspicion of an epic mode that for Woolf belongs to the partisans of virility, the literary he-goats. In this respect the hostility toward Joyce converges with her hostility toward Milton.

The substance of Milton is all made of wonderful, beautiful and masterly descriptions of angels' bodies, battles, flights, dwelling places. He deals in horror and immensity and squalor and sublimity but never in the passions of the human heart. Has any great poem ever let in so little light upon one's own joys and sorrows? I get no help in judging life; I scarcely feel that Milton lived or knew men and women.

Then she immediately adds, "He was the first of the masculinists."[5] This construal of Miltonic epic as the genre of the masculinist and the implied construal of Joycean epic in the same terms let us secure a link already implied in *To the Lighthouse*. Mr Ramsay imagines himself as soldier and hero, "the leader of the doomed expedition" (p. 57), struggling through the philosophic alphabet while bearing the weight of human ignorance. The opposition between epos and domesticity with which George Eliot begins *Middlemarch* repeats itself at the opening of Woolf's novel, where Mr Ramsay, in "the exaltation and sublimity of his gestures" (p. 58), takes on the aspect of the epic quester obliged to wander far from the beauties and consolations of home. The problem of male egotism and the problem of epic grandeur thus immediately show themselves as two faces of the same problem.

At the end of the ninth book of *Paradise Lost*, Adam and Eve, having been tempted, having yielded, having eaten, having ensured their fall, turn upon one another and quarrel bitterly. In the final lines of the book, Milton summarizes their unhappy new condition.

> Thus they in mutual accusation spent
> The fruitless hours, but neither self-condemning,
> And of their vain contest appeered no end.[6]

The tenth book opens with a radical dislocation of perspective.

> Meanwhile the hainous and despiteful act
> Of *Satan* done in Paradise, and how
> Hee in the Serpent had perverted *Eve*,
> Her Husband shee, to taste the fatal fruit,
> Was known in Heav'n; for what can scape the Eye
> Of God All-seeing, or deceave his Heart
> Omniscient . . .(lines 1–7)[7]

There follows a heavenly council at the "Throne Supream" where the "most High/Eternal Father" speaks from his "secret Cloud." This sudden enlargement of perspective diminishes the carping between Adam and Eve, causing its bitterness to dwindle against the background of divine equanimity. Milton's God omniscient restores events to the wide compass of heavenly space and time, and we might take this as distinctive of the epic temper, for which the opening of wider contexts does not threaten individual dignity but ratifies it, by displaying the frames beyond frames that keep inner meanings in place.

The penultimate chapter of *Ulysses*, "Ithaca," achieves a similar perspectival shift, not by a literal change in physical standpoint but by a tonal ascension to what Kenner has aptly called the view of a "cosmic intelligence."[8] What Milton achieves through God omniscient, Joyce effects through the omniscience of language, the capacity of our verbal apparatus to prescind from experience as we live it and to secure our meager private lives within the expansive forms of collective speech — as in the opening of "Ithaca" which might be taken as the Joycean counterpart to the opening of Milton's tenth book.

What parallel courses did Bloom and Stephen follow returning?

Starting united both at normal walking pace from Beresford place they followed in the order named Lower and Middle Gardiner streets and Mountjoy square, west: then, at reduced pace, each bearing left, Gardiner's place by an inadvertence as far as the farther corner of Temple street: then, at reduced pace with interruptions of halt, bearing right, Temple street, north, as far as Hardwicke place. Approaching, disparate, at relaxed walking pace they crossed both the circus before George's church diametrically, the chord in any circle being less than the arc which it subtends.[9]

To arrive at this chord subtending the arc of a circle is to glimpse Joyce's version of the Miltonic heaven: not a cosmological dwelling-place but a continually present resource of language that can degrade or redeem human experience by translating it into other terms – geometry here, but as "Ithaca" goes on, also astronomy, orthography, hydraulics, musical notation ("a mathematico-astronomico-physico-mechanico-geometrico-chemico sublimation of Bloom and Stephen").[10] As Joyce puts it, "all events are resolved into their cosmic physical, psychical, etc. equivalents,"[11] and more than anything Bloom does or anything done to him, it is a change in the descriptive epithets that gain him a "passport to eternity."[12] Much like James's exploitation of metaphor and typification, the "equivalents" inhering in language become for Joyce an elaborate translation apparatus, translation in its etymological connotation, a "carrying across" of Bloom into new linguistic regions, until he and Stephen become "heavenly bodies, wanderers like the stars at which [they] gaze."[13] Indeed what binds Joyce most firmly to the epic tradition may be just this gesture toward the *consolations of distance*, achieved here through an expanding linguistic web which encloses folly, malice, weakness, doubt, within an endlessly reticulating verbal design.

The "Time Passes" section at the center of *To the Lighthouse* produces a similarly radical shift in perspective, a similarly daunting juxtaposition of human limits and extra-human powers, finite human time and the infinite and infinitely patient timelessness of eternity. As Adam and Eve are swallowed in divine immensity, as Bloom and Stephen melt into the analogies that exalt them, so the lives of the Ramsays

170

are reduced to parenthetical asides within time's endless monologue. But even to invoke these connections is to distinguish sharply between Woolf and the epic tradition. When Woolf raises her angle of vision, she broadens her frame as suddenly and as thoroughly as Milton or Joyce, but unlike these two she finds no consolation in the widening view. If a distinctive formal movement of the epic is the opening of general contexts that will secure local meanings, Woolf engages in the counter-epical act of enlarging her background as a way of diminishing those left wandering in the foreground. In passages like the following, "Time Passes" might be read as a parody of Miltonic justification.

It seemed now as if, touched by human penitence and all its toil, divine goodness had parted the curtain and displayed behind it, single, distinct, the hare erect; the wave falling; the boat rocking, which, did we deserve them, should be ours always. But alas, divine goodness, twitching the cord, draws the curtain; it does not please him; he covers his treasures in a drench of hail, and so breaks them, so confuses them that it seems impossible that their calm should ever return or that we should ever compose from their fragments a perfect whole or read in the littered pieces the clear words of truth. For our penitence deserves a glimpse only; our toil respite only. (p. 193)

It is customary to speak of Woolf as a lyrical novelist, where "lyrical" refers primarily to the fine musicality in a passage such as this. But in the present context Woolf's lyricism suggests more than a quality of her prose rhythms; it positions her work within an unstated but active play of opposing genres. Specifically, it represents an attempt to escape from the prestige of epic, the very shape of which, she suggests in *A Room of One's Own*, fails to conform to the sensibility of women.

The problem posed by Lily Briscoe's art, as well as the problem posed by Lily's life, is how to exist outside an epic conception of art and self that construes both the significant life and the significant work as expanding outward, continually extending the domain of its values. Two extraordinary passages in *To the Lighthouse* suggest the struggle towards a contending view. The first occurs during Nancy Ramsay's meditation on the beach, when she wanders off from the others and studies a pool of water collecting on the sand.

171

Brooding, she changed the pool into the sea, and made the minnows into sharks and whales, and cast vast clouds over this tiny world by holding her hand against the sun, and so brought darkness and desolation, like God himself, to millions of ignorant and innocent creatures, and then took her hand away suddenly and let the sun stream down. Out on the pale criss-crossed sand, high-stepping, fringed, gauntleted, stalked some fantastic leviathan (she was still enlarging the pool), and slipped into the vast fissures of the mountain side. And then, letting her eyes slide imperceptibly above the pool and rest on that wavering line of sea and sky, on the tree trunks which the smoke of steamers made waver upon the horizon, she became with all that power sweeping savagely in and inevitably withdrawing, hypnotised, and the two senses of that vastness and this tininess (the pool had diminished again) flowering within it made her feel that she was bound hand and foot and unable to move by the intensity of feelings which reduced her own body, her own life, and the lives of all the people in the world, for ever, to nothingness. So listening to the waves, crouching over the pool, she brooded. (pp. 114–15)

"So much depends," thinks Lily, "upon distance" (p. 284). To lift one's eyes toward the horizon – whether spatially or temporally conceived – is to suffer a violent diminishment, in line with the perception that "distant views seem to outlast by a million years . . . the gazer and to be communing already with a sky which beholds an earth entirely at rest" (p. 34). The alternative to distant views – what we may think of as the lyric alternative to epic expansion – is the evocation of a world in miniature, as in Nancy's transformation of a pool of water into a dense universe or (in a second pertinent image) Mrs Ramsay's vision of the fruit centerpiece on the dining table.

What had she done with it, Mrs Ramsay wondered, for Rose's arrangement of the grapes and pears, of the horny pink-lined shell, of the bananas, made her think of a trophy fetched from the bottom of the sea, of Neptune's banquet, of the bunch that hangs with vine leaves over the shoulder of Bacchus (in some picture), among the leopard skins and the torches lolloping red and gold. . . Thus brought up suddenly into the light it seemed possessed of great size and depth, was like a world in which one could take one's staff and climb hills, she thought, and go down into valleys. (p. 146)

An entire world in tiny places, a world as richly articulated as the great world beyond, but without raising the perils of infinite expanse – this is the powerful attraction of the Woolfian miniature that exerts its charms all through the novel.

More subtly differentiated than epic grandeur, it escapes the annihilation of distance by reducing the vast world in order to bring it close at hand. Then in a second gesture the micro-universe is enlarged until it becomes a counterpart world, one responsive to imaginative will, growing and shrinking as imagination requires, and in this way avoiding the horror of the world's real unassimilable sublime immensity. When Nancy converts minnows into whales, or when the light lets Mrs Ramsay see grapes and pears as a landscape fit for hiking, the two implicitly affirm the dignity of the lyric miniature. Of Joyce too it must be said that he finds dignity in small places. But one great labor of Joycean epic is to recover the "strand-entwining" link between the contingent detail and the rest of the universe, to pass through contingency on the way to mythic necessity. As the elevation of Nancy's gaze makes plain, the rest of the universe is for Woolf the enemy of lyric satisfaction.

A third image sits uneasily alongside Nancy's pool and Mrs Ramsay's mountainous bowl of fruit: it is Lily's picture of the self as a hive, an enclosed interior containing the muted hum of personality. "How," asks Lily, " did one know one thing or another thing about people, sealed as they were? Only like a bee, drawn by some sweetness or sharpness in the air intangible to touch or taste, one haunted the dome-shaped hive, ranged the wastes of air over the countries of the world alone, and then haunted the hives with their murmurs and their stirrings; the hives, which were people" (pp. 79–80).

This vision of the Other marks as severe an epistemological crisis as Marlow's exasperated solitude in *Heart of Darkness* or Dowell's weary solipsism in *The Good Soldier*. But for Woolf, it should immediately be added, the problem is not how to know what the Other knows but how to be where the Other is. In this respect the representation of the self in *To the Lighthouse* becomes another and privileged example of the novel's studied miniaturism. Like a pool of water or a bowl of fruit, the self can become the object of such complete imaginative absorption that in its tininess it becomes a large world. And as Mrs Ramsay imagines strolling among the pears, so Lily imagines not Dowell's knowing "the heart of another," but being within another's heart: "What art was there, known to love or cunning, by which one pressed through into those secret chambers? What device for becoming, like waters poured into one jar, inextricably the same, one with the object one adored?" (p. 79) Here the fantasy of the capacious miniature merges with the fantasy of perfect intersubjectivity, the dream of a thorough mutuality, transparency, and finally identity between distinct selves.

In writing of James's ghost stories, Woolf once remarked that "the visionary imagination was by no means his. His genius was dramatic, not lyric."[14] This comment recalls the long-standing difficulty of defining the novel in relation to traditional genres, and it also suggests, much more immediately, Woolf's own difficult task of distinguishing her novelistic lyricism from contending modernisms, the Jamesian drama as well as the Joycean epic. In "The Narrow Bridge of Art," published in the same year as *To the Lighthouse*, she imagines a novel of the future that will "make little use of the marvellous fact-recording power"; that "will have little kinship with the sociological novel or the novel of environment"; that will instead give "the relation of the mind to general ideas and its soliloquy in solitude."[15] This makes plain that not only the divine scale of classical epic but also the social scale of drama is at odds with the visionary lyric rather astonishingly conceived as a figure for the new novel. Admittedly, the identification of "lyric" with "visionary" is vague, but it should not obscure the distinctive emphasis on what I am calling the miniature, whether it take the form of an inanimate object secreting imaginative possibility or a human subject dense with hidden emotion. The world in small places – nowhere better exemplified than in the close space of the lighthouse itself: "For how would you like to be shut up for a whole month at a time, and possibly more in stormy weather, upon a rock the size of a tennis lawn?" (pp. 11–12) – is an invitation to lyric intensity, and while it offers the deepest consolations to the soliloquizing self, it also raises difficulties of which Woolf is keenly aware.

Woolf confided to her diary the fear that *To the Lighthouse* would be called "sentimental,"[16] and one might say that sentimentality is her lyric temptation. The caressing of the

174

miniature, the invention of another world inside our larger one, the visionary gleam within the endless dark – these characteristics of Woolf's lyricism indeed raise the threat of a sentimental attachment to the lyric fragment as a way of avoiding the blank unlovely cosmos. The specter of un-earned lyricism haunts *To the Lighthouse*; the novel is in flight from the luscious emotionalism that fascinates it. In the midst of her extended reverie on the terrors and consolations of life, Mrs Ramsay suddenly thinks, "We are in the hands of the Lord." Then, "instantly she was annoyed with herself for saying that. Who had said it? Not she; she had been trapped into saying something she did not mean" (p. 97). This is the sentimental lure. Mrs Ramsay's momentary self-deception, Mr Ramsay's self-pity, James's self-will, Lily's self-mortification – each represents an excess of sentiment uncorrected by irony. In considering how the novel resists its own lure, how it keeps the solitary ego from luxuriating in its inner world, we can take as a starting point Andrew Ramsay's description of his father's philosophic concern – "Subject and object and the nature of reality" (p. 38) – and as our guiding metaphor we may take the vicissitudes of a rectangle.

The title of part one, "The Window," gives a first rectangular image suggesting, among many other things, a transparency between perceiving self and perceived world. In Ramsayan terms, if there is only a window between subject and object, then it will be possible to see the "nature of reality" without distortion. All through the opening phase of *To the Lighthouse* the high ambitions of realist epistemology are allowed to test their strength. In the novel's first incident Mr Ramsay looks through the drawing-room window and tells his son James that the next day's weather won't be fine, in this way dashing hopes for a trip to the lighthouse. The act of looking through the window becomes a figure for examining facts without the veil of illusion.

What [Mr Ramsay] said was true. It was always true. He was incapable of untruth; never tampered with a fact; never altered a disagreeable word to suit the pleasure or convenience of any mortal being, least of all of his own children, who, sprung from his loins, should be aware from childhood

175

that life is difficult; facts uncompromising; and the passage to that fabled land where our brightest hopes are extinguished, our frail barks founder in darkness (here Mr Ramsay would straighten his back and narrow his little blue eyes upon the horizon), one that needs, above all, courage, truth, and the power to endure. (pp. 10–11)

The intellectual severity of the realist promises a toughened temperament, braced by an unblinking gaze through the window, calloused by collisions with the real. But in fact, as the passage suggests, it creates emotional needs which clear sight cannot satisfy – not only in the Ramsay children but in Ramsay himself. Having stared too long at the futility of his life, Ramsay will long for "sympathy, and whisky, and some one to tell the story of his suffering to." (p. 57) And under the pressure of these needs, the metaphor of the window is redrawn. The transformation occurs in the middle of supper.

Now all the candles were lit, and the faces on both sides of the table were brought nearer by the candle light, and composed, as they had not been in the twilight, into a party round a table, for the night was now shut off by panes of glass, which, far from giving any accurate view of the outside world, rippled it so strangely that here, inside the room, seemed to be order and dry land; there, outside, a reflection in which things wavered and vanished, waterily. (pp. 146–7)

The window loses its transparency. An "accurate view of the outside world" becomes an unapproachable goal. The rectangle gives only a reflected image of things. In effect a window transforms into a mirror, and as the novel moves into its central section, the figure of the mirror describes another temptation in our dealings with the external world. In place of a dream of ideal transparency, there appears a dream of perfect reflection which stirs the thought that our values are images of a valuable world.

In those mirrors, the minds of men, in those pools of uneasy water, in which clouds for ever turn and shadows form, dreams persisted, and it was impossible to resist the strange intimation which every gull, flower, tree, man and woman, and the white earth itself seemed to declare (but if questioned at once to withdraw) that good triumphs, happiness prevails, order rules; or to resist the extraordinary stimulus to range hither and thither in search of some absolute good, some crystal of intensity, remote from the known pleasures and familiar virtues, something alien to the processes of domestic life, single, hard, bright, like a diamond in the sand, which would render the possessor secure. (p. 199)

176

The figure of the window suggests an ideal of objectivity according to which one might learn to see things as they are and to submit to the destinies which inhere in the objects themselves. The mirror, on the other hand, suggests that truth develops on the photographic plate of human subjectivity. The window offers the truth of being, and the mirror the truth of seeming.

Alternatively Woolf reverses the image — this is the virtue of a mirror — and locates the reflecting power not on the surface of the mind but on the surface of the world. Here the emphasis falls on our inclination "to marvel how beauty outside mirrored beauty within" (p. 201) and our eagerness to have "the world reflect the compass of the soul" (p. 193). It should be clear that while there are important differences of emphasis in the metaphors of window and mirror, they both suggest congruity between the perceptions of the self and the world perceived. It is not surprising, then, that the promise of the mirror will prove as disappointing as the promise of the window. Passing time — this is the lesson of the novel's middle — brings death and war, and shatters the illusion of reflection that had replaced the illusion of transparency.

Did Nature supplement what man advanced? Did she complete what he began? With equal complacence she saw his misery, condoned his meanness, and acquiesced in his torture. That dream, then, of sharing, completing, of finding in solitude on the beach an answer, was then but a reflection in a mirror, and the mirror itself was but the surface glassiness which forms in quiescence when the nobler powers sleep beneath? Impatient, despairing yet loth to go (for beauty offers her lures, has her consolations), to pace the beach was impossible; contemplation was unendurable; the mirror was broken. (pp. 201–2)

Here, then, is another rupture in the history of a metaphor. First, the window clouded over and became a mirror; then, reflection showed itself to be an illusion. The mirror breaks, and in breaking allows for a final transformation, a third and last construal of the rectangular image and a last metaphoric interpretation of subject, object and the nature of reality. The window, having lost its transparency and the mirror having ceased to reflect, the painter's canvas comes into prominence and becomes the occasion for a new meditation on the figure of the rectangle. The canvas suggests a third possible relation between subject and object: neither transparency nor reflection but a more complex condition suggested in the following passage.

Then, as if some juice necessary for the lubrication of [Lily's] faculties were spontaneously squirted, she began precariously dipping among the blues and umbers, moving her brush hither and thither, but it was now heavier and went slower, as if it had fallen in with some rhythm which was dictated to her (she kept looking at the hedge, at the canvas) by what she saw, so that while her hand quivered with life, this rhythm was strong enough to bear her along with it on its current. Certainly she was losing consciousness of outer things. And as she lost consciousness of outer things, and her name and her personality and her appearance, and whether Mr Carmichael was there or not, her mind kept throwing up from its depths, scenes, and names, and sayings, and memories and ideas, like a fountain spurting over that glaring, hideously difficult white space, while she modelled it with greens and blues. (p. 238)

What she sees dictates a rhythm to her, and yet she loses consciousness of outer things. She forgets her name, personality, and appearance, but fragments of her past, "scenes" and "memories" and "ideas," fill the space of the painting. The difficult suggestion is that the world and the ego together lose their conventional aspect, and that we can no longer speak of negotiations between subject and object because in their encounter on the painterly canvas, the terms have changed beyond recognition. Much as Mrs Ramsay appears in the picture as a purple shadow — Lily "had made no attempt at likeness" (p. 81) — so Lily's own tense emotional career shows itself as masses in a pictorial relation. One can no longer usefully debate the merits of objectivism or subjectivism, now that reality and subjectivity have collided on this last rectangular field, each annihilating the pretensions of the other. Not the look of outer things but their rhythm, not the identity of the personality but its liberated emotional history — these meet on the canvas and create something which is neither of the world nor of the self but a third thing composed in their mutual unveiling.

The danger of sentimentality which Woolf rightly feared, the threat of unrestrained emotion created by lyric effusion, is met by this *chafing* between self and world, which is chiefly, but not uniquely, exemplified in the act of painting. The translation of experience into the form of art defeats the illusion of self-mastery but also defeats the tyranny of the world. If one takes the definition of the sentimentalist that Stephen Dedalus borrowed from Meredith − "The sentimentalist is he who would enjoy without incurring the immense debtorship for a thing done" (p. 164) − then it is possible to see *To the Lighthouse* as haunted by the spectre of unearned lyricism. Central to the novel's conception of art is the sense that in the torment of creation, all debts must be acknowledged; and, in general, art appears as that form of "combat" showing most plainly that "one was bound to be worsted" (p. 236) and that the best measure of one's triumph is the number of wounds one can bear. The distinctive rhythm of the novel is a rhythm of sentiment paid for and then enjoyed and then paid for again: "the vision must be perpetually remade" (p. 270). Every gain comes framed in loss, and one loves while one mourns.

II

At the end of *A Portrait of the Artist as a Young Man* Stephen Dedalus places himself against the sentimentality of dogma, the sentimentality of faith not paid for and consolations not earned. In the last conversation recorded in the novel, Cranly prods him to acknowledge that in abandoning God he is choosing Satan. Stephen willingly accepts the implication, stubbornly posing for a portrait of the artist as a young blasphemer. As *Ulysses* begins, however, the Satanic mask is worn not by Dedalus but by Mulligan, who now firmly occupies the role of verbal antagonist. The shift from strained intimacy with Cranly to strained intimacy with Mulligan is a significant one, reflecting Joyce's own effort to adjust the mode of his fiction by redefining the contending values. At the end of *Portrait* Stephen opposes himself to the sentiments of orthodoxy, but at the opening of *Ulysses* his task is to disentangle himself from Mulligan's blasphemous parody. This change corresponds to a movement from the quarrel with Catholicism of the earlier book, at the center of which lay the assertion of freedom against authority, to the conversation with Homer in the later book. In *Ulysses*, the question is not whether a fiery

179

autonomous subjectivity can blaze, but whether a tremulous intersubjectivity might be fanned into being. As Cranly gives way to Mulligan and orthodoxy gives way to blasphemy, Stephen is liberated from the burdens of Satanic opposition to become an opponent of the devil's parody and so to move back toward the modal and moral center where he will encounter Bloom.

In the terse appraisal of Mulligan that ends "Telemachus," Stephen names his towermate "Usurper" (p. 19), a judgment referring to both the physical and cultural dispossession that Stephen has endured from him. But as *Ulysses* unfolds, "usurper" comes to have a still broader implication that reveals Mulligan as a more dangerous adversary. For its first nine episodes the method of the novel remains under the dominance of its two leading characters, and (though this puts it too neatly) when Bloom is in the foreground, the problem is how to find words to fit experience, and when Stephen is prominent, the task is to find experience to fit the words. It might be said that the novel's celebrated turn after the ninth episode is not merely a turn away from stream of consciousness but a turn from the project of linking words and an experience external to them.

When we read that Bloom "liked thick giblet soup, nutty gizzards, a stuffed roast heart, liverslices fried with crustcrumbs, fried hencods' roes" (p. 45), we taste with the hungry man. But when we read in "Sirens" that "Bloom ate liv as said before" (p. 223), we get no sensory assurance; and in place of the circumstantiality of a world, we confront the circumstances of language. As Litz has put it, "From 'Wandering Rocks' and 'Sirens' onward, the 'reality' to be processed into art is both the imitated human action and the rich artistic world already created in the earlier and plainer episodes. Technique tends more and more to become subject-matter."[17] And as the book begins to put world-making in the second place, and to point in the first place to the girders and rivets that will hold the world together, and also to the false facades and the brass wire, then the dominant method of the book becomes what Joyce called "*scorching*" – a fiery assault on existing conventions that the artist uses and then ruthlessly uses up. Or as Joyce quaintly put it, "each successive episode, dealing with some province of artistic culture (rhetoric or music or dialectic), leaves behind it a burnt up field."[18]

What is this but to say that the method of the book starts to become the method of Mulligan? As first intimated in "Wandering Rocks" and culminating in "Oxen of the Sun," the governing modality is parody in ways that it was not before, and as the book shifts from a concern with the relation between words and experience to a concern with the experience of words, the movement occurs under the sign of the Buck. When Joyce writes that "Since I wrote the *Sirens*, I find it impossible to listen to music of any kind,"[19] he is acknowledging the dark power of parody celebrated by Mulligan, the sense of a fatality inherent in our conventions that, once exposed, will cause them to yield their last secrets and then shrivel and die. The ear for verbal absurdity, the eye for moral weakness, the insatiable appetite for pun and paradox, the willingness to amuse until amusement irritates, the incessant unrepentant theatricality – these central features of Mulligan's sensibility become dominant features at the center of *Ulysses*. Mulligan thus becomes a "usurper" in another sense than Dedalus had intended. He usurps, or threatens to usurp, the mode of *Ulysses*, infusing it with his parodic temper until other modes and tones grow inaudible.

Much as sentimentality is the temptation of Woolfian lyric, parody tempts the Joycean epic. The decision to make Bloom's odyssey also an odyssey of style (as Karen Lawrence has well emphasized),[20] the resolve to give "each adventure . . . its own technique,"[21] invites a relativizing of form in which every style, each technique, displays its excesses and reveals its susceptibility to parodic assault.

In "Oxen of the Sun," it is plain, the temptations of parody have become irresistible; by its close the series of prose pastiches has so thoroughly historicized style that it is no longer possible to dream of a natural relation between a self and the language it happens to speak. And yet the opening episodes of the work had often dreamed precisely this dream. The stream-of-consciousness experiments in the early sections must surely be seen (and have habitually been seen) as part of an

181

effort to reach past the prevailing conventions of psychological representation in order to find the natural language of mental life. The transformations in the late chapters do not simply ignore the technical ambitions of stream-of-consciousness virtuosity; they reinterpret what that virtuosity had in fact achieved. This is perhaps clearest in the second half of "Nausicaa" where the once familiar rhythms of Bloom's inner speech abruptly reappear: "Did me good all the same. Off colour after Kiernan's, Dignam's. For this relief much thanks. In *Hamlet*, that is. Lord!" (p. 305) But now, after so many other techniques governed by other conventions, the old Bloomian tune cannot be taken as the one true sound of his voice. Within *Ulysses* itself, stream-of-consciousness changes its valence, transformed from a weapon wielded against dying conventions to another mortal instance in the history of prose styles.

A consequence of this stylistic relativity is that character risks losing the usual marks of its individuality. As forms, conventions, tones and modes loom up and disappear, the customary differentiae of personality loom and disappear with them. On Nausicaa's beach Cissy Caffrey appears as a careless tomboy, "one of the bravest and truest hearts heaven ever made" (p. 290), but in Nighttown, under harsh light and harsh sentence rhythms, she names herself "a shilling whore" (p. 479). Who (or which) is Cissy Caffrey? The question has no sense because identity has been made relative to the vicissitudes of style: depending on the mode at hand, she is tomboy or prostitute, and there is no place outside style where one might resolve the ambiguity. A risk in the novel is that Cissy Caffrey's fate will become general, that as a name is immersed in a new prose medium, what it names will change, that the parodic temper will convert individuality into a mere effect of style. And by the time "Oxen of the Sun" has taken the name of Bloom through a thousand years of tonal inflections, *Ulysses* has reached a formal crisis in which the stylistic discontinuity, the relativity of convention, the parodic scorching of natural speech, threaten to dissolve identity into a succession of unrelated phases.

The dispersal of personality and the muting of individual

voice — these are the consequences of the book's approach to a thoroughgoing Mulliganism that reaches a climax in "Oxen of the Sun" where the parodic stylist approaches the limits of his art and brings the work toward a formal cul-de-sac. Part of the achievement of "Circe" is that it invents a way out of the cul-de-sac, a way past parody. In so doing it recovers a value for personality, not by reassembling its scattered pieces, but by scattering them still further.

The events of history, Stephen had once conceded, "are not to be thought away. Time has branded them and fettered they are lodged in the room of the infinite possibilities they have ousted. But can those have been possible seeing that they never were? Or was that only possible which came to pass?" (p. 21) The surmise suggests that the history from which Stephen is trying to awake must be taken in the large sense of contingent reality as such — not only, that is, the history of the historians, but that of all those fictionalists, Joyce included, who had identified the real with the actual and who, in painting a scene, sought to persuade us (in Woolf's phrase) that "It happens precisely so."[22] To see this is to see that the ousting of the possible occurs in fiction as well as history and that, as the succession of styles in *Ulysses* makes plain, every convention delimits a new region of the real and trounces another region of the possible.

In "Scylla and Charybdis" Stephen "ponders things that were not: what Caesar would have lived to do had he believed the soothsayer: what might have been: possibilities of the possible as possible: things not known: what name Achilles bore when he lived among women" (p. 159). What Stephen once merely contemplates is rendered in "Circe": the possibilities of the possible as possible. The actual, the contingent, and the conventional are overwhelmed in a new modality that, challenging the distinction between the real and the imagined, registers every event, no matter how improbable, as a rightful bearer of possibility. This not only represents a psychological liberation — Bloom set free to be a visionary as well as a voyeur, a woman as well as a man, a potentate as well as an abject slave — but also, perhaps more profoundly, a formal liberation. The dominance of the parodic temper is broken in "Circe" where parody is displayed as only one mode among many and where it must vie on equal terms with comedy, sentimentality, melodrama, romance and countless other tonal shades. In "Circe" Joyce's stated program of devising a new stylistic technique for each new episode takes the form of a style whose leading feature is that it can incorporate every other style.

Joyce remarked of Bloom that he was a "complete man," a "good man,"[23] and it is evident that in *Ulysses* these two characteristics come to imply one another. Goodness is complete, completion is good. In "Circe," where the imaginable wins its revenge over the actual, and the dream of infinite possibility exceeds the nightmare of meager history, then the morality of completeness appears in its most vivid form. No matter how exalted or degraded Bloom becomes, no matter how violent the tonal shifts − from the song and dance of the soap to the vision of a dead son − every new possibility can rightfully claim a place in the moral encyclopedia that makes totality a first virtue.

This is the reparation *Ulysses* offers for the ravages it has inflicted upon integral subjectivity. Having redefined the individual as an effect of style, having dispersed personality among its divergent techniques, it now imagines a Bloom swollen large enough to comprise all those "possibilities of the possible as possible" that he has been made to endure. Here then is the measure of Joycean epic character: not the strength to control destinies in the realm of historical events but the gift of expanding in the realm of fictive possibility. That Bloom can find a role to play in any imagined scene, though it be a role of the most humiliating kind, is the mark of his peculiar grandeur. The Joycean epic hero is the one who can sail through every change of mode and tone, and who can establish a homestead in every style.

III

The psychological counterpart to the epic synthesis is Bloom's androgyny: in the Circean guise of the "new womanly man" Bloom achieves a sexual fusion giving particular force to the image of a "complete man." The question of the solitary ego takes on an adventurous new form when it is a matter of one individual accommodating the aspects of two sexes, and it is just at this point that Joyce's experiments lead us back to those of Woolf.

As late as November 1926, in an essay called "Life and the Novelist," Woolf intensifies the clichés of Victorian sexuality in order to cast the struggle between art and life in terms of the struggle between dangerously incompatible sexual habits. "Stridently, clamorously," she writes,

life is forever pleading that she is the proper end of fiction and that the more he [the novelist] sees of her and catches of her the better his book will be. She does not add, however, that she is grossly impure; and that the side she flaunts uppermost is often, for the novelist, of no value whatever. Appearance and movement are the lures she trails to entice him after her, as if these were her essence, and by catching them he gained his goal.[24]

Still, it is impossible, Woolf goes on, "to retire to one's study in fear of life." The novelist must approach the great blaze and endure its fascination: "He must expose himself to life; he must risk the danger of being led away and tricked by her deceitfulness; he must seize her treasure from her and let her trash run to waste. But at a certain moment he must leave the company and withdraw, alone, to that mysterious room where his body is hardened and fashioned into permanence."[25]

This strange imagistic rendering of the creative process — art as a seduction, an arousal, a withdrawal and an excited abstinence — offers a satiric heightening of erotic conventions, but it gives no way beyond the depressingly limited sexual antitheses that are figures for the equally depressing antithesis of life and art. It is useful to think of *To the Lighthouse* as attempting to re-imagine the view developed in the discursive essay contemporaneous with it.

It does so first by readjusting the relations between art and life. The studied and much-noted similarity between the activity of the mother (Mrs Ramsay) and the activity of the painter (Lily), and the neglected connection between both of these and the work of the domestic (Mrs McNab), suggest that

aesthetic experience is not fundamentally a matter of the independent conventions of an artistic tradition, but that it arises
out of the immediate desire merely to organize the materials
of the world into some form of equilibrium. Mrs Ramsay's
arrangement of lives, Lily's arrangement of pictorial masses,
Mrs McNab's arrangement and recovery of a decaying house
– these acts are placed in profound continuity. Mrs Ramsay,
thinks Lily, "resolved everything into simplicity," converted
"silliness and spite" into "friendship and liking"; and the
memory of this achievement "stayed in the mind affecting one
almost like a work of art" (pp. 239–40). Woolf brings the
aesthetics of everyday life as close as possible to the domain
of art, but her "almost" marks the fissure that keeps nearness
from becoming identity. *To the Lighthouse* struggles with the
difficult thought that art emerges out of everyday
aesthetics,[26] and the still more difficult thought that at some
point it outgrows its vital sources.

Here is where *To the Lighthouse* makes a second amendment
to "Life and the Novelist." The severe sexual opposition in
the essay returns in the first part of Woolf's novel, interpreted
here in the terms of husband and wife rather than ascetic and
harlot. But it is still cast in similarly strict metaphoric antitheses: husbandly scimitars and wifely fountains, male girders
and female auras. It will be no news to say that the tendency
of *To the Lighthouse* is toward an overcoming of these stark
differences and that the following description of Lily's
painting brings the conventional figures for gender into an
unconventional fusion: "Beautiful and bright it should be on
the surface, feathery and evanescent, one colour melting into
another like the colours on a butterfly's wing; but beneath
the fabric must be clamped together with bolts of iron"
(p. 255).

Elegant though the synthesis appears, it has a less obvious
and less consoling aspect. This appears, for instance, in a subtle
parallel between Ramsay's philosophy and Lily's painting. The
task of the philosopher is presented as the "seeing of angular
essences," the "*reducing* of lovely evenings, with all their
flamingo clouds and blue and silver to a white deal four-legged
table" (p. 38, my emphasis). Although this may seem far

removed from the concretions of the aesthetic act, we soon find Lily's painting defended on the ground that "A mother and child might be *reduced* to a shadow without irreverence" (pp. 81–2, my emphasis). Art here partakes of the same abstraction and reduction that animates philosophy, and this is what breaks any easy continuity between art and life. One might say that it is the philosopher within the artist who inserts the "almost" between Mrs Ramsay's arranging of marriages and the arrangement of Lily's canvas.

Within the allegory of human possibility that *To the Lighthouse* unmistakably weaves, aesthetic experience and philosophy, left to themselves, stare blankly at one another, antagonists within a drearily traditional sexual symbology. The aim of the narrative, when it takes up the allegorical thread, is to find a third term capable of surpassing the dualism.

Marriage offers itself as just such a third term, but while married life gives moments of blinding glory, it never disables the essential antagonism. It provides complementarity but not unity. The story of the Ramsay marriage is the story of the erratic convergence of embodied beauty and disembodied idea, each acknowledging the value of the other, but each engaged in a tense struggle to protect its identity from the pressures of its counterpart. Art, on the other hand, is a rival third term, composed out of the same dualism but (at least in Lily's understanding) dedicated to overcoming the isolation of its rival parts. The sensual immediacy of aesthetic experience, identified throughout with the female domain, becomes recognized as art only when it merges with male philosophy — merges, that is, with the ability to reduce immediate experience to underlying forms. Marriage in this novel is always haunted by the possibility that husband and wife might better realize their gifts apart, but art can no more be separated into its "male" and "female" components than painting can be separated into form and color.

Because of the focus upon Lily Briscoe it might easily appear that Woolf is concerned with defining the question only from a woman's point of view and that the opposition between aesthetic experience and philosophy, and the rival mediations of marriage and art, apply only to the aspirations of the female artist. In the context of these concerns, however, the figure of Augustus Carmichael takes on an importance out of proportion to his narrative stature. He enters the final section of the novel in the guise of a celebrated poet, and it is easy to forget his earlier incarnation described only in passing. In the first pages of the novel Mrs Ramsay has let us know that "He should have been a great philosopher . . .; but he had made an unfortunate marriage" (p. 19). The movement from philosophy through a failed marriage to successful poetry represents, in effect, an approach to art which is the reverse of Lily Briscoe's, an approach from the male domain, the realm of abstraction.

The meeting of the two in the book's final scene not only echoes and reinterprets the Ramsays' climactic moment at the end of part one; it also suggests how Lily and Carmichael have worked their way toward the *middle* which is art. This is not only a matter of Carmichael's reversing Lily's movement from domestic aesthetics to the formality of art, by making his journey from philosophic abstraction to poetic rhythm. Carmichael's change of vocation also carries, though elusively, its own erotic tinge. His affections, to the extent that we know them, have turned from his estranged wife to Andrew Ramsay (Mrs Ramsay "thought how devoted he was to Andrew, and would call him into his room, and, Andrew said, 'show him things' ") (p. 145); and after Andrew's death in the war, Carmichael is said to have "lost all interest in life" (p. 289). Chaste though we must take this connection to be, it nevertheless hints at the drift away from sexual polarity, a drift clearly associated with the mediations of art. It also encourages us to consider how the androgynous turn was prepared in the longer novelistic trail followed through this study.

James's Strether and Conrad's Marlow are marked by their distance from erotic demands, their fastidious withdrawal from the colliding bodies around them. In seeking a context for their studied subduing of passion, we should heed Ann Ardis's suggestion that the New Woman of the English nineties exerted pressures on the development of modernism persistently neglected in histories of the period. The independence, the sexual daring, the direct challenge to male authority, all these much publicized features of the New Womanly revolt might be seen as descending underground in many canonized modern fictions. Kurtz's African bride, Strether's *grandes dames*, Ford's New England adventuress, may give transformed expression to the provocation of the New Woman, and although no causal tie is drawn between the assertion of female desire and the sexual abstentions of Marlow, Strether and Dowell, we have reason to surmise the connection.

Within the set of novels under scrutiny, Forster's Schlegel sisters give the least displaced version of the New Woman. While they ultimately become reformed cases of the cultural type, who abandon urban wilfullness for rural domesticity, they still unsettle the conventions of male sexuality, if only by so thoroughly taming Henry Wilcox, that man's man. What is unstated, perhaps unconscious, in James, Conrad and Ford, becomes a direct struggle between the principals of *Howards End*. Still, Forster's most extreme reflections on gender occur as little more than graffiti scrawled on the margins of the plot. In opposing the female domain of the Schlegels to the male region of the Wilcoxes, Forster toys with the thought of what happens when an individual is born into a realm dominated by the other sex. Tibby Schlegel, the feminized brother, and Evie Wilcox, the masculinized sister, are perfect reverse images of one another. Although they are both presented in distinctly negative terms and left out of the novel's final resolution, they suggest the submerged but insistent line of development: a redistribution of the marks of gender, and the creation of unprecedented new composites.

In the late stages of Lewis's *Tarr*, "woman" is defined as the amorphous beginning of all experience: diffuse, emotional, and, in the highest personalities, obsolete. Such dull misogyny is only relieved by Tarr's perception that most of his male acquaintances are " 'true' women," while Anastasya herself has broken out of the category altogether – leading Tarr to suppose that "he would not be a pervert because he had slept with her, but more than that would be peculiar" (p. 328). In *Tarr* this reflection remains just part of the noisy idling of the Nietzschean machinery, but it does suggest how obtrusive the instability of gender has become. Lawrence, who took theories of androgyny far more seriously, writes in his "Study of Thomas Hardy" that "every man comprises male and female in his being,"[27] and in *Women in Love* he gives us a Birkin who wants to complete himself by balancing a "perfect relationship" with a man against the perfection of his marriage to a woman. Yet what is most telling about Birkin's erotic maneuverings is that they leave him less with a double gender than with no gender at all. "Birkin in love," not women in love, is the subject of the novel, but he turns to his love objects by placing himself beyond the distinction between them, until he reaches a kind of erotic vanishing point where he can feel sexual desire without possessing a sexual identity. Still, we can see Birkin's negation of gender as a preparation for the experiments in androgyny made by Joyce and Woolf. When Woolf writes in *A Room of One's Own* of a properly androgynous imagination as "man-womanly" or "woman-manly,"[28] the phrases echo the description of Bloom as "a finished example of the new womanly man" (p. 403). One useful way of arranging the historical narrative is to see Bloom and Lily as completing an erratic movement from the inversion of sexual types to their complex convergence.

It is tempting then to see Lily as Bloom's counterpart, the new manly woman, the son who survived — as he is her missing mother. But it is worth remarking that Lily at least could not see things in this way. She sees herself not as combining or transcending sexual distinctions, but as failing even to qualify for the sexual category that biology assigns to her. When the emotionally promiscuous Ramsay demands sympathy for the loss of his wife, Lily is left without a response to his groaning sorrow, although "any other woman in the whole world would have done something, said something — all except myself, thought Lily, girding at herself bitterly, who am not a woman, but a peevish, ill-tempered, dried-up old maid, presumably" (p. 226).

The judgment is unnecessarily harsh, but it preserves the sharp contrast between Bloom and Lily, between the cuckold as epic hero and the old maid as lyric heroine. The cuckold and the old maid have stood as cruel traditional paradigms of sexual failure, but they exist in only spurious symmetry. The male cuckold has had and lost, while the unmarried woman — to release her from the oppressive epithet — is condemned by convention "to want and want and not to have" (p. 300). The cuckold, one might say, has had too much experience, but it is Joyce's vocation to convert that "too much" into just enough and to make sexual degradation a coherent part of moral completeness. Bloom's indignity becomes a means to self-completion; having been husband and cuckold, he has experienced male possession and female dispossession; and cuckoldry becomes another approach to epic totality.

Too little experience, on the other hand, is the fate traditionally and ungenerously reserved for the respectable single woman, and Woolf's act of transformation is to take, not a heart of darkness, but a "centre of complete emptiness" (p. 266), and to see it as a prod to aesthetic ingenuity. The absence left by unsatisfied desire becomes a formal difficulty for the painter, susceptible to pictorial solutions. In a moment of great strain, when Lily feels the "horror," the "cruelty," the "unscrupulosity" of love, she remembers her painting and thinks with relief that "she need not marry, thank Heaven: she need not undergo that degradation. She was saved from that dilution. She would move the tree rather more to the middle" (p. 154).

Art is a solution to the problem of desire — not because it eliminates the press of want, but because it changes the objects of desire and the terms of satisfaction. A center of emotional emptiness can be confronted by moving a tree to the middle of the canvas. Hold this thought one way and it shows art in flight from the heat of sexuality. Hold it another way and it shows sexuality as itself fleeing the stresses of form. *To the Lighthouse* gazes at both sides of the thought, art as a compensation for unsatisfied desire and art as a critique of desire's usual (and vulgar) satisfactions. The work is the androgyne; the artist is the self-described old maid; and *To the Lighthouse* builds to a double perception of wholeness in a painting and partiality in a life. The insufficiencies assigned to the unmarried woman appear side by side with the self-sufficiency of the female artist, her private marriage of male and female within the artifact she builds in solitude.

IV

During the "Aeolus" episode of *Ulysses* Bloom consults with Red Murray about the Alexander Keyes advertisement that so tediously occupies the working hours of his day. "Of course, if he [Keyes] wants a par," says Murray, "we can do him one." "Right," says Bloom aloud, but silently he clings to Murray's offhand assumption of community. In the one-word line that concludes the short section, Bloom repeats to himself the longed-for pronoun: "We" (p. 97). It is a terse statement of his dread of solitude and his yearning for solidarity, but it should not be interpreted simply in terms of the Homeric theme of exile. What makes Bloom's situation even more difficult than Odysseus' is that he not only suffers exile from Penelope; he is exiled from a community of fellows and followers who might sustain him until he reaches home. Later in "Aeolus" when he leaves the newspaper offices, a group of newsboys trail after him, parodying his walk in a grotesque mockery of discipline and fidelity. The minor incident dramatizes perhaps the most basic difference between Bloom and Odysseus: in Dublin Bloom has no common culture whose destiny he projects. Put simply, he has no crew.

And yet, the novel does not rest with the isolation of its besieged protagonist; it continues to aspire to a form of epic community. It does so, however, not by locating these comrades in the space around Bloom but by discovering them in time. The avatars with whom he is associated, Odysseus of course, but also Elijah, Parnell, Christ, Shakespeare, become another kind of crew, a community achieved through the recovery (or the construction) of a tradition. When Bloom makes his indignant reply to the Jew-baiting citizen, he characteristically responds by conjuring an army of precedents: "Mendelssohn was a jew and Karl Marx and Mercadante and Spinoza. And the Saviour was a jew and his father was a jew" (p. 280). By the end of the novel Bloom is moving through a Dublin night crowded with his complex ancestry, and although he stumbles through space, he arrives home in time.

The issue is not simply a matter of the self finding a community of historical others; it is perhaps more profoundly a question of the self distributing and then collecting its temporal identity. Stephen's antic reflections on his successive selves — "I, I and I. I" (p. 156) — and Bloom's more somber meditation — "Me. And me now" (p. 144) — express the condition of value in *Ulysses*, the acknowledgment that human character can only know itself and show itself as it extends through time.

The crisis in Stephen's character, his fall towards a vain aesthetic posturing, is relieved only by the intermittent reminder that the movement of time can break his paralysis. When Mulligan casually remarks that Dedalus "is going to write something in ten years" (p. 205), he is still mocking the artist's pose, but as attentive readers pertly note, the span of ten years directs us to 1914 and to the beginning of Joyce's work on *Ulysses*. While this link cannot authorize the identity of character and author, it does give Stephen a tie to the outside of the book and to a future "I" that might cancel the humiliations of the present. Or as Stephen puts it in "Scylla and Charybdis": "in the future, the sister of the past, I may see myself as I sit here now but by reflection from that which then I shall be" (p. 160). In this episode, as Kellogg has justly said, "Joyce tells his reader in effect: 'I, too, am the father, the older man whom this young artist would one day become.' "[29] From within its pages Dedalus briefly swells to contain the novel containing him.

The thought can be extended by noting that Stephen is made to bear the fatigue of Joyce's own progress and his march through the literary genres. Stephen scrawls a tense little lyric as he walks along the beach; he recites his "Parable of the Plums" on the way to a pub; in the library he delivers his speculative chapter in the biography of Shakespeare. May we not see these as Joyce's parodic summary of his own early career? The lyric looks back to (and criticizes) *Chamber Music*; "The Parable of the Plums," as others have pointed out, is a jaundiced variant on the stories in *Dubliners*; and the reinvention of Shakespeare's life amounts to another *Portrait of the*

Artist. In the unfolding of the sequence Stephen is sacrificed to Joyce's ritual dis(re)membering of his creative history, each attempt in each genre now coolly registered as a phase of creative adolescence. But in being sacrificed he is given his one chance of redemption, which lies in extending his life through time, following the path charted by Joyce's own. The future convergence of Stephen and Joyce remains only one possible outcome, but as long as the possibility lives within the work, then Stephen's failures can lay claim to being the apprenticeship of genius. His late undramatic departure from the work might be seen as taking him outside the novel in preparation for becoming the author of his past.

At the same time, however, in one of Joyce's sternest gestures, the artist who aspires to contain the characters of his novel is himself swallowed by them. In "Eumaeus" Bloom absorbs Stephen (and his fine tenor voice) into his fantasy of a new triumph on the local musical circuit. Managed by Bloom, partnered with Molly, Stephen will become, not a world historical artist, but a Dublin novelty. Bruns sees this vision as marking Stephen's catastrophe: "Bloom's entrepreneurial fantasy is Stephen's endgame; it is the vision of the Dedalus played out once more, this time, however, not in a young man's fervid soul, but upon the bourgeois fields of Bloom's comic fancy."[30]

It is that, and more than that. The assimilation of Stephen to Bloom's commonplace ambition is, on the one hand, a defeat for certain ideals of artistic purity. On the other hand, it is a reconsideration of the values and consequences of art. The artist, in being absorbed into common life, becomes a powerful instrument in the imaginative life of non-artists. In the last moments of "Circe" when Stephen mutters fragments from Yeats's "Who Goes with Fergus?," Bloom mishears Fergus as Ferguson, interpreting it as the name of Stephen's lover. We may take this as another sign of art's vulnerability to the cultural philistine. But it is worth recalling that the novel's next event is the uncanny appearance of Bloom's dead son Rudy, and it seems right to say that if Bloom's encounter with Stephen has not given him a fine appreciation of poetry, it has engendered a visionary moment important for the workings of ordinary love, if not for the advance of extraordinary art.

The most important example, and the one that completes this line of thought, occurs late in Molly's soliloquy. Bloom, in casting up the advantages of introducing Stephen to his wife, has pictured the benefits to Molly as "disintegration of obsession, [and] acquisition of correct Italian pronunciation" (p. 570). The former, it is fair to say, is the more important, and in Molly's final reverie, the leading and dangerous obsession is the erotic infatuation with Boylan. If by the end of the day Bloom has not yet made Stephen a lodger in his household, he has done something more fundamental: he has lodged Stephen in his wife's consciousness. Chattering of his plans, he has insinuated the image of Dedalus, poet and professor, into Molly's rich fantasy life, with the result that by the end of the soliloquy, Stephen has come into sexual prominence. No more than her husband does Molly coincide with Stephen's aesthetic temperament, but like Bloom she unhesitatingly adopts the figure of the artist to imaginative purposes of her own. Having projected herself into a romance with Stephen, Molly begins her climactic last sentence with a savage critique of Boylan from the standpoint of art: Boylan is "the ignoramus that doesnt know poetry from a cabbage" (p. 638).

With this stroke an obsession disintegrates. Stephen changes the course of a reverie, dislodges Boylan from his place of privilege, and leaves Molly wondering what to do with her new lover now that she has found a newer. The danger of erotic obsession has been not merely that it poses a threat to marriage; it also poses a threat to that expansive sense of life history which is a fundamental condition of value in *Ulysses*. Molly's anticipation of a next romantic tryst binds her to the immediate future — "O Lord I cant wait till Monday" (p. 621) — and restricts and recasts her sense of the marital past. The loosening of Boylan's hold on her imagination, the dissolution of this fixed erotic idea, which occurs erratically through her reverie and then climactically when Stephen replaces Boylan, unfreezes her experience of time and lets her rove backwards toward Bloom. When anticipation stutters between two lovers, it opens to allow retrospection, and her last ecstatic breath, "yes I said yes I will Yes," is among other things a celebration of time's tenses — an utterance in the present ("Yes") that stands as a memory ("I said") of an anticipation ("I will"), so that present, past and future are folded together in a dense temporality.

Bloom's accumulation of historical precedents; Stephen's projection into an artistic future coincident with his author's; Molly's overcoming of the immediate urgencies of passion until she can mix memory and desire — these turns of character express the high value of constantly expanding time, of epic time. And at this point it is appropriate to introduce a last large distinction that bears on a general problem in narrative form and at the same time pertains to the question of individual life history. The distinction is between what one may call "configurational" and "serial" form. The first of these coincides with a traditional and well-established definition of form, a definition frequently taken as the last word on the subject. A standard observation, for instance, is that form is "the successful combining of all parts into an artful whole."[31] "Multeity in unity" is the most celebrated formulation, but in *A Portrait of the Artist as a Young Man*, Stephen Dedalus himself offers a fluent version of the view.

Then, said Stephen, you pass from point to point, led by its formal lines; you apprehend it as balanced part against part within its limits; you feel the rhythm of its structure. In other words the synthesis of immediate perception is followed by the analysis of apprehension. Having first felt that it is *one* thing you feel now that it is a *thing*. You apprehend it as complex, multiple, divisible, separable, made up of its parts, the result of its parts and their sum, harmonious. That is *consonantia*.[32]

This scholastic principle serves as an epitome of the dominant construal of aesthetic form, form as the form of the harmonious whole, the whole as the happy integration of its several elements.

The provocation of serial form is that it depends not on the relation of parts to a superintending whole, but rather on the relation of parts to one another. The difference can be visualized in geometric terms as the difference between, say, a triangle and a set of parallel lines. As a closed form the triangle can accommodate no new line without losing its structure; parallel lines, on the other hand, can accommodate any number of additions without jeopardizing the pattern, as long as each new element stands in the appropriate relation to the preceding. A classical haiku can receive no new syllable, but a poem in heroic couplets has no stipulated number of lines. A sonnet resists a fifteenth line, but a sonnet series may continue indefinitely. And (a more complex example) a tragedy may not move past the fall of a protagonist to a new rise, while a diary can follow every vicissitude in the life of its author and can digest any novelty without compromising the integrity of its form.

Indeed the diary can be regarded as a paradigm of serial form, a form that remains open to any addition, and that does not aim to the satisfactions of a configurational whole but to the quite different satisfactions of an unfolding series. And yet to say that the diary offers the clearest example of narrative series is not to imply that serial form remains peripheral to the workings of the novel. The establishing of part–part relations, in principle continuing without end, is a formal tendency exerting pressure on all narrative art, a tendency that erupts to prominence in the picaresque (and other episodic forms) but that also seems to have a place at the very origins of our yearning for narrative.

A prevailing and cogent argument in the theory of fiction has been that the impulse toward narrative represents an attempt to organize the disorder of our ordinary lives. As Frank Kermode has put it in the most influential statement of this position, "Men, like poets, rush 'into the middest,' *in medias res*, when they are born; they also die *in mediis rebus*, and to make sense of their span they need fictive concords with origins and ends, such as give meaning to lives and poems."[33] Narrative in this view presents a way for those who live in time to achieve the refuge of *consonantia*; it offers the "satisfying consonance" of coherent patterns in the midst of flux.

Such a speculation has much to recommend it, but the persistence of serial form suggests that another and rival yearning may underlie the will to narrative. Grant (however tentatively) that the integrity of form can attach not only to the marriage between part and whole but to the unconsummated friendship of part and part, and then it becomes reasonable to suppose that we invest our imaginations in storytelling not just for the sake of the bounded configuration but also for the sake of the (potentially) unbounded series. That the story might continue, that the adventures of the protagonist might be resumed, that a next generation might be chronicled — these familiar readerly longings are too common to be seen as merely vulgar or as incidental to the experience of fiction. And if it be objected that in the tradition of the novel the invitation to continue a finished tale is rarely accepted, one can respond, first of all, that in the tradition of popular narrative — in the tales of Hercules, say, or Punch and Judy — the protagonists are regularly resuscitated and sent off to a sequence of new episodes that arrive at no definite conclusion; and second, one may recall such instances as Crusoe's *Farther Adventures*, the return of Sherlock Holmes, and closer to home, Joyce's prying open of the frame of the *Portrait* to allow Stephen Dedalus to walk again in *Ulysses*. All of these examples suggest another and contending motive for narrative: the desire to provide an ongoing record of ongoing experience, to register not finality but continuity, to match the unfolding of time with the unfolding of story. Seen in these terms, the aim of narrative is not simply to give shape, to establish bounds, or to impose order, but *to keep narrating*.

It would be absurd to hold that series is more fundamental or more essential than configuration, or that the secret aim of fiction was to set story free from the tyranny of shape and to leave narrative unbound. On the other hand, it seems right to say that both patterns inform the structure of narrative and that our desire for integral wholes is shadowed by a desire for the ceaseless expansion of story without end. Henry James glances at just such a shadow when he asks in the preface to *Roderick Hudson*: "Where, for the complete expression of one's subject, does a personal relation stop — giving way to some other not concerned in that expression?" He then answers that "Really, universally, relations stop nowhere, and the exquisite problem of the artist is eternally but to draw, by a geometry of his own, the circle within which they shall happily *appear* to do so."[34]

One way to express a difference between Jamesian form and the forms of Woolf and Joyce is to notice how the latter are willing to leave the circle open. Both take the proposition that "relations stop nowhere" and bring it into the fiction as a condition of experience. How an individual can construct a life in the face of this perception is the question looming over this chapter, a question which first brings Woolf and Joyce together and then drives them apart.

Homer, it is clear, gave Joyce two inviting ways to draw the Jamesian circle, which one may think of as Bloomwise and counter-Bloomwise. The first conforms to the Homeric precedent in which the narrative closes on the successful return of the protagonist, the defeat of the suitors, and reunion with wife and son; and the second represents an ironic reversal in which the returning hero returns to homelessness. *Ulysses*, it is generally agreed, is no simple anti-Odyssey, but plainly as "Penelope" begins, the movement is sharply counter-Bloomwise, and the prospect of narrative closure brings with it the threat of Boylan's erotic ascension and Bloom's domestic decline. And yet, during the course of her night-thoughts, Molly's memory floats back to her husband, and the temptation is to see the novel as finally melting into harmony with its Homeric source.

What will be Bloom's condition on June 17, 1904? This is how the question of interpretation has customarily been posed, but to seek Bloom's fate in the context of a succeeding *day* is already to expose a difficult ambiguity. On the one hand, the fact that *Ulysses* takes a day as its first temporal domain opens it, we know, to an almost unimaginable density of experience. On the other hand, that it takes the *Odyssey* as its chief historical precedent suggests a significantly different narrative rhythm. The *Odyssey*, whether we see it as a dignifying parallel or ironic counterpoint, plots a long curve from exile to return. This curve may exist in parallel with Bloom's daily round, but its satisfactions depend on invoking broader patterns of life than the pattern of a single day. To ask how Odysseus and Penelope will feel on the next morning is to ask an incomprehensible question, one which simply fails to engage with the Homeric scale of time. If we see Joyce's decision to compress events as just an ingenious appropriation of the epic tradition, then we miss the extent to which the Homeric paradigm struggles against the paradigm of a single day. A day, after all, is a unit in a potentially infinite series, a repeatable unit that makes us acknowledge that another day might bring another density, another precedent, another outcome.

Molly Bloom's final "Yes" participates in this same demanding condition, since it stands at once as a sign of culmination and a mark of punctuation. It culminates in the sense that it gives as devout a narrative consummation as any wandering husband could wish; it punctuates in the sense that it conforms to the idiosyncratic syntax developed in the course of the soliloquy, a syntax organized by the repetitions of Yes acting as hinges in the movement of mind. The rhythm of Molly's thought is marked out by her recurrent Yes, and the more it recurs the more inimical it becomes to any last decisive instance bringing repetition to an end. Much as with the submerged tension between Homer and a single day, Molly's Yes sets finality against the pressures of repetition. The allure of resolution must contend with the dread of the "tone of closure" — a contest that may lie deeper than the ambiguity between Homer sincere and Homer ironic.

When Joyce writes that the real end to *Ulysses* comes in its penultimate episode, "Ithaca," and that "Penelope" cannot conclude the work because it "has no beginning, middle or end",[35] he is trying to capture the difficult image of a novel that continues past its proper ending and concludes with the inconclusiveness of the infinite. It is a good thing to have the satisfactions of Homeric finality, but it is another, and for Joyce perhaps a finer, thing to make one's peace with infinity. When Bloom finally re-enters his marriage bed, we read:

If he had smiled why would he have smiled?

To reflect that each one who enters imagines himself to be the first to enter whereas he is always the last term of a preceding series even if the first term of a succeeding one, each imagining himself to be first, last, only and alone whereas he is neither first nor last nor only nor alone in a series originating in and repeated to infinity. (p. 601)

The catechetical question that follows is "What preceding series?", and the response is to list the names of twenty-five men and to end with the phrase "and so on to no last term" (p. 602).

This list has recently become controversial, the difficulty being that if we take it as giving the names of Molly's lovers (as one did for so long), then it is dangerously misleading. Kenner makes the strong case that of those on the list, only Boylan is indisputably a bedmate, and Hayman has pointed out, just as damagingly, that the list fails to mention Lieutenant Gardner, whose erotic charge becomes evident in "Penelope."[36] All this is important. And yet, if we become too fascinated with detecting the stains on Molly's sheets, then we miss the force of the book's meditation on fantasy and desire as independent of their satisfaction. Not the lovers Molly has had, but the lovers she has fancied, or the ones who have fancied her, or those whom Bloom has fancied for her — these give the series with no last term. And when Molly thinks, "I'd like a new fellow every year" (p. 625), she makes clear how the problem of the infinite series in *Ulysses* is more than a matter of narrative form, and also how it cannot be disarmed by arguments for June 16 as the unique occasion of Molly's marital infidelity. Wanting a new man every year, Molly suggests what Bloom's fantasies have already implied, that human desire is endlessly mobile, replacing its objects in a ceaseless progression, pursuing the logic of a series that knows no resting point, "originating in and repeated to infinity."

What remains for marriage? Is it possible to acknowledge the condition of the boundless series and still keep a place for the finality of marriage? No, it is not. The ideal of love "first, last, only and alone" shatters irreparably; only a professional matchmaker would insist otherwise. Still, marriage in *Ulysses* is not a value denied; it is a value transvalued. What is finally most telling in Molly's night-thoughts is not that they end with Bloom, but that in their erratically curving course they have returned to him repeatedly, and then have withdrawn, and have returned again, only to withdraw again. A long series of men passes through her reverie, but what distinguishes Bloom from the others is not that he can halt the movement of erotic fantasy and attract all desire to himself, but that through all the movements of her mind his image reappears. In the series stretching to infinity, the others – Mulvey and Gardner, Boylan and Stephen – loom up and recede, but it is Bloom's privilege, not to persist, but to recur. This might almost count as a Joycean definition of a husband or a wife: not to be alone and only, first and last, but to be the repeated unit in an endless series. Molly's late turn toward Dedalus must be seen as another step in the series with no last term. It eliminates any claim of Boylan to be a resting point for mobile desire; and in advancing beyond Boylan, it allows for another lurch back to Bloom, the eternal husband content to recur, who lets the infinite do his dirty work.

Here, if not before, it becomes obvious how the idea of serial form comes into close relation with the value of the fully temporalized life. The Jamesian precept, that the novel must always simulate the tone of finality, clearly contends with the deep temporal commitments inherent in novelistic form, and when Joyce talks of Bloom's "eternity" or Molly's "infinity" he is struggling to sustain the infinitude of novelistic time in the face of the finite configuration inevitably implied by the shape and heft of a book. The series of suitors (real or imagined), like the series of narrative styles, like a day, like Yes, points to no concluding term but instead projects an unfolding pattern of experience – a form for narrative that imitates the form of a life. In the Dublin of *Ulysses* the response to individual constraint is not another place but another time or, more accurately, all time. The temporalized self is the novel's answer to the moral paralysis that Joyce first identified in *Dubliners*, and as such it stands in telling contrast to the chief source of value and the most important imaginative figure in *To the Lighthouse*.

V

In one of her commentaries on *Ulysses* Woolf wrote in her diary that having been "amused, stimulated, charmed, interested," by the first two or three chapters, she became "puzzled, bored, irritated, & disillusioned as by a queasy undergraduate scratching his pimples." She describes the novel as the "illiterate" accomplishment of a "self taught working man," and later adds "brackish," "pretentious," and "under-bred," to the list of wounding epithets.[37] If in one emphasis Woolf's image of Joyce as histrionic egotist coincides with the image of the father realized in Mr Ramsay, in this second aspect the picture of Joyce as one of the untamed intellectual rabble finds its embodiment in Ramsay's emotionally unkempt pupil Charles Tansley. This is not to suggest some elaborate and perverse allegory of Woolf's hostility to Joyce, but it is to insist again upon the congruence between her fictive rendering of male provocation and the relation of the novel itself to its most celebrated modernist antecedent.

This congruence suggests a way of formulating the problem which Woolf (and because of her, Lily Briscoe) had to encounter; it suggests that the emergent female self has two converging dangers to negotiate. The first, represented by Mr Ramsay, might be described as the theatrical patriarch, who stands as the boisterous custodian of the cultural past, hoarding its treasures and turning them to purposes of his own. The second, represented by Tansley, is the jeering upstart − self-taught, underbred, brackish − who emanates from the lower orders, laying claim to the cultural future. Woolf's Joyce combines these figures of theatrical patriarch and jeering upstart, and through the connection of Ramsay and Tansley *To the Lighthouse* registers this double provocation. If Woolf's portrait of the artist as an aging woman locates her so firmly in the middle class, that is in significant part because the old intellectual aristocracy and the new intellectual proletariat, the civilized past and the semi-civilized future, are seen equally as male preserves, alien lands for female creativity. The Joycean project, the epic project, of restoring the self to its place in cultural time, has no purchase in *To the Lighthouse* where such time is the time of dispossession.

To the Lighthouse contains its own image of serial form, which appears most accessibly in the finite sequence of the alphabet, used in the novel to represent the strength of human thought moving on a scale from A to Z. Mr Ramsay, who remains pinned at Q, draws an opposition between those plodders like himself who try to "repeat the whole alphabet in order, twenty-six letters in all, from start to finish" and those "who miraculously, lump all the letters together in one flash – the way of genius" (p. 55). At the end of the novel's first phase, this opposition is transposed into a distinction between husband and wife, and at the same time a distinction between literary kinds.

Mr Ramsay, who has connected the neglect of Scott to his own coming obscurity, sits down to read *The Antiquary*, and in being delighted by the novel, he overcomes his unease about himself. But then, as he finishes the chapter, he feels immediately that he must read the entire novel again, because "he could not remember the whole shape of the thing. He had to keep his judgment in suspense" (p. 180). Mrs Ramsay, on the other hand, who is reading Shakespeare's sonnet ninety-eight, arrives at a significantly different sensation. As she finishes the poem, she feels that "there it was, suddenly entire; she held it in her hands, beautiful and reasonable, clear and complete, the essence sucked out of life and held rounded here – the sonnet" (p. 181). The difference between novel and sonnet, as it is suggested in this episode, reenacts the difference between plodder and genius, and also the difference between serial and configurational form. The classic novel, composed out of a succession of chapters, repeats those units of form in such a way as to resist any direct appropriation of its "whole shape." The decisive encounter with Scott has to be postponed; another chapter follows this one, eluding the comprehensive glance, suspending the will to judgment. The sonnet, on the other hand, might be taken as a paradigm of configurational form; it displays the completeness, the whole shape, that the novel teasingly withholds. These are, of course, generalities open to question, but in *To the Lighthouse* they exist for purposes other than literary theoretical illumination.

What makes Woolf's presentation startling is that, unlike the extensive reach of novelistic form, the powers associated with the sonnet – the power to disclose an essence and to reveal a totality – are so evidently high values in *To the Lighthouse*. Here is a novel which raises doubts about novelistic form from the standpoint of the sonnet – what are we to make of this? Woolf frequently contemplated an overcoming of the barriers between prose and verse, novel and poetry; and while this ambition is most obvious in the rhythm of her prose, its most radical expression is the effort to write a novel that achieves the self-containment of a lyric poem. Moreover, the problem of formal integrity is in this case entirely congruent with the problem of personal integrity. The attempt to assimilate the extended serial forms of the novel into the configuration of the lyric miniature is at one with the attempt (in Forster's terms) to convert life in time into life by values. How can we live in time and still be whole?

Wyndham Lewis's *Time and Western Man* has at least this fact to recommend it: that beneath its grinning bitterness and its cranky jocularity, it bluntly returned the questions of space and time to central analytic consideration. That the modern mind is a "Time-mind," that this condition leads to a decadent obsession with flux and process, that it links Joyce, Proust, Lawrence, Bergson, Charlie Chaplin and numerous others, that Lewis himself represents a rival "space-mind" – these claims appear with a heuristic simplicity captured in one of Lewis's opening remarks:

The main characteristic of the Time-mind from the outset has been a hostility to what it calls the "spatializing" process of a mind *not* a Time-mind. It is this "spatializing" capacity and instinct that it everywhere assails. In its place it would put the Time-view, the flux. It asks us to see everything *sub specie temporis*.[38]

It is really an accident of history that Woolf was not a principal target of the polemic in *Time and Western Man*. Had *To the Lighthouse* appeared even a year earlier, it might have been the centerpiece of Lewis's showy display, because however one characterizes the elusive Time-mind, no one can doubt that it finds its way into Woolf's novel. Part of Lewis's contention is that the temporal imagination finds organic process everywhere, and further that it anthropomorphizes natural process, endowing inorganic matter with sentience and finally with intelligence. Indeed Woolf's attempt to find metaphors for time seems a telling confirmation of Lewis's speculative thesis. In the "Time Passes" section of the novel, where time becomes the leading character, it enters in this way.

Only through the rusty hinges and swollen sea-moistened woodwork certain airs, detached from the body of the wind (the house was ramshackle after all) crept round corners and ventured indoors. Almost one might imagine them, as they entered the drawing-room, questioning and wondering, toying with the flap of hanging wall-paper, asking, would it hang much longer, when would it fall? Then smoothly brushing the walls, they passed on musingly as if asking the red and yellow roses on the wall-paper whether they would fade, and questioning (gently, for there was time at their disposal) the torn letters in the waste-paper basket, the flowers, the books, all of which were now open to them and asking, Were they allies? Were they enemies? How long would they endure? (pp. 190–1)

Here the movement of time appears as "certain airs," elsewhere as the remorseless sea eating away at the land, but always as a knowing fluidity.

In *Men Without Art* (1934) Lewis made good his neglect of Woolf, turning his polemic and his misogyny in the direction of her critical essays, which he described as crystallizing "*the feminine* — as distinguished from the feminist — standpoint."[39] In itself, the judgment is uninteresting and unpersuasive; but in ways that Lewis surely did not intend, in ways that leave his misogyny behind, the remark about femininity comes into interesting relation to the earlier comments about time. For in *To the Lighthouse* the distinction between men and women is cast precisely in terms of solidity and flux. This point, everywhere apparent and much remarked, may be evoked through a single illustration, Mrs Ramsay at the dinner table acknowledging the failure of community.

Nothing seemed to have merged. They all sat separate. And the whole of the effort of merging and flowing and creating rested on her. Again she felt, as a fact without hostility, the sterility of men, for if she did not do it nobody would do it. (p. 126)

Mrs Ramsay, we elsewhere learn, is a column of spray, a fountain of life, whereas her husband is an arid scimitar and a stake in the channel. Taken alone, the sexual metaphorics may seem disappointingly conventional, but when placed in the context of the play of related metaphors, the conventions are exploited so thoroughly that they change their shape and their force.

Women and time share a metaphor. This is the first uncanny perception, certainly not unique to Woolf's novel: that women and time are composed of the same metaphoric stuff, that they both merge and flow, as airs and as waters. What makes this parallel so charged is that for Woolf unlike Joyce – indeed unlike the epic tradition more generally – to extend temporal perspective to its broadest reach is not to collect new meanings; it is to pass beyond the domain of meaning. Closer in this respect to Lawrence, she envisions the natural world set free of its human interpreters, and she does so by raising the angle of vision until she sees time before and after civilization – until she realizes, that is, that the "very stone one kicks with one's boot will outlast Shakespeare" (p. 56). The problem we need to confront may be put as follows. If women and time derive from a common fund of metaphors, metaphors of fluidity, and if time is rendered as complacently destructive, then are women implicated in the destructions of time?

We may say this: that men in the novel cling to permanence as to a stake in the channel. Ramsay's anxiety that the satisfactions in Scott will fade (and by easy implication, that his own achievement will blur then disappear); his son James's adolescent obsession with the trauma of his childhood; Tansley's assertion of a universal law of gender ("Women can't write, women can't paint"); all express a refusal to accept the workings of time, which will undo all fixities. Women, on the other hand – at least those three importantly associated women, Mrs McNab, Mrs Ramsay, Lily Briscoe – know intimately the ravages of time. Listening to the ocean Mrs Ramsay reflects that the waves "like a ghostly roll of drums remorselessly beat the measure of life, made one think of the destruction of the island and its engulfment in the sea, and warned her whose day had slipped past in one quick doing after another that it was all ephemeral as a rainbow" (pp. 27–8). Watching the house deteriorate through the years, Mrs McNab tersely notes that "Things were better then than now" (p. 206). And Lily at the novel's climax concedes without regret that her painting will be "hung in the attics," that it will be "destroyed" (pp. 309–10). The distinction here, roughly put, is between those who battle the current of time in a gesture of fierce denial, and those who, in a spirit of acceptance, learn to swim with the tide. Indeed Mrs McNab, dusting and sweeping, looks "like a tropical fish oaring its way through sun-lanced waters" (p. 200), while Lily's painting itself becomes a form of swimming: "Down in the hollow of one wave she saw the next wave towering higher and higher above her" (p. 236). Alternatively, Mr Ramsay, when he is not a stake in the channel, is an awkwardly amphibious sea lion.

The radicalism of *To the Lighthouse* lies in its refusal to take civilization as the basis for our values, its suggestion that values emanate from a deeper source, and that civilization must seek a foundation outside its own architecture. This perception receives clearest expression in "Time Passes," when the house (emblem of civilization) has come to the verge of annihilation and "would have turned and pitched downwards to the depths of darkness," had not Mrs McNab, with Mrs Bast, "stayed the corruption and the rot; rescued from the pool of Time that was fast closing over them now a basin, now a cupboard; fetched up from oblivion all the Waverley novels" (pp. 208–9). That the Waverley novels, the novel's focus of the fragility of culture, have been saved from the pool of Time by a tropical fish — this fact not only dramatizes the dependent status of canonical cultural artifacts, it renders the paradoxes of life in time, value in time, by constructing a paradoxical conceit. How can a fish save books from the rot of dampness?

An approach to the conundrum can be made through a passage appearing early in the work, where Lily has a moment of recognition during a conversation with the scientist William Bankes.

Suddenly, as if the movement of his hand had released it, the load of her accumulated impressions of him tilted up; and down poured in a ponderous avalanche all she felt about him. That was one sensation. Then up rose in a fume the essence of his being. That was another. (p. 39)

Two phrases in this passage must be brought together: "accumulated impressions" and "essence." What the passage tells us is that impressions accumulated over time may suddenly cohere into an essence, and the question that this raises, a question central for understanding the condition of character and value in *To the Lighthouse*, is how passing time allows for the perception of essences. Woolf's notion of the "moment of being" has become worn intellectual property, as has its foreign relations to such modernist ideas as image, impression, epiphany, vortex. But what remains puzzling, and what collects so many of the novel's diverse concerns, is the connection between the privileged moment and passing time.

A key to the difficulty is provided by the fine-grained description of Lily's act of painting, where we read at one point that

Lily stepped back to get her canvas — so — into perspective. It was an odd road to be walking, this of painting. Out and out one went, further and further, until at last one seemed to be on a narrow plank, perfectly alone, over the sea. And as she dipped into the blue paint, she dipped too into the past there. (p. 256)

Soon after we learn that "She went on tunneling her way into her picture, into the past." Her picture, the past. Woolf's decision to make her woman artist a painter must not be reduced to an act of homage to her sister or to her own reticence about the activity of writing. The distribution of shapes, colors and lines in pictorial space becomes a vivid sign for the novel's sense of how passing time might yield up significant moments. Put most concisely, the proposal is that time should be converted into space.

Early in the work Lily braces herself to endure Bankes's judgment of her painting and takes consolation in the thought that "if it must be seen, Mr Bankes was less alarming than another. But that any other eyes should see the residue of her thirty-three years, the deposit of each day's living mixed with something more secret than she had ever spoken or shown in the course of all those days was an agony. At the same time it was immensely exciting" (p. 81).

As the "residue" of thirty-three years, as the "deposit" of daily living, the painting stands as the *spatial representation of a life-history*, time projected onto a surface. All through the novel's final sequence Lily remembers in order to paint and paints in order to remember. The austere opposition between space and time, so crucial to Lewis's indictment of literary modernity, is drained of its ultimacy, as space and time are displayed not as rival categories of experience but as aspects of an underlying continuity – a continuity well dramatized by the disembodied voice in "Time Passes": "But what after all is one night? A short space . . ." (p. 192)

This motif, far more prevalent than any enumeration of examples can suggest, is no idiosyncrasy; it is part of an intricate and rigorous meditation on the conditions of value in a world of flux. If time past and time future belong to the stones that will outlast Shakespeare, how can we secure meaning in time present? The answer, I have started to say, lies in overcoming the barrier between time and space, in conceiving space as time cohering into order, time structured. Here one may usefully recall Woolf's most cherished metaphor, the wave, which belongs to the fluid ocean (the figure for passing time), which indeed is nothing other than the fluid medium, but which represents fluidity in the act of finding its shape. And as the wave is the sea discovering form, so – on a more abstract plane – space is time's significant form. As Lily performs the work of mourning that allows her to paint, she remembers Mrs Ramsay saying

"Life stand still here"; Mrs Ramsay making of the moment something permanent (as in another sphere Lily herself tried to make of the moment something permanent) – this was of the nature of a revelation. In the midst of chaos there was shape; this eternal passing and flowing (she looked at the clouds going and the leaves shaking) was struck into stability. Life stand still here, Mrs Ramsay said. "Mrs Ramsay! Mrs Ramsay!" she repeated. She owed it all to her. (pp. 240–1)

"In the midst of chaos there was shape" – all through this novel, in an ingenious variety of ways, the epiphanic instant, the "moment of being," discloses itself, not as a disembodied experience of value, but as a spatial perception, the arrangement of "disorderly sensations" and "unrelated passions" into some visually extended form, whose final realization is the pictorial surface. Time, left to itself, allows night and day, month and year, to run "shapelessly together" (p. 203). Love, almost as provoking as time, has a "thousand shapes" (p. 286). But at those instants of poise, one finds a simplicity "as clear as the space which the clouds at last uncover – the little space of sky which sleeps beside the moon" (p. 78). Mr Ramsay, who can never see "the whole shape of the thing" (p. 180), must stride blindly forward, "as if he were leaping into space" (p. 308). It is not for the artist alone to see that "beneath the colour there was the shape"; it is an imperative for anyone who "demand[s] an explanation" for the short mystery of life, anyone who hopes that "the space would fill; [that] those empty flourishes would form into shape" (p. 268). Lily's painting then derives from a more primitive recognition that harks back to the moral impressionism associated earlier with Conrad's Marlow. It too implies the recognition that aesthetics and ethics converge in some aboriginal intuition of balance, harmony and proportion that Woolf locates not in the Conradian sensorium of taste, smell and touch, but in the perception of space as such, shape in itself.

Woolf well knows that we always only live in space. There is no better place. But the feeling that we infrequently see the spatial medium and only rarely recognize the shapes it contains — this is the thought that runs deep in the imagination of *To the Lighthouse*. That the world is extended, that objects are distinct, that things have forms — these are recognitions so rudimentary that it is difficult to formulate them, difficult to express the extraordinary satisfactions they offer. But repeatedly through the novel, at moments of the highest tension, the feeling of space and shape, independent of any particular manifestation, signals the possibility of apprehending value within the valueless ooze of passing time. Or as Lily puts it with no longer suppressed fervor, "Heaven be praised for it, the problem of space remained" (p. 255).

At this point the question of gender returns. For if women in *To the Lighthouse* mimic time, if they merge and flow and spray like the watery years themselves, they are also the novel's agents of spatial form, of dry shape. Lily's struggle with pictorial balance — "It was a question . . . [of] how to connect this mass on the right hand with that on the left" (p. 82) — stands in precise analogy to Mrs Ramsay's arrangement and rearrangement of the guests at her dinner table; and both Lily's yearning for masses in relation and Mrs Ramsay's mania for marriage find a further reflection in Mrs McNab's efforts to restore structure to a house drowning in a pool of time.

211

Far from contradictory, these two roles, swimmer in time and sculptor in space, come to imply one another. Because Woolfian space is not distinct from Woolfian time (no more distinct than wave from ocean), and because an acceptance of passing time — Mrs Ramsay's acknowledgment of death, Lily's mourning, Mrs McNab's direct encounter with time's ravages — is the condition of making shape, only those who immerse themselves in time (like fish in water) can see (or invent) the shapes that time allows.

How can one live inside marriage? This might be taken as the question of questions in *Ulysses* where marriage implies not just the intimacy of a couple but the overcoming of social contrast within some common culture. In the face of the many obstacles — human desire, cultural provincialism, political narrowness, historical blindness — the extensions of time offer the best chance for the marriage of differences. This is not because patience will finally secure an ecstatic union, but because in the endlessness of time, exile and return can continually succeed one another. The characterization I have offered of Bloom's marital condition, the husband as the recurrent term in an endless series, might serve to describe the general relations between the exorbitant ego and its sluggish society. Much as Bloom's stubborn domestic strength is shown not by his power to win back the loyalty of his wife but merely by his ability to turn up repeatedly in her imaginings, so his importance to Dublin resides not in his influence upon it, but his recurrence within it. And because he recurs, however unconsciously and however ambiguously, as successor to such as Odysseus, Elijah, Shakespeare, etc., his case suggests that the gifted exceptions will give us not just one chance to welcome them, but that they will follow diverse series of their own, disappearing and reappearing, but irrevocably married to the cultural tradition.

How can one live outside marriage? This is a question for the single woman not the uxorious cuckold, but as in *Ulysses* marriage in *To the Lighthouse* becomes a general figure for relations between self and society. Bloom's task is to live out his solitude in the spirit of community, but Lily faces the reverse labor of living in community without jeopardizing her solitude. The "soliloquy in solitude" that Woolf takes as one high aim of the new novel requires that her heroine overcome not social estrangement but the blandishments of social integration. The last phase of *To the Lighthouse* shows how it may be possible for the aesthetic isolate to forswear marriage, to choose solitude, and to invent an ego.

Reflecting on Carmichael, Lily muses on "how many shapes one person might wear" (p. 289) — a thought which seems to suggest an irreducible multiplicity in human character. *To the Lighthouse*, however, generates the many shapes of individuality only as a prelude to the great labor that falls to Lily in its final phase, the attempt to find the shape of one's shapes, to discover a form which (however briefly) gives equilibrium to the dispersed fragments of a self cast up by a single life history.

Time is the novel's great engine of multiplicity. Passing as it does, it dissolves the myth of unity and leaves a succession of faces that it would take a "thousand eyes" to see. To have a life history is to suffer a disgregation of coherence. But the novel's most ingenious trope, we have seen, is the conversion of time into space; the form of a painting is the consummate figure for the possibility that shows itself teasingly throughout the book; and when Lily speaks of her painting as the "residue" of her life, the "deposit" of her experience, she is gesturing toward the ideal contained in that dominant trope, the ideal of the spatialized ego. To project that ego into pictorial form is to take all the fragments that time has dispersed and to find the shape of their accumulated shapes. It is the prospect of the leavings of time brought into spatial array, life history transposed onto a surface, a prospect animating the final section of *To the Lighthouse*, suggesting that even our incomplete lives might suddenly encounter their proper wholeness.

All through this study a chronic ache has recurred in the unsteady relations between the ego figured as a suffusive whole and the ego figured as a yearning part, the individual as its own richly populated world or as a broken limb severed from the corporate body. Woolf would not put the question in precisely this way. She would put it better, as she does in a long passage from the late memoir "A Sketch of the Past" where she has been describing her vulnerability to shock.

And so I go on to suppose that the shock-receiving capacity is what makes me a writer. I hazard the explanation that a shock is at once in my case followed by the desire to explain it. I feel that I have had a blow; but it is not, as I thought as a child, simply a blow from an enemy hidden behind the cotton wool of daily life; it is or will become a revelation of some order; it is a token of some real thing behind appearances; and I make it real by putting it into words. It is only by putting it into words that I make it whole; this wholeness means that it has lost its power to hurt me; it gives me, perhaps because by doing so I take away the pain, a great delight to put the severed parts together. Perhaps this is the strongest pleasure known to me. It is the rapture I get when in writing I seem to be discovering what belongs to what; making a scene come right; making a character come together. From this I reach what I might call a philosophy; at any rate it is a constant idea of mine; that behind the cotton wool is hidden a pattern; that we — I mean all human beings — are connected with this; that the whole world is a work of art; that we are parts of the work of art. *Hamlet* or a Beethoven quartet is the truth about this vast mass that we call the world. But there is no Shakespeare, there is no Beethoven; certainly and emphatically there is no God; we are the words; we are the music; we are the thing itself. And I see this when I have a shock.[40]

The opening of this passage gives another brave statement of solitary aesthetic heroism. The vulnerable but resilient artist suffers shocks, puts the severed parts together, discovers order. The artist makes the whole; here is another case of triumphant loneliness; and then without a transition being signalled, the passage gives us a whole that is no longer made but found, no longer something composed by the lonely artist, but something that composes the artist, even something that annihilates artistic sovereignty. A movement has occurred from the personal, even idiosyncratic, history of a shock-receiving, whole-restoring individual to the existence of a webbed whole, a web of words, the art of the universe that particular works can disclose but not create.

It is true. As Lily makes her central stroke, she performs a radically individuating act, identifying herself as a third term, like a Marlow, like a Strether, but poised now not between two cultures but between two sexes, an androgyne, an artist, neither left nor right, but a central, centered, middle thing. At this point it appears that the fiction could not be further from the life of the community, from all the non-artists and all the married couples. Lily seems even lonelier than those connoisseurs of privacy, Marlow, Strether and Dowell. The struggle of Marlow to communicate his experience, the nervous turns of Strether inside the labyrinth of dialogue, the appeals of Dowell to his silent reader — these acts of desperation seem cheerfully social when set against Lily's perception: that her painting will be neglected, discarded, destroyed. Her visionary moment is only a moment and only her own; "my vision" is the novel's final and uncompromising phrase.

And yet, as we know, during the act of painting, and by extension during any real imaginative flight, the self is not the author of its visions. After the false promise of the window to give the truth of being, and the false promise of the mirror to give the truth of seeming, the canvas makes no promises. It repudiates both the authority of subjectivity and the authority of the world; and if the painting is the residue of a life history, this is a life history inevitably contaminated with a world that precedes and exceeds it, with other lives and their other histories. To identify Lily with the line drawn in the middle, as everything encourages us to do, is to see her no longer simply as compositor of the work, but as a thing composed. It is to recognize, in Woolf's terms, that "the whole world is a work of art; that we are parts of the work of art."

"It was a question, she remembered, how to connect this mass on the right hand with that on the left" (pp. 82–3). Lily Briscoe enters the solitude of creative labor and finds — what? — not a bedrock of subjectivity, but colors, lines, shapes, shadows. No forms could be more general, and in generalizing as they do, they collect the circumstances and the metaphors of other lives. Subject and object, man and woman, self and other, time and space, land and water — these conspicuous dualisms marching through the work are collected under the aspect of Lily's two masses. Mr Ramsay's epistemological pair (the knower and the known), and Mrs Ramsay's marital pair (the eligible man and the eligible woman) receive a formal summary in the structure of Lily's design. In its very simplicity, the painting hints at something like the conditions of sociality. The single line taking its place among the masses, the severed parts finally joining, the adjusting of all the elements for the sake of the whole — abstract though this be, it suggests a rudimentary form of human community.

Two things needing to meet, a line drawn between them — on this lofty pinnacle of pictorial formalism, the last sentences of the novel gather what preceded them and show how a novel might aspire to lyric totality, where the configuration of the whole seems to show its form in a single instant. Mr Ramsay, that plodder through the alphabetic series, had imagined the genius who merges the letters in "one flash." Here it occurs, when in the book's final motion, the drawing of a line, *To the Lighthouse* transforms its linear progress into one perceptible shape, and a soliloquy in solitude becomes the collective voice of the novel. Then it does what this book of mine can only dream of doing: it shows its whole shape as it ends.

Notes

1 TWO CULTURES AND AN INDIVIDUAL

1. Henry James, *The Notebooks of Henry James*, ed. F. O. Matthiessen and Kenneth B. Murdock (New York: Oxford University Press, 1947), pp. 227–8.
2. Henry James, *The Ambassadors*, 2 vols., New York Edition (1909; rpt New York: Charles Scribner's Sons, 1937), I, p. 137. References to this edition will be cited parenthetically within the text.
3. Joseph Conrad, *Heart of Darkness*, ed. Robert Kimbrough (New York: W. W. Norton, 1988), p. 41. All references to this work will be cited by page parenthetically within the text.
4. For an important discussion of Conradian dislocation see J. Hillis Miller, *Poets of Reality* (Cambridge MA: Belknap Press of Harvard University, 1965).
5. Albert J. Guerard, *Conrad the Novelist* (Cambridge MA: Harvard University Press, 1958), pp. 33, 39. For other psychological interpretations of the novel, see Frederic Crews, "The Power of Darkness," *Partisan Review*, 34 (Fall 1957), pp. 507–25; Bernard Meyer, *Joseph Conrad: A Psychoanalytic Biography* (Princeton NJ: Princeton University Press, 1967), pp. 154–9; Thomas Moser, *Joseph Conrad: Achievement and Decline* (Cambridge MA: Harvard University Press, 1967), pp. 80–1.
6. Early statements of this position appeared in J. Hillis Miller, *Poets of Reality*, pp. 20–6; and James Guetti, *The Limits of Metaphor* (Ithaca NJ: Cornell University Press, 1967), pp. 58–67. For a deconstructionist version of the approach, see Arnold Krupat, "Antonymy, Language, and Value in Conrad's *Heart of Darkness*," *The Missouri Review*, 3 (Fall 1979), pp. 63–85.
7. Tzvetan Todorov, "Connaissance du Vide," *Nouvelle Revue de Psychanalyse*, 11 (Spring 1975), p. 152.
8. Perry Meisel, "Decentering *Heart of Darkness*," *Modern Language Studies*, 8 (Fall 1978), pp. 25, 26.
9. In the course of arguing that *Heart of Darkness* is a "decentered" narrative, Meisel refers to the movement from London to Rome to the Congo, *ibid.*, p. 23. Said, too, invokes the concept of a shifting center defined by its "radiating significance" rather than by time or geography. While this emphasis is helpful, I am arguing that it achieves its due force only when linked

to the opposing topos. Edward Said, *The World, the Text, and the Critic* (Cambridge MA: Harvard University Press, 1983), p. 96.

10. James Clifford, "On Ethnographic Self-Fashioning," in *The Predicament of Culture* (Cambridge MA: Harvard University Press, 1988), pp. 21–54.

11. H. G. Wells, *Boon, The Mind of the Race, the Wild Asses of the Devil, and the Last Trump* (New York: George H. Doran, 1915), pp. 106, 108.

12. See David Lodge's discussion of the use of "heightened cliché." Lodge, "Strether by the River," in *The Language of Fiction: Essays in Criticism and Verbal Analysis of the English Novel* (London: Routledge & Kegan Paul, 1966), p. 196.

13. John Paterson, "The Language of 'Adventure' in Henry James," *American Literature*, 32 (November 1960), pp. 291–301.

14. See William Bysshe Stein, "*The Ambassadors*: The Crucifixion of Sensibility," *College English*, 17 (February 1956), pp. 289–92; and J. A. Ward. "*The Ambassadors* as a Conversion Experience," *Southern Review*, n.s. 5 (Spring 1969), pp. 350–74.

15. I owe this last insight to Professor Richard Begam of the University of Wisconsin.

16. Austin Warren's consideration of mythic knowledge in James continues to be highly pertinent: "The Jamesian equivalent of myth lies . . . in the metaphors." Warren, "Myth and Dialectic in the Later Novels," *The Kenyon Review*, 5 (Autumn 1943), p. 556.

17. Henry James, "Miss Prescott's 'Azarian'," in *Notes and Reviews* (Cambridge MA: Dunster House, 1921), pp. 18–19.

18. *Ibid.*, p. 29. The distinction between individual speaker and the speech community stands in obvious parallel to the Saussurean distinction between *parole* and *langue*. Perhaps a more suggestive analogy can be found in J. L. Austin's notion of ordinary language as a source of philosophic illumination:

our common stock of words embodies all the distinctions men have found worth drawing, and the connexions they have found worth marking, in the lifetimes of many generations: these surely are likely to be more numerous, more sound, since they have stood up to the long test of the survival of the fittest, and more subtle, at least in all ordinary and reasonably practical matters, than any that you or I are likely to think up in our arm-chairs of an afternoon – the most favoured alternative method.

Austin, "A Plea for Excuses," in *Philosophical Papers*, ed. J. O. Urmson and G. J. Warnock, 2nd edition (London: Oxford University Press, 1970), p. 182.

19. Ruth Bernard Yeazell has argued persuasively that "in James's late fiction, the metaphoric imagination works with its most feverish intensity when faced with knowledge that is both deeply desired and profoundly terrifying." This insight is essential to an understanding of James's metaphors, but before they can be psychologically illuminating, the metaphors must first establish the domain out of which individual psychology, and much else, can be constructed. The psychological per-

tinence of specific metaphors is a central instance of the general phenomenon that I am pursuing here. Ruth Bernard Yeazell, *Language and Knowledge in the Late Novels of Henry James* (Chicago IL: University of Chicago Press, 1976), p. 54.

20. Ralph Waldo Emerson, "Nature," *The Collected Works of Ralph Waldo Emerson*, ed. Alfred R. Ferguson and Robert E. Spiller (Cambridge MA: Belknap Press of Harvard University Press, 1971), I, p. 29.

21. James, *The Notebooks*, pp. 226, 227.

22. Henry James, "Project for *The Ambassadors*," *The Notebooks*, p. 374.

23. Henry James, *Roderick Hudson*, New York Edition (1907; rpt. New York: Charles Scribner's Sons, 1935), pp. xi, x.

24. J. L. Austin, *Sense and Sensibilia*, reconstructed from the manuscript notes by G. J. Warnock (Oxford: Oxford University Press, 1962), p. 8.

25. Henry James, "Project for *The Ambassadors*," p. 397.

26. Henry James, preface to *The Spoils of Poynton* (New York: Charles Scribner's Sons, 1908), p. xv.

27. Henry James, *The Letters of Henry James*, ed. Percy Lubbock (New York: Charles Scribner's Sons, 1920), II, p. 245.

28. Immanuel Kant, *Critique of Pure Reason*, trans. Norman Kemp Smith (1929; rpt New York: St. Martin's Press, 1965), p. 171.

29. Henry James, "Project for *The Ambassadors*," p. 410.

30. Joseph Conrad, *Letters to William Blackwood and David S. Meldrum*, ed. William Blackburn (Durham NC: Duke University Press, 1958), pp. 36, 37.

31. For a synopsis of the revisions see Jonah Raskin, "*Heart of Darkness*: The Manuscript Revisions," *Review of English Studies*, n.s. 18 (1967), pp. 30–9.

32. Joseph Conrad, *Letters From Joseph Conrad 1895–1924*, ed. Edward Garnett (New York: The Bobbs-Merrill Co., 1928), p. 150.

33. Joseph Conrad, *Letters to William Blackwood and David S. Meldrum*, p. 43.

34. Joseph Conrad, *Last Essays* (New York: Doubleday, Page & Company, 1926), p. 17.

35. Conrad seems unduly apologetic in his response to Graham. He suggests that his original "idea" has become "increasingly wrapped up in secondary notions" – a reversal of the metaphor in which the meaning of Marlow's tales is said to be "outside" like a haze rather than inside like a kernel – and insists that Graham will still be able to find "the right intention" if he examines the episodes carefully. It is almost as though Conrad, startled at how far he has strayed, were trying to reclaim his story for his original political design. *Joseph Conrad's Letters to R. B. Cunninghame Graham*, ed. C. T. Watts (Cambridge: Cambridge University Press, 1969), p. 116.

36. The other two types of social domination are patriarchal (or traditional) authority and charismatic authority – of which more later. Max Weber, *Economy and Society*, ed. Guenther Roth and Claus Wittich (New York: Bedminster Press, 1968).

37. *Ibid.*, p. 988.

38. Max Weber, *Max Weber on Law in Economy and Society*, ed. Max Rhein-stein (Cambridge MA: Harvard University Press, 1954), p. 351.
39. From a 1909 speech, quoted in Reinhardt Bendix, *Max Weber* (New York: Doubleday, & Company, 1962), p. 464.
40. Weber, *Economy and Society*, pp. 1115, 1113, 1112.
41. *Ibid.*, p. 1117. Yet the pathos of charisma, and the pathos of Weber's sociology, is that quotidian needs make an inexorable return: "Every charisma is on the road from a turbulently emotional life that knows no economic rationality to a slow death by suffocation under the weight of material interests: every hour of its existence brings it nearer to this end." Moments of ecstasy yield to enduring social structures. Institutions reform and traditions reestablish themselves. There occurs a "routinization of charisma," in which it "recedes as a creative force" and changes "from a unique, transitory gift of grace . . . into a permanent possession of everyday life." No longer a supernatural endowment disclosed by revelation, it is appropriated by the king, the priest, or the bureaucrat, who invoke its aura in virtue of their office not in virtue of their mission. *Ibid.*, pp. 1120, 1146, 1121.
42. V. J. Emmett makes a passing reference to Weber's notion of charisma in the context of his discussion of Conradian heroism in relation to Carlyle. See "Carlyle, Conrad, and the Politics of Charisma: Another Perspective on *Heart of Darkness*," *Conradiana*, 7 (1975), pp. 145–54.
43. Lillian Feder, "Marlow's Descent Into Hell," *Nineteenth-Century Fiction*, 9 (March 1955), p. 290.
44. Peter Brooks has recently written that, "More than a masterful, summary, victorious articulation, 'the horror!' appears as minimal language, language on the verge of reversion to savagery, on the verge of a fall from language." Brooks is certainly right to point to the liminal character of Kurtz's final words, but we can see them as ascent quite as readily as descent; language as it emerges from sensation, from wordless reflex to reflective word. Peter Brooks, *Reading for the Plot* (New York: Alfred A. Knopf, 1984), p. 250.
45. Frederic Jameson has written of the "perceptual vocation of Conrad's style" which "offers the exercise of perception and the perceptual recombination of sense data as an end in itself." No doubt the activity of perception carries its own justification for Conrad, but that activity receives sufficient warrant only through its contribution to the moral vocation of the style. Marlow may not be an articulate moralist, but he has a moral style. *The Political Unconscious* (Ithaca NY: Cornell University Press, 1981), pp. 231, 230.
46. For a useful discussion of Conradian metaphor see William W. Bonney, "Joseph Conrad and the Betrayal of Language," *Nineteenth-Century Fiction*, 34 (September 1979), p. 128.
47. For a good general discussion of naming in *The Ambassadors*, see Mary Cross, " 'To Find the Names': *The Ambassadors*," *Papers on Language and Literature*, 19 (Fall 1983), pp. 402–18.
48. James, "Project for *The Ambassadors*," p. 396.

49. Paul Rosenzweig has a useful discussion of "being right" in relation to pastoral motifs in *The Ambassadors*, but he unnecessarily insists that the term loses its moral connotations. "James's 'Special-Green Vision': *The Ambassadors* as Pastoral," *Studies in the Novel*, 13 (Winter 1981), p. 383.

50. Henry James, "A French Critic," in *Notes and Reviews*, p. 105.

51. Typically, "being right" suggests "being correct," in the sense in which one can be correct about any fact at all. There is no essential connection between being right and being good or just or decent.

52. Joseph Conrad, *Lord Jim*, ed. Thomas Moser (New York: W. W. Norton, 1968), p. 47.

53. Seymour Chatman discusses such Jamesian expletives in *The Later Style of Henry James* (New York: Barnes and Noble, 1972), pp. 72–6.

54. G. P. Baker and P. M. S. Hacker, *Understanding and Meaning* (Chicago: University of Chicago Press, 1980), p. 222.

55. "La 'subjectivité' dont nous traitons ici est la capacité du locuteur à se poser comme 'sujet'. . . nous tenons que cette 'subjectivité', qu'on la pose en phénoménologie ou en psychologie, comme on voudra, n'est que l'émergence dans l'être d'une propriété fondamentale du langage. Est 'ego' qui *dit* 'ego.' Nous trouvons là le fondement de la 'subjectivité', qui se détermine par le statut linguistique de la 'personne'." Emile Benveniste, *Problèmes de linguistique générale* (Paris: Editions Gallimard, 1966), p. 260.

56. Henry James, *Wings of the Dove*, 2 vols., New York Edition (1909; rpt. New York: Charles Scribner's Sons, 1937), II, p. 25.

57. Benveniste, "Le langage est ainsi organisé qu'il permet à chaque locuteur de *s'approprier* la langage entière en se désignant comme *je*." *Problèmes*, p. 262.

58. Henry James, *Portraits of Places* (New York: Lear Publishers, 1948), pp. 115–16.

59. James, "Project for *The Ambassadors*," p. 415.

2 LIBERALISM AND SYMBOLISM IN *HOWARDS END*

1. E. M. Forster, *Howards End*, Abinger Edition, vol. 4 (1910; London: Edward Arnold, 1973), p. 37. Subsequent references to this edition will be represented by page number parenthetically within the text.

2. Matthew Arnold, *Culture and Anarchy*, in *The Complete Prose Works of Matthew Arnold*, vol. 5, ed. R. H. Super (1869; Ann Arbor MI: University of Michigan Press, 1965), p. 112.

3. Lionel Trilling, *E. M. Forster* (1943; New York: New Directions, 1964), p. 118.

4. *Ibid.*, pp. 118, 135. Cyrus Hoy also presents a useful reading of *Howards End* "in terms of conflicting principles whose reconciliation serves to define the novel's meaning." "Forster's Metaphysical Novel," *PMLA*, 125 (March 1960) p. 126.

5. Trilling, *E. M. Forster*, p. 118.

6. E. M. Forster, "What I Believe," *Two Cheers for Democracy*, Abinger Edition, vol. 11 (1951; London: Edward Arnold, 1972), p. 72. See

Frederick C. Crews for an exposition of the background to Forster's liberalism. *E. M. Forster: The Perils of Humanism* (Princeton NJ: Princeton University Press, 1962), pp. 7–36.

7. L. T. Hobhouse, *Liberalism* (New York: Henry Holt, n.d.), pp. 224, 134, 54, 47, 129.

8. *Ibid.*, pp. 100, 67.

9. *Ibid.*, pp. 127, 147, 128.

10. John Sayre Martin, *E. M. Forster* (Cambridge: Cambridge University Press, 1976), p. 109.

11. Hobhouse, *Liberalism*, p. 136.

12. *Ibid.*, pp. 133, 232–3.

13. "He declares for the autonomy of the work; for co-essence of form and meaning; for art as 'organic and free from dead matter'; for music as a criterion of formal purity; for the work's essential anonymity. Like all art, he thinks the novel must fuse differentiation into unity, in order to provide meaning we can experience; art is 'the one orderly product that our race has produced,' the only unity and therefore the only meaning. This is Symbolist." Frank Kermode, "The One Orderly Product (E. M. Forster)," in *Puzzles and Epiphanies: Essays and Reviews 1958–1961* (London: Routledge & Kegan Paul, 1962), p. 80.

14. F. R. Leavis, "E. M. Forster," in *The Common Pursuit* (London: Chatto & Windus, 1952), p. 269.

15. Leavis, "E. M. Forster," p. 262. Malcolm Bradbury has argued that the standard opposition between "comic" and "poetic" emphases conceals a third form, Forsterian irony, and "that irony is of the essence, for it is a mediating presence between the parts of the book that are preeminently social comedy and those concerned with the poetic, which is also the infinite." *Possibilities: Essays on the State of the Novel* (Oxford: Oxford University Press, 1973), p. 100.

16. Alan Wilde, *Art and Order: A Study of E. M. Forster* (New York: New York University Press, 1964), p. 123.

17. Ludwig Wittgenstein, *Philosophical Investigations*, trans. G. E. M. Anscombe, 3rd ed. (New York: Macmillan, 1971), p. 206.

18. *Ibid.*, pp. 193, 195, 206, 202.

19. *Ibid.*, p. 208.

20. *Ibid.*, p. 196.

21. Bradbury calls the problem of duality "very close to the entire question of Forster's temperament" and shrewdly compares Forster to Hawthorne on this point. *Possibilities*, p. 97.

22. Gérard Genette, *Narrative Discourse: An Essay in Method*, trans. Jane E. Lewin (Ithaca NY: Cornell University Press, 1980), p. 161.

3 CHARACTER IN *THE GOOD SOLDIER*

1. Ford Madox Ford, "Impressionism and Fiction," in *Critical Writings of Ford Madox Ford*, ed. Frank MacShane (Lincoln NE: University of Nebraska Press, 1964), p. 43.

2. Ford Madox Ford, "Impressionism and Fiction," pp. 44–5, my emphasis.

3. Ford Madox Ford, *The Good Soldier: A Tale of Passion* (1915; rpt. New York: Vintage, 1955), p. 240. Subsequent references to this edition will appear parenthetically within the text.

4. Samuel Hynes, "The Epistemology of *The Good Soldier*," *Sewanee Review*, 69 (Spring 1961), p. 233. Robert Green, on the other hand, argues that the novel "mediates a conflict between received conventions and urgent passional drives." Robert Green, *Ford Madox Ford: Prose and Politics* (Cambridge: Cambridge University Press, 1981), p. 98.

5. Carol Ohmann, for instance, writes that "Dowell is not only incapable of sexual relationship with a woman; he is deeply afraid of it. . . Unconsciously, he attempts to prove himself not a mature man but one who is *absolutely* chaste, whose feelings towards women are entirely innocent and childlike." Carol Ohmann, *Ford Madox Ford: From Apprentice to Craftsman* (Middletown CT: Wesleyan University Press, 1964), p. 88. Jo-Ann Baernstein discusses the "unconscious but recurrent transference of male and female roles" in the novel. See her essay, "Image, Identity, and Insight in *The Good Soldier*," *Critique*, 9 (1966), p. 30.

6. Seymour Chatman, *Story and Discourse* (Ithaca NY: Cornell University Press, 1978), p. 126.

7. Anthony Trollope, *Barchester Towers* (1857; London: Oxford University Press, 1966), p. 126.

8. Moser calls Dowell's tone "an almost indescribable combination of irony, sentimentality, cynicism and bafflement." Thomas Moser, *The Life in the Fiction of Ford Madox Ford* (Princeton NJ: Princeton University Press, 1980), p. 155.

9. Mark Schorer, "An Interpretation," (1951), rpt in *The Good Soldier*, p. x.

10. John Meixner, *Ford Madox Ford's Novels* (Minneapolis MN: University of Minnesota Press, 1962), p. 159.

11. Hynes, "Epistemology," p. 230.

12. Ford, "Impressionism and Fiction," p. 41.

13. Ford, "Joseph Conrad," in *Critical Writings*, p. 72; "Impressionism and Fiction," p. 42.

14. As reported by Jean Renoir in *Renoir, My Father*, trans. Randolph and Dorothy Weaver (Boston MA: Little, Brown, 1958), p. 174.

15. Austin characterizes the theory of sense-data in this way: "We never see or otherwise perceive (or 'sense'), or anyhow we never *directly* perceive or sense, material objects (or material things), but only sense-data (or our own ideas, impressions, sensa, sensations, perceptions, percepts, etc.)." J. L. Austin, *Sense and Sensibilia*, reconstructed from the manuscript notes by G. J. Warnock (Oxford: Clarendon, 1962), p. 2. See also Ian Watt, *Conrad in the Nineteenth Century* (Berkeley CA: University of California Press, 1979), pp. 169–72.

16. A. J. Ayer, "Has Austin Refuted Sense-Data?" in *Symposium on J. L. Austin*, ed. K. T. Fann (London: Routledge & Kegan Paul, 1969), pp. 284–308.

17. Isaiah Berlin, "Austin and the Early Beginnings of Oxford Philosophy," in *Essays on J. L. Austin* (Oxford: Clarendon, 1973), pp. 10–11.
18. Lilla Cabot Perry, "Reminiscences of Claude Monet from 1889 to 1909," *The American Magazine of Art*, 18 (March 1927), pp. 119–25; rpt in Linda Nochlin, *Impressionism and Post-Impressionism 1874–1904* (Englewood Cliffs NJ: Prentice-Hall, 1966), pp. 35–6.
19. Albert Wolff, review of the April 1876 Impressionist exhibition in *Le Figaro*, rpt Maria and Godfrey Blunden, *Impressionists and Impressionism*, trans. James Emmons (New York: The World Publishing Company, n.d.), p. 110.
20. Ford, "Impressionism and Fiction," p. 46.
21. Schorer, "An Interpretation," p. vii.
22. Paul L. Wiley, *Novelist of Three Worlds: Ford Madox Ford* (Syracuse NY: Syracuse University Press, 1962), p. 200; Schorer, "An Interpretation," p. xi.

4 LEWIS'S *TARR*

1. Because of the greater availability of the 1927 text, all references will be to this later version of the novel. Wyndham Lewis, *Tarr* (Harmondsworth: Penguin, 1982), p. 17. Subsequent citations will appear parenthetically within the text.
2. Alan Munton, "Wyndham Lewis: The Transformations of Carnival," in *Wyndham Lewis*, ed. Giovanni Cianei (Palermo: Sellerio Editore, 1982), p. 152; Valerie Parker, "Enemies of the Absolute: Lewis, Art and Women," in *Wyndham Lewis: A Revaluation*, ed. Jeffrey Meyers (Montreal: McGill-Queen's University Press, 1980), p. 213; Thomas Kush, *Wyndham Lewis's Pictorial Integer* (Ann Arbor MI: University Microfilms International, 1981), p. 69; Frederic Jameson, *Fables of Aggression: Wyndham Lewis, the Modernist as Fascist* (Berkeley CA: University of California Press, 1979), p. 99.
3. William H. Pritchard has discussed the relations of Lewis and Lawrence in the context of the dispute between Leavis and Eliot. "Lawrence and Lewis," *Agenda*, 7–8 (Autumn-Winter 1969–70), pp. 140–7.
4. Wyndham Lewis, "The Meaning of the Wild Body," in *The Complete Wild Body*, ed. Bernard Lafourcade (Santa Barbara CA: Black Sparrow Press, 1982), p. 157. For a fine discussion of absurdity in the Wild Body stories see Bernard Lafourcade, "The Taming of the Wild Body," in *Wyndham Lewis: A Revaluation*, pp. 68–84.
5. Lewis, "The Meaning of the Wild Body," p. 157.
6. *Ibid.* pp. 157–8. Lewis opens the essay by observing that "to assume the dichotomy of mind and body is necessary here, without arguing for it."
7. John Holloway has provided a very useful basis for addressing the problem of humanity and dehumanization in Lewis, a problem that obviously bears quite closely on the issue of mind and body. "Machine and Puppet: A Comparative View," in *Wyndham Lewis: A Revaluation*, pp. 3–14.

8. On this point see Roger B. Henkle, "The 'Advertised' Self: Wyndham Lewis's Satire," *Novel*, 13 (Fall 1979), pp. 95–108.

9. T. S. Eliot, "Tarr," *Egoist*, 5 (September 1918), p. 106.

10. Pritchett, for instance, has called Kreisler an "almost tragic character" who is prevented from a "tragic apotheosis" only by a "lack of feeling on the author's part." V. S. Pritchett, *Books in General* (New York: Harcourt, Brace, 1953), p. 250. Davies, on the other hand, calls the work a Nietzschean novella (in the lineage of Mann and Rilke) which cannot be judged in terms of tragic conventions. Alistair Davies, "*Tarr*: A Nietzschean Novel," in *Wyndham Lewis: A Revaluation*, pp. 107–19.

11. In the essay "Inferior Religions" of 1917 Lewis describes his characters as "intricately moving bobbins . . . all subject to a set of objects or one object in particular." *The Complete Wild Body*, p. 147.

12. In an interesting essay Ian Duncan locates Lewis in a post-Darwinian context. "Towards a Modernist Poetic: Wyndham Lewis's Early Fiction," in *Wyndham Lewis*, ed. Giovanni Cianei, pp. 67–85.

13. Love proves to be just as dangerous as hatred: "It was certainly a sort of passion he had for him! But – mystery of mysteries! – because he loved him he wished to plunge a sword into him, to plunge it in and out and up and down!" (p. 278).

14. Wyndham Lewis, *Rude Assignment* (London: Hutchinson, 1950), p. 151.

15. *Ibid.*, p. 164.

5 "THE PASSION OF OPPOSITION" IN *WOMEN IN LOVE*

1. D. H. Lawrence, *Women in Love* (1920; Harmondsworth: Penguin, 1982), p. 71. Subsequent references to this edition will be cited parenthetically within the text.

2. Here I follow Daleski who has written that "the problem, as it presents itself in both its personal and social aspects, is primarily concerned with the difficulty of achieving a self. . . It is the failure to consummate a self that undermines life." H. M. Daleski, *The Forked Flame: A Study of D. H. Lawrence* (Evanston: Northwestern University Press, 1965), pp. 161–2.

3. *The Letters of D. H. Lawrence*, ed. Aldous Huxley (New York: Viking, 1932), p. 199.

4. Albright cannily points out that Birkin's distrust of language and his longing for silent communion is the "linguistic analogue" of his fantasy of the clean humanless world. *Personality and Impersonality: Lawrence, Woolf, and Mann* (Chicago IL: University of Chicago Press, 1978), p. 51.

5. D. H. Lawrence, *Women in Love* (Harmondsworth: Penguin, 1976), p. viii. For discussion of Lawrence's use of repetition, see, for example, H. M. Daleski, *The Forked Flame*, p. 131; Frank Kermode, *D. H. Lawrence* (New York: Viking, 1973), pp. 65–7; David Lodge, *The Modes of Modern Writing: Metaphor, Metonymy, and the Typology of Modern Literature* (Ithaca NY: Cornell University Press, 1977), pp. 160–4; Marc

Schorer, "Women in Love," in *The World We Imagine* (1948; rpt. New York: Farrar, Straus and Giroux, 1968), pp. 118–19.

6. Brooks and Warren have offered the canonical description of the well-formed paragraph. "In itself every sound paragraph has unity: it deals with one aspect of the subject or serves one function. It is coherent: that is, it hangs together; it is not a jumble. Finally, it often has its own emphasis or high point – it peaks at some point of stress. In sum, the paragraph resembles an essay in miniature." Cleanth Brooks and Robert Penn Warren, *Modern Rhetoric*, 4th edition (New York: Harcourt Brace Jovanovich, 1979), p. 217.

7. Richard Drain studies the disruption of "a continuous time flow" caused by the alternation of "momentary" and "fixed" images in *Women in Love*. "*Women in Love*," in *D. H. Lawrence: A Critical Study of the Major Novels and Other Writings*, ed. A. H. Gomme (Sussex: Harvester Press, 1978), p. 76.

8. Cornelia Nixon, *Lawrence's Leadership Politics and the Turn against Women* (Berkeley CA: University of California Press, 1986), p. 22.

9. Compare too Birkin's reflection in "Moony": "What did the small privacies matter?" p. 322.

10. On a related issue, both Nixon and Colin Clarke have argued persuasively and at length that corruption, decay, reduction, dissolution, etc. are essential to the positive moral vision of the work. As Clarke tersely puts it, "paradoxes about corruption are dramatized at *every* level." *River of Dissolution, D. H. Lawrence and English Romanticism* (New York: Barnes and Noble, 1969), p. xi; Nixon, *Lawrence's Leadership Politics*.

11. Quoted in Stephen Miko, *Toward Women in Love: the Emergence of a Lawrentian Aesthetic* (New Haven: Yale University Press, 1972), pp. 268–9.

12. Virginia Woolf, *To the Lighthouse* (1927; New York: Harcourt Brace Jovanovich, 1955), p. 186.

13. Leo Bersani, *A Future for Astyanax* (Boston MA: Little, Brown, 1976), p. 182.

14. Donaldson is surely right to say that when Birkin discusses life outside the marriage tie he is "conflating and confusing two quite distinct things: his need for other people, and his need for Gerald." George Donaldson, "Men in Love? D. H. Lawrence, Rupert Birkin, and Gerald Crich" in *D. H. Lawrence: Centenary Essays*, ed. Mara Kalnins (Bristol: Bristol Classical Press, 1986), p. 47.

15. Compare this remark from "The Crown": "it is the fight of opposites which is holy. The fight of like things is evil." *Reflections on the Death of a Porcupine and Other Essays* (Bloomington IN: Indiana University Press, 1963), p. 18.

16. See Moynahan on the distinction between Birkin's and Ursula's *becoming* and Gerald's and Gudrun's *coming apart*. Julian Moynahan, *The Deed of Life: The Novels and Tales of D. H. Lawrence* (Princeton NJ: Princeton University Press, 1963), p. 81.

6 FROM THE EPIC *TO THE LIGHTHOUSE*

1. Irving Babbitt, *The New Laokoon* (New York: Houghton Mifflin Company, 1910), p. 249; T. E. Hulme, "A Lecture on Modern Poetry," in *Further Speculations*, ed. Sam Hynes (Lincoln NE: University of Nebraska Press, 1962), p. 69; James Joyce, Notebook in Lockwood Memorial Library of the University of Buffalo, cited in Richard Ellmann, *James Joyce* (New York: Oxford University Press, 1959), p. 510.

2. Virginia Woolf, *The Diary of Virginia Woolf*, vol. 2, *1920–1924*, ed. Anne Olivier Bell, assisted by Andrew McNeillie (London: The Hogarth Press, 1978), p. 202.

3. *Ibid.*, p. 199.

4. Virginia Woolf, *To the Lighthouse* (1927; New York: Harcourt, Brace & World, 1955), pp. 40, 226, 72, 227, 274, 71. Subsequent references to this edition will be cited parenthetically within the text.

5. Virginia Woolf, *The Diary of Virginia Woolf*, vol. 1, *1915–1919*, ed. Anne Olivier Bell (London: The Hogarth Press, 1977), p. 193.

6. John Milton, *Paradise Lost*, in *The Poetical Works of John Milton*, vol. 1, ed. Helen Darbishire (Oxford: Clarendon Press, 1952), p. 212.

7. *Ibid.*, p. 213.

8. Hugh Kenner, "Molly's Masterstroke," *James Joyce Quarterly*, 10, 1 (Fall 1972), p. 23.

9. James Joyce, *Ulysses: The Corrected Text*, ed. Hans Walter Gabler with Wolfhard Steppe and Claus Melchior (New York: Random House, 1986), p. 544. Subsequent references to this edition will be cited parenthetically within the text.

10. James Joyce, *Letters*, vol. 1, ed. Stuart Gilbert (New York: The Viking Press, 1966), p. 164.

11. *Ibid.*, p. 159.

12. *Ibid.*, p. 160.

13. *Ibid.*, p. 160.

14. "Henry James's Ghost Stories," in *Collected Essays*, vol. 1 (London: Hogarth Press, 1966), p. 287.

15. Virginia Woolf, "The Narrow Bridge of Art," in *Collected Essays*, vol. 2 (London: Hogarth Press, 1966) p. 225.

16. Woolf, *Diary*, vol. 3, p. 107.

17. A. Walton Litz, "Ithaca," in *James Joyce's Ulysses*, ed. Clive Hart and David Hayman (Berkeley CA: University of California Press, 1974), p. 386.

18. Joyce, *Letters*, vol. 1, p. 129.

19. *Ibid.*

20. Karen Lawrence, *The Odyssey of Style in Ulysses* (Princeton NJ: Princeton University Press, 1981).

21. Joyce, *Letters*, vol. 1, p. 147.

22. Virginia Woolf, "Phases of Fiction," in *Collected Essays*, vol. 2, p. 58.

23. Reported in Frank Budgen, *James Joyce and the Making of 'Ulysses'* (Bloomington IN: Indiana University Press, 1960), p. 17.

24. Virginia Woolf, "Life and the Novelist," in *Collected Essays*, vol. 2, p. 135.
25. *Ibid.*, p. 136.
26. I owe this formulation to Professor Austin Quigley.
27. D. H. Lawrence, "Study of Thomas Hardy" in *Phoenix*, ed. Edward D. McDonald (Harmondsworth: Penguin Books, 1974), p. 481.
28. Virginia Woolf, *A Room of One's Own* (New York: Harcourt Brace Jovanovich, 1957), p. 102.
29. Robert Kellogg, "Scylla and Charybdis," in *James Joyce's Ulysses*, ed. Clive Hart and David Hayman, p. 167.
30. Gerald L. Bruns, "Eumaeus," in *James Joyce's Ulysses*, p. 383.
31. R. B. West and R. Stallmann, *The Art of Modern Fiction* (New York: Rinehart & Company, 1949), p. 647.
32. James Joyce, *A Portrait of the Artist as a Young Man* (1916; Harmondsworth: Penguin Books, 1976), p. 212.
33. Frank Kermode, *The Sense of an Ending* (Oxford: Oxford University Press, 1966), p. 7.
34. Henry James, *Roderick Hudson*, New York Edition (1907; rpt. New York: Charles Scribner's Sons, 1935), p. vii.
35. Joyce, *Letters*, vol. 1, p. 172.
36. See David Hayman, *Ulysses: The Mechanics of Meaning* (Madison WI: University of Wisconsin Press, 1982), p. 117; and Hugh Kenner, *Ulysses* (Baltimore MD: The Johns Hopkins Press, 1987). Kenner describes the list as "a list of past occasions for twinges of Bloomian jealousy" (p. 142).
37. Woolf, *Diary*, vol. 2, pp. 188–9, 199.
38. Wyndham Lewis, *Time and Western Man* (1927; Boston MA: Beacon Press, 1957), p. xv.
39. Wyndham Lewis, *Men Without Art* (London: Cassell & Company, 1934), p. 160.
40. Virginia Woolf, "A Sketch of the Past," in *Moments of Being*, ed. Jeanne Schulkind (New York: Harcourt Brace Jovanovich, 1976), p. 72.

Index

229